David Bade

Epistemologies of Rape and Revelation

International Association for the Integrational Study of Language and Communication

International Association for the Integrational Study of Language and Communication

2015
David Bade, Rita Harris, Charlotte Conrad. *Roy Harris and Integrational Semiology 1956-2015: A bibliography.*

2020
Sinfree Makoni. *Language in Africa. Selected papers* vol. 1
David Bade. *Efficiencies and Deficiencies: Cataloging and Communication in Libraries.*
Sinfree Makoni. *African Applied Linguistics. Selected Papers*, vol. 2
David Bade. *Integrational Linguistics for Library & Information Science: Linguistics, Philosophy, Rhetoric and Technology*
Sinfree Makoni. *Linguistic Ideologies, Sociolinguistic Myths and Discourse Strategies in Africa. Selected Papers*, vol. 3
Sinfree Makoni. *Languages and Language Planning in Zimbabwe. Selected Papers*, vol. 4
David Bade. *Making Mongolians: Linguistics, Historiography, Fiction*
Lars Taxén. *Exploring the Relation between Biomechanical and Macrosocial Factors: Integrationism meets Neuroscience and Information Systems*

2021
David Bade. *Epistemologies of Rape and Revelation*

In preparation
Cristine Severo and Sinfree Makoni. *Language in Lusophonia: Perspectives from Bakhtin, Southern Theory and Integrational Linguistics*
Talbot J. Taylor. *Collected Papers* (in four volumes)

The International Association for the Integrational Study of Language and Communication

The IAISLC was founded in 1998. It is managed by an international Executive Committee, whose members are:

Adrian Pablé (University of Hong Kong), Secretary
David Bade (University of Chicago, retired)
Charlotte Conrad (Dubai)
Stephen J. Cowley (University of Southern Denmark)
Daniel R. Davis (University of Michigan)
Dorthe Duncker (University of Copenhagen)
Jesper Hermann (University of Copenhagen)
Christopher Hutton (University of Hong Kong)
Peter Jones (Sheffield Hallam University)
Nigel Love (University of Cape Town)
Sinfree Makoni (Penn State University)
Rukmini Bhaya Nair (Indian Institute of Technology)
Jon Orman (Brighton)
Talbot J. Taylor (College of William & Mary)
Michael Toolan (University of Birmingham)

Anyone wishing to join the Association can do so by email apable@hku.hk or by sending their name and address to the Secretary:

Dr Adrian Pablé
School of English
Run Run Shaw Tower
Centennial Campus
The University of Hong Kong
Hong Kong S.A.R

For my grandson Chinguun Warren Bilguun
May he grow to love the world even more than his grandfather does

This collection ©2021 David Bade.

To those who do not smile ©2001 Originally published in *The Chicago Maroon*, 25 May 2001.
Signs, Language and Miscommunication: An Essay on Train Wrecks ©2011 Originally published in *Language Sciences,* v.33, nr.4, p.713-724
Signs Unsigned and Meanings not Meant: linguistic theory and hypothetical, simulated, imitation, and meaningless language ©2012 Originally published in *Language Sciences* v.34, nr.3, p. 361–375
Signs Unfounded and Confounded (with Adrian Pablé) ©2012 David Bade and AdrianPablé. Originally published in *RASK, International tidsskrift for sprog og kommunikation* v.35, p.43-85
Respondeo etsi mutabor: Eugen Rosenstock-Huessy and Linguistic Theory ©2014 Originally published in Darrol Bryant (ed.), *Eugen Rosenstock-Huessy, Then and Now*. Waterloo, Ontario, Canada: Eugen Rosenstock-Huessy Society, 2014, p. 20-50
Humanist Machines: An Integrationist Critique of Mechanical Models ©2017 Originally published in *Critical Humanist Perspectives: The Integrational Turn in Philosophy of Language and Communication.* New York: Routledge, 2017. p.154-170
Edward Said, Roy Asked, and the Peasant Responded: Reflections on Peasants, Popular Culture and Intellectuals. ©2021 Originally published in: Sinfree Makoni, Deryn Phillips Verity and Anna Kaiper-Marquez (eds.), *Integrational Linguistics and Philosophy of Language in the Global South*. New York: Routledge, 2021, pages 18-29.

Contents

Preface..1
I. *Respondeo etsi mutabor: Eugen Rosenstock-Huessy and Linguistic Theory*..5
II. *Signs Unfounded and Confounded* (with Adrian Pablé)......63
III. *Language and Historiography*...109
IV. *How Not to Study Swahili: Hannah Arendt, the Encyclopædia Britannica and the Violence of Authority*..129
V. *Signs, Language and Miscommunication: An Essay on Train Wrecks*...165
VI. *Signs Unsigned and Meanings not Meant: Linguistic Theory and Hypothetical, Simulated, Imitation and Meaningless Language*.......................205
VII. *Humanist Machines: An Integrationist Critique of Mechanical Models*..255
VIII. *Epistemologies of Rape and Revelation*........................283
IX. *Edward Said, Roy Asked and the Peasant Responded: Reflections on Peasants, Popular Culture and Intellectuals*..299
X. *To Those Who Do Not Smile*..317

Preface

This volume is comprised of papers that chart my attempts to understand language as an engagement with the world around and within us. They reflect my long-standing interests in language, history, philosophy, technology, the political responsibility of speaking and working in the everyday world, and the relationship between love and knowledge. While much of my writing focused on language in the library—the world in which I worked for 35 years—these papers, most of which were written during the sixth decade of my life, are rooted in the passionate engagements of my high school/college/graduate school years during the 1970s, and are most fittingly indicated by the title of a previously unpublished paper written in 2014 which I have also used for the title of this collection.

The first paper took me almost 20 years to write. I credit Rosenstock-Huessy with preparing me for my later encounter with Roy Harris by turning my head away from the linguistics that I had studied in the university and towards language as encounter and communication: people speak, he insisted, because they have something to say, because they have been spoken to. Yet Rosenstock-Huessy's philosophy of language baffled and sometimes infuriated me as I struggled to understand how to put it all together. Reading Harris almost a decade after Rosenstock-Huessy I immediately grasped the profound reorientation of linguistics that Harris had accomplished, and this recognition I credit in large part to Rosenstock-Huessy: I doubt that I would ever have paid any attention to Harris, much less understood him, had I not previously been reoriented by Rosenstock-Huessy. Yet Harris's critique of the Language Myth caused me even more trouble than ever in trying to understand Rosenstock-Huessy! After a decade of rereading the latter in light of Roy Harris's critique of the language myth and integrational semiology, conversations with Paul Mendes-Flohr and corresponding with Roy Harris and Wayne Cristaudo, I was finally led to new appreciations of both philosophers, and the first paper, an attempt to indicate my understanding of and debt to both, was a great breakthrough for me after two decades of struggle.

The second paper (written with Adrian Pablé) was a response to Søren Lund's complete misunderstanding of the writings of Roy Harris and integrational linguistics. That paper, like the third printed here, was written in exasperation and irritation, for neither Lund nor McCullagh (in the third paper) were worth reading. Nevertheless, having read them, I responded.

The third and fourth papers have not been previously published: 'Language and historiography' was a response to C. Behan McCullagh's review of Roy Harris's *The Linguistics of History*, while 'How not to study Swahili' was prompted by my studies of ontologies in information science and how these were being advocated as supports for research by librarians as well as computer scientists. Hannah Arendt's use of the *Encyclopaedia Britannica* seemed to provide a perfect example of the disastrous consequences of grounding research in 'accepted knowledge' rather than rigorous critical examination, and the even more disastrous consequences of designing research tools and digital libraries that would be based upon and directed by the wisdom of the crowd and a Bayesian understanding of truth—all of that hidden behind the scenes and 'under the hood' of our increasingly monocultural and myopic information systems.

The fifth paper takes integrational semiology into the heart of socio-technical systems in operation, focusing on railroad communication systems. Understanding machines in use requires understanding why they are made, who uses them and how, which is to say that mechanical models of machines can never be of any help in understanding machines since they are objects born within and formed by social practices. The question that led both to and from this fifth paper I am still exploring: whether mechanical models can explain anything. Roy Harris and Erik Hollnagel were the principal catalysts motivating me to reconsider machines, while Bernard Charbonneau and Gilbert Simondon were equally influential in my later thinking. It is an area that I hope to continue to explore in what future I may have left.

The sixth paper looks at both the presence of nonsense and the making of sense in linguistic theory, the use of information technologies, and modern life. How people make sense of a world as nonsensical and absurd as the one in which I have lived has been the question that has oriented much of my thinking for the past 40 years and owes as much to Jacques Ellul and Lewis Mumford—who introduced me to the study of technique and technology as the expression, incarnation and operation of social desires, fears and forces when I was still a high school boy—as to Roy Harris who reoriented me again thirty years later.

The final three papers were, like the first paper, all conference papers written after my retirement from the University of Chicago. The reader may find their relation to linguistics to be tenuous at best, but those who have taken the trouble to grapple with the profound insights of Eugen Rosenstock-Huessy and Roy Harris will understand that language both arises from and acts upon our lives together, and thus issues of epistemology, politics and the ideas that orient and guide us in all our actions—in short, our religion—present unavoidable and necessary question marks for understanding the language and worlds we make together.

The letter to the editor which closes the volume goes into the streets and takes theory to task in a confrontation with race, class, gender, selfrighteousness and hatred. As in the second and third papers above, it was provoked by something I had read that appalled me. Short and unpleasant, it nevertheless provides a glimpse into my attitudes and orientations prior to my encounter with the writings of Roy Harris. With Harris, linguistics went from a stultifying 'Move alpha' to a politics of engagement which has oriented me ever since, but I had, and continue to have, more vital concerns than linguistics, concerns indicated in the title of this volume.

David Bade
Rachel's Farm
2 July 2020

I

Respondeo etsi mutabor:
Eugen Rosenstock-Huessy and Linguistic Theory

Abstract
Rosenstock-Huessy argued that language originates—always and everywhere—from the need to respond to a world that addresses us and calls us by name. Thus in his view, unlike much contemporary theory which concerns itself with an autonomous system, language is understood as a human activity, a social phenomena or power brought into existence by social forces and involving the varied capabilities of the human mind and body. In this paper Rosenstock-Huessy's philosophy of language is briefly presented and questioned from the perspective of Integrational linguistics, an approach to language and semiology that stresses social relations and time in the making of meaning.

0. Introduction.

Eugen Rosenstock-Huessy was neither a semiologist nor a linguist by training, by profession or by reputation. To my knowledge he has left no discernible mark whatsoever on the history of linguistics and semiology, at least as that history is to be judged from the histories so far written and the bibliographies and references that one may encounter in the literatures of linguistics and semiology of the past century. His lectures on linguistics in 1966 (published under the title *The Lingo of Linguistics*) were not well-received by the linguists in attendance who assured him that they had no interest in language as he understood it. Nevertheless his writings on language, education, poetry, singing, liturgical rites, marriage, law, treaties, royal insignia, sports, clothing and fashion constitute a way of thinking about language and semiology that is radically different from the linguistic and semiological theories current during his lifetime. In light of the integrational semiology developed by Roy Harris and his students after the death of Rosenstock-Huessy, the latter's writings on language and semiology provide an exceptionally well-grounded critique of any and all linguistic theories that assume language to be an autonomous system of signs.

One of the most important differences between Rosenstock-Huessy's philosophy of language and other theories of his time is his denial of the autonomy of the sign and indeed his refusal to develop an autonomous science of signs and language at all. This in itself makes it difficult for anyone trained in modern linguistics to grasp what he is doing in theoretical terms, and he adds to this difficulty with a writing style in which the theoretical terms of the linguistics of his time have no place at all.[1] His

---

[1] It is not just the linguistic terminology of his time that he ignores, but as Jakubowski noted, the terminology of sociology as well: "Terms such as culture, citizenship, individual, society, structure, strata, groups, roles, status, actors, public life, and many others which form the core sociological con-

rare references to individual linguists are usually curt dismissals with little if any discussion. Additional difficulties arise with his use of older terms, his discussions of the categories of traditional grammar and a focus on names and naming. Yet by far the greatest obstacle that he throws in the way of even the most sympathetic reader is his insistence on beginning and ending with matters that other theories of language reject as political, sociological, metaphysical or religious matters which are not considered to be within the province of linguistics proper. What I have attempted to do in this paper is to set out as clearly and concisely as I can the questions that oriented and formed Rosenstock-Huessy's approach to language and how he responded to the questions that moved him. The first section will discuss the theoretical world to which he responded as a writer, and the current situation of linguistics within which we must read his works.

1. Rosenstock-Huessy's philosophy of language in light of his predecessors, contemporaries and successors

> Without Engels, no Marx. (Rosenstock-Huessy 1956: I, 12)

Rosenstock-Huessy's relation to linguistics is generally critical and dismissive, but not always. While he nowhere responds at length to any linguist—either in critical analysis or agreement—there are scattered references in his writings that note points of agreement as well as disagreement.[2] Since most of his writings

---

cepts appear rarely, if ever, in the writings and recorded lectures of Rosenstock-Huessy." (Jakubowski 2011a: 114)

[2] The closest Rosenstock-Huessy ever comes to a sustained discussion of any one linguist is in his 1962 essay "'Es regnet' oder die Sprache steht auf dem Kopf", a response to the "blasphemy" of Alan Gardiner's (1932) claim to get at the mysteries of language through an analysis of the sentence "It rains." As it happens, Michael Toolan (1996: 148-154) has also discussed Gardiner's raining examples from an integrationist perspective which makes for an ex-

on language are sociologically and philosophically oriented, the authors to whom he responds are more often sociologists, philosophers, anthropologists and statesmen than linguists, and less frequently, psychologists, economists, theologians and biologists. He often puts himself in opposition to Parmenides, Plato, Aristotle, Aquinas, Descartes, Herder and Kant while aligning himself with Heraclitus, Augustine and Hamann. Although Rosenstock-Huessy offers the biologist Adolf Portmann in defence of his claim that language is not a natural object (Rosenstock-Huessy 1962) and the biologist Jakob von Uexkuell as well as the sociologist Robert MacIver as indications that his rejection of the subject-object dualism is in agreement with the most recent biological and sociological theory (Rosenstock-Huessy 1970b: 5), he discusses none of these thinkers in any depth anywhere.

In his book *Speak that I may see thee!*—a book dedicated to Rosenstock-Huessy—Stahmer (1968: 109) suggested as Rosenstock-Huessy's intellectual precursors "St. John, Saint-Simon, Paracelsus, Hamann, Jacob Grimm, Wilhelm von Humboldt, Friedrich von Schlegel, Otto Gierke, B.G. Niebuhr and William James" as well as Feuerbach, and Stahmer's book itself includes chapters on some of Rosenstock-Huessy's contemporaries who influenced him as he influenced them, namely Martin Buber, Franz Rosenzweig and Ferdinand Ebner.[3] These latter thinkers were the principal figures behind the journal *Die Kreatur*, to which Rosenstock-Huessy also contributed, and his statement about the journal and its contributors applies to him as well:

---

cellent comparison between Rosenstock-Huessy's "speech-thinking" and integrationist thinking.
[3] Stahmer also notes that while Rosenstock-Huessy has been compared to Heidegger and vice versa, "they differ dramatically, precisely because, for example, of the asocial origin of Heideger's thought (Stahmer 1968: 118).

Die Kreatur pulled together the sum of the struggles of Kierkegaard, Feuerbach, Dostoevsky, Nietzsche and William James. They had all discovered that no one has anything to say if they are all saying the same thing. The human being does not speak like God does. A man does not speak like a woman, nor a Christian like a Jew, or a child like a professor. For that reason and that reason alone are they able to and must speak to one another" (Rosenstock-Huessy 1947: 210)

At the time that Rosenstock-Huessy was developing his ideas, linguistics was regarded as within the province of anthropology, and his readings in anthropology were extensive, influencing not only his thinking on language but on history and society as well. In the footnotes to *The Origin of Speech* we learn that his writings on the origins of language were informed by readings of Francis La Flesche, Everard Ferdinand im Thurn, Alfred Ernest Crawley, Alfred Kroeber, Wilhelm Schmidt, Eduard Norden, Edward Sapir, Wilhelm Schulze, Lev Trachtenberg, Carl Meinhof and Clyde Kluckhohn, and many more anthropologists are cited throughout his *Soziologie* of 1956-1958. In that work he wrote of the anthropologist A.P. Elkin "I accord him an honourable place here," and quoted him: "We then realize that we are not using language as a tool—rather it is "using" us, acting upon us just as other forms of behaviour do" (Rosenstock-Huessy 1956: II, 323; Elkin's quote is from *The American Anthropologist*, N.S. 43 (1941), p. 89). In the 1945 essay "How language establishes relations" Malinowski is credited with "the discovery among the primitives that the language they speak is denotation of actions" (Rosenstock-Huessy 1970a: 122), a major point for Rosenstock-Huessy. In *The Origin of Speech* we also learn of the many European and non-European, ancient and modern languages that he studied during the development of his ideas on the subject,[4] and on page 77 we read his negative appraisal of several of the 19th century's important writers on language:

> Wundt, Grimm, Bopp, Durkheim and Humboldt never completely separated names from words. Thus the dictionary, that cemetery of language, with its definitions of terms, became the normal starting point for linguistics as well as psychology. The political role of speech was treated as secondary, as built on an already existing language. But speech originates in a group through the names with which its members are addressed! Names are not words. With words we speak of things; we speak to people by names. (Rosenstock-Huessy 1981a: 77)

Aside from the anthropologist-linguists, Rosenstock-Huessy mentions a number of other more theoretical linguists, but rarely with praise.[5] In the essay "In defense of the grammatical method" we read of "Magnusson's brilliant Ph.D. thesis" (Rosenstock-Huessy 1970a: 20) and in a later essay in the same collection "Articulated speech" he elaborates on Magnusson's work of 1893, referring to him as being the only grammarian who "has made grammar the philosophy of time and space which it is" (Rosenstock-Huessy 1970a: 52). Also in that essay we read that Otto Jespersen's merit was in having reasserted that "In articulated speech, we create a variation of the existing ling-

---

[4] On page 130 he mentions in addition to most of the European languages and Sanskrit, Hebrew, Syriac, Arabic, Egyptian, fifteen Ugro-Finnic languages and twenty African languages.

[5] In some autobiographical remarks quoted in Stahmer (1968: 118-119) Rosenstock-Huessy provides a few paragraphs about his early love of philology and lists some of his reading from the period 1902-1912, during which time he had not yet suffered the crisis of the war. His criticism of 19th-early 20th century philology would be developed during the war and published afterwards.

uistic tradition" and that the neglect of "this feature in all speech ... has made an understanding between grammarians and thinkers impossible for thousands of years." (Rosenstock-Huessy 1970a: 49)[6] but that Josef Schaechter's *Prolegomena zu einer kritischen Grammatik* (1935) is "a little masterpiece of this dissecting and reducing method which just because it is perfect makes one feel that we are all going to give up the spirit soon because language is illogical, stupid and always wrong against logic" (Rosenstock-Huessy 1970a: 57). In the 1935 essay "University of logic, language, literature" we read of Karl Buehler that his "investigations fit into our own discoveries. However, it cannot be the purpose of this paper to deal with his studies in detail since he separates thought and language throughout" (Rosenstock-Huessy 1970a: 96). While W. von Humboldt was castigated in the quotation above, we find Rosenstock-Huessy also writing that an "attempt like the present to unify the cosmos of thought, literature, speech, can find no better patronage than the name of Wilhelm von Humboldt. ... he believed that the structure of language contained the secrets of national individuality, of history, of man's creative destiny. He treated languages ... not for their own sake but for a complete picture of the possibilities of the human mind" (Rosenstock-Huessy 1970a: 67).

---

[6] The variation of which Rosenstock-Huessy speaks is not what is commonly meant by the term in e.g. sociolinguistics. He is referring to the situation in which a speaker and interlocutor speak about something, each in their own way. Thus "When we answer, we neither repeat merely what the first speaker has said nor do we start in our own language. ... The language, the linguistic materials which are to be used, is prescribed by the first speaker. It makes no sense to answer a man in a language in which he does not want to talk, but inside this framework I am free to introduce variations, to enrich, to specify, in short to articulate" (Rosenstock-Huessy 1970a: 48). The following passage is indicative of what impressed Rosenstock-Huessy in Jespersen's writing: "The essence of language is human activity—activity on the part of one individual to make himself understood by another, activity on the part of that other to understand what was in the mind of the first..." (Jespersen 1992: 17)

In the 1945 essay "How language establishes relations" Joseph Vendryes is credited with recognizing the error of "using the term 'Copula' for the word 'is,' which is one of the most inveterate signs of the fact that grammar has not been treated as a science of society" (Rosenstock-Huessy 1970a: 119) but a few pages later in the same volume, in an earlier 1944 essay "The listener's tract" Vendryes is castigated for publishing a treatise on language in which "the words that signify the acts of hearing, listening, obeying, understanding are not to be found, even the word 'oreille,' the ear, is missing" (Rosenstock-Huessy 1970a: 135). A few years later in volume I of his 1956 *Soziologie* Rosenstock-Huessy repeated these remarks on Vendryes, with additional remarks on Brice Parain's 1942 PhD thesis *Recherches sur la nature et les fonctions du langage*, a thesis directed by Vendryes. Of these two works Rosenstock-Huessy remarked :

> Philology structured itself on the processes of phonetics and, from that vantage point, around saying, speaking, writing. But neither 'calling,' nor 'calling on the phone,' 'calling into office,' 'calling into being,' nor 'calling into life' have any place in the textbooks. For those expressions make it almost impossible to overlook the intimate connection between a call and its aural perception on the part of a hearer. Acts of hearing are reserved for other disciplines of study or perhaps left to chance. In academic military training, questions of obedience, the psychology of comprehension, the acoustic nature of hearing, and learning and teaching are treated. But these departments remain silent about linguistics. (Rosenstock-Huessy 1956-1958: I, 141)

Rosenstock-Huessy's thinking on language was already fully developed in his 1925 *Soziologie* with his later writings largely working out and elaborating the themes set out therein.[7] The major movements of 20th century linguistics, philosophy of language and semiotics after the publication of Pierce, Saussure and Wittgenstein had hardly any echo at all in his writing: in his entire published writings Saussure is mentioned only once ("The most recent language scrutineers—Revesz, Louis H. Gray, Meillet, Saussure, Sapir, Alan Gardiner—all dilate on the origins of language. But the index entry, name, does not occur in any of their works." Rosenstock-Huessy 1956-1958: I, 178).[8] While Wittgenstein gets an entire encyclopedia entry, Pierce and Whorf fare even worse: Rosenstock-Huessy never mentions them.[9] Yet that he continued to read linguistics is evident in his remarks on publications by Meillet, Schaechter, Gebser and Parain during the 1930-1940s, numerous works on classical and Biblical languages published in the 1940-1960s, and Gardiner's works from 1932 through 1961 as well as a wide range of publications on ancient Egyptian language, texts and archaeology of the same period. It is also clear that he was reading Jakobson in

---

[7] While the 1925 *Soziologie* presents the range of his ideas together for the first time, the main reorienting ideas had already been the subject of conversations between Rosenstock-Huessy and Rosenzweig prior to their July 1913 encounter that led to Rosenzweig's conversion to Judaism. D'Antuono (1999: 189) describes Rosenstock-Huessy's philosophy of that early date as a "philosophy of revelation" arising from his reflection on language, "the *organon* of the disolution of ontology" in which revelation is understood to involve "an adherance to the point of view of the interlocutor."

[8] There is probably an oblique reference to Saussure in his brief remarks against the arbitrariness of names in Rosenstock-Huessy (1946: 8-9): "Every American college student feels safe, as far as I can see, behind the barbed wire of this argument: words and names both are 'arbitrary.' They have confused 'transient' and 'arbitrary.'"

[9] Cristaudo (2012: 66-71) devotes several pages to Rosenstock-Huessy's comments on Wittgenstein, while Meredith Cargill claims in an unpublished conference paper from 2006 that Rosenstock-Huessy was definitely an adherent of the Sapir-Whorf view of language but cites no references to Whorf in Rosenstock-Huessy's writings or lectures (notes on the paper are available at http://www.erhsociety.org/links/).

1962 for there is a footnote to Jakobson's paper "Why 'Mama' and 'Papa'"? that was added to "Im Prägstock eines Menschenschlags oder der tägliche Ursprung der Sprache," the revised German version of a work from the 1940's prepared later in the same year as the work cited—1962—and published in 1964 (Rosenstock-Huessy 1964; the citation to Jakobson's paper is to the version published in the latter's 1962 *Selected Works* and appears in footnote 2 on p. 453).

That Rosenstock-Huessy never tackled Saussure (or Whorf) is puzzling to say the least, given both the apparent similarities and sharp contrasts between those theorists' interest in speakers and society. One of Saussure's translators—Roy Harris—noted in his introduction to his translation of the *Cours de linguistique générale* that "*Langue* and *parole* are thus both defined by reference to the mental faculty involved (*le langage*), and *not* by reference to the community or to the community's speech practices (which differ from one country to another)" (Saussure 2013: xxxi). For Saussure, *langue* is a structure, its properties structural properties (Harris and Taylor 1997: 209), but the question of how that structure exists in and among human beings is not so straightforwardly indicated. Harpham noted that

> Saussure is relentless in attacking those who regard language as natural or organic, but is for some reason unable to weed out all references to nature from his own discourse, ... Indeed, the entire fifth chapter of the Introduction is conducted in the key of biology, with references to "*l'organisme intérieur de l'idiome*," "*la vie des langues*," "*l'organisme grammatical*" (compared to "the inner organism of a plant"), "*le développement naturel, organique d'un idiome*," "*l'organisme linguistique interne*," and so forth. ... And throughout, the social product of language, the invention of the collective mind, is,

for reasons never articulated, described in biological and merely organic terms. (Harpham 2013: 29)

Harpham went on to note that Saussure's science of language offers language as a kind of system in which "despite a general sense of individual freedom (in the production of speech), each element is subject to the rule of the system, or langue, from which it derives its identity; and that the names of politics and history must not be spoken" (Harpham 2013: 31). Saussure himself plainly stated (in the Harris translation) "the rules a community accepts are imposed upon it, and not freely agreed to" (Saussure 2013: 82). The contrast with Rosenstock-Huessy in this matter could hardly be overstated.

While the various schools of thought drawing upon Saussure each dealt differently with the biological and social aspects of language, all have had in common the notion of language as an autonomous system operating in some connection with the brain, the social aspects of language arising as a result of using that system. A description of this system is the primary object of linguistic theory; what happens after the system generates language is a topic for another discipline.

Nearly all of Rosenstock-Huessy's publications were written prior to Chomsky's *Aspects of the Theory of Syntax* (1965) and he nowhere gives Chomsky or any of his followers any attention, but the chief theoretical issues that Rosenstock-Huessy rejects in the theorizing of his predecessors and his contemporaries appear unaltered in most linguistic theory that has appeared since his death in 1973. Language for the nineteenth century linguists as for Chomsky and today's cognitive linguists is and always has been a natural phenomenon, a matter of biological structures, physiological functions and physical evolution. The rules of a linguistic community are imposed upon it by this genetic/neurological/biological inheritance, as is clear in

Chomsky's famous statement about "a completely homogeneous speech-community":

> Linguistic theory is concerned primarily with an ideal speaker-listener, in a completely homogeneous speech-community, who knows its language perfectly and is unaffected by such grammatically irrelevant conditions as memory limitations, distractions, shifts of attention and interest, and errors (random or characteristic) in applying his knowledge of the language in actual performance. (Chomsky 1965: 3)

Chomsky later defined his research more and more narrowly as a biological science. In a 2009 lecture he remarked that "the physical sciences are not studies of phenomena. Rather they are studies of the principles and processes that underlie phenomena" and with this move he supposes that he has freed himself from the necessity of dealing with any actual linguistic—much less social—phenomena. In his attempt to develop linguistics from a behavioral science into a physical science, "to integrate the study of language and cognitive processes generally, human thought and understanding," Chomsky inaugurated biolinguistics, "the study of language as a biological capacity, pursued much as we study, for example, the nature of the human visual system or the insect visual system or other capacities of organisms. ... The only way known to study the capacity is to develop computational theories that attribute the computations to the mind of the insect and ask the question of what these capacities are in the insect, how do they develop, and how they are used" (Chomsky 2009: 6-7). In a paper written with Berwick and published two years later the authors were more blunt in their definition of language: "human language, a particular object of the biological world" (Chomsky and Berwick 2011: 19).

Language is a natural system to be studied as an object of natural science: that was the assumption that oriented linguistics in the 19th century as it did during the 20th century and continues to do so today. Ironically Chomsky's desire to develop a "hard science" of linguistics has been strenuously defended in a recent textbook which declares grammar to be "magic": "syntax has a biological base, and that human beings, from whatever language community, sociocultural background, or millennium, are all bound together by the same basic grammatical magic" (Hall 2005: 197).

There is, however, one important school of linguistics that flourishes as an exception, a group of dissenting voices against theorizing language as a natural biological system. In his theoretical writings since 1973 Roy Harris has elaborated an approach to language—called variously Integrationism, Integrational Linguistics or Integrational Semiology—that constitutes a sustained critique of language as a system and adherents to this school of thought insist that language can only be understood within a broader theory of human communication and social relations. In the discussion that follows Rosenstock-Huessy's writings will be poked, prodded and investigated in light of Integrationist theory.[10]

2. Language and social relations.

In his 1945 essay "How language establishes relations" Rosenstock-Huessy began by warning the reader that he did not plan to discuss language through the study of the history of language, of phonetics or semantics but instead would "try to explain speech as a function of the various elementary social relations, just as breathing is a function of respiration" (Rosen-

---

[10] The reader unfamiliar with the work of Roy Harris and others inspired by his writing will find a bibliography and a few short pieces by Harris introducing Integrationism on his website, http://www.royharrisonline.com/index.html as well as a database of integrationist oriented publications at http://www.integrationistsrepository.com/

stock-Huessy 1970a: 117). He followed this introduction by offering the reader four types of social relations established in the act of speaking:

> 1. The speaker and the listeners are unanimous, of one spirit. They agree.
> 2. The speaker and the listener are "dubious," split, and of two spirits. They are strangers.
> 3. The speaker depends on the listener, whom the speaker expects to act on what he has to say.
> 4. The listener depends on the speaker because the speaker has acted already. (Rosenstock-Huessy 1970a: 117)

That language establishes relationships is not an idea unique to Rosenstock-Huessy, but the latter's emphasis on social relationships as indicated in the passage just quoted is something quite different from other well-known discussions. We may, for example, contrast Rosenstock-Huessy's approach with Rorty's comment in the latter's essay "Pragmatism and romanticism":

> When Nietzsche says that a thing conceived apart from its relationships would not be a thing, he should be read as saying that since all language is a matter of relating some things to other things, what is not so related cannot be talked of. Language establishes relationships by, for example, tying blood in with sunsets and full moons with tree trunks. Lack of describability means lack of relations, so our only access to the indescribable must be the sort of direct awareness that the empiricist has of redness and that the mystic has of God. Much of the history of Western philosophy, from Plotinus and Meister Eckhart

down to Husserl and Russell, is the history of the quest for such direct awareness. (Rorty 2007: 118)

In Rorty's examples the "relationships" established are between two "things" that are themselves "words that are no more than the creation of finite human creatures in response to finite human needs" (Rorty 2007: 119). Rorty's relationships are relationships between words, not social relationships. Rosenstock-Huessy on the other hand insists that not only do "The fundamental classifications of grammar and the fundamental classifications of social relations coincide" but that "Grammatical classifications in themselves would remain arbitrary without such empirical backing by social reality" (Rosenstock-Huessy 1970a: 117). The full measure of how far Rorty is from Rosenstock-Huessy on the matter of language establishing relationships is made clear in a comment in the last paragraph of Rorty's essay: "a pragmatist outlook ... would complete the process of secularization by letting us think of the desire for non-linguistic access to the real as as hopeless as that for redemption through a beatific vision" (Rorty 2007: 119). For Rosenstock-Huessy, it is Rorty's 'real' that moves us to speak—love, hatred, desire, need, war and revolution—and in his view a beatific vision may indeed lead to redemption. We speak of the real because our first-order experience of the real is what moves us, and our vision of the future may lead us to our redemption through speaking new social relationships into existence.

For Rosenstock-Huessy, first-order experience of language begins when we are spoken to: the proper order of the pronouns is not 1st person *I*, 2nd person *you* and 3rd person *he/she/it*; rather our linguistic experience begins not with our *I* speaking at all but with hearing ourselves addressed by name, as someone else's *you*.

> Out of a thousand cares, impressions, and influences which surround, flow around, and beset it, a child gradually stakes out its borders as an independent entity. Its first discovery on its own, therefore, is that it is neither world, nor mother or father, nor God, but *something else*. The first thing that happens to the child—to every person—is that it is spoken to. It is smiled at, entreated, rocked, comforted, punished, given presents, or nourished. *It is first a "you"* to a powerful being outside itself—above all to its parents. ...
>
> Hearing others say that we exist and mean something to them, and that they want something from us, precedes our articulating that we ourselves exist and our articulating what we ourselves are. We develop self-consciousness by receiving commands and by being judged from outside. (Rosenstock-Huessy 1988: 16)

It is this address from without, not our biological inheritance, that brings us into language. Here Rosenstock-Huessy departs from modern linguistics entirely: language is not the product of an internal organ or cognitive mechanism, but comes from without as a gift. Yet not as a gift produced elsewhere by others and handed to us ready made, but a gift such as friendship which establishes the conditions for its own existence through an act of friendship. *Respondeo etsi mutabor*: speaking changes both the speaker and the one spoken to; through the act of speaking both interlocutors make themselves into human beings.[11] "Man's language aims at something not aimed at by apes or nightingales: it intends to form the listener into a being which did not exist before he was spoken to" (Rosenstock-Huessy 1981a: 4. The German edition of this book was interestingly entitled *Im Prägstock eines Menschenschlags oder der tägliche Ursprung*

---

[11] On this Stahmer remarks "With Kierkegaard, Rosenstock-Huessy would insist that humanity is a task and not a fact." (Stahmer 1968: 132).

der Sprache). Man is not human, he wrote later on in this same essay (Rosenstock-Huessy 1981a: 80), unless he manages to integrate into a unity his determined material body and his "undetermined social organ" (his temporal character), an integration that is effected through ritual language. He contrasts this becoming human through language with the situation of an animal:

> Nobody tells the animal of its origin. But we, the churches and the tribes of time immemorial, have lifted all human beings from their dependence on mere birth. We have opened their eyes to their origins, to their predecessors. We have transformed their mere births so that they became a succession of precedents well-known and well-established. And we have transformed their mere deaths into a precedent leading to an emancipation of their successors. We have made men know their origins by originating one tongue for them. The origin of human speaking is the speaking of human origin! Speaking one tongue, men have become and can continue to become Man. (Rosenstock-Huessy 1981a: 21)

Adherents of the view that language is an autonomous system of signs—biological or otherwise—will immediately object that in order "to speak of origins" language would already have to exist, so Rosenstock-Huessy has explained nothing about the origin of language. This is a crucial point, the foundation of Rosenstock-Huessy's understanding of language. How does he deal with this question?

He never addresses that question directly, but argues that the social conditions that give rise to speech—and the origin of speech is a social event, not a biological evolution—are the same now as in the first speech event in human history. He proceeds with his argument by making a distinction between pre-formal, formal and informal speech. Pre-formal speech is

> A method of showing a man the direction to the next farm on the road or a way of stopping a child from crying. Then it comes in with gestures, smiles, and tears, and then the apes and the nightingales are our masters. There is no doubt in my mind that, in our daily chatter and prattle, our speech serves the same purposes as animal sounds. ... There are areas in our life where we share the conditions under which animals emit sounds of courtship, warning, etc. When we use sounds in these same areas they bear some resemblance to the languages sounded by animals. (Rosenstock-Huessy 1981a: 1)

Formal speech on the other hand signifies

> the power to sing a chorale, to stage tragedy, to enact laws, to compose verse, to say grace, to take an oath, to confess one's sins, to file a complaint, to write a biography, to make a report, so solve an algebraic problem, to baptize a child, to sign a marriage contract, to bury one's father. (Rosenstock-Huessy 1981a: 1-2)

After making this distinction he introduces informal speech and relates this form of speech to pre-formal and formal speech:

> Informality is a rebellion against formality. Never can "informal" be called pre-formal. ... After forms have been created and perhaps grown stale, we may become informal. To be informal means to neglect forms which exist. ... Logically and historically, the formal precedes the informal, and it succeeds animal speech. In anticipation of our result, we may say 1. pre-formal animal speech, 2. formal human speech, 3. informal, low brow speech. (Rosenstock-Huessy 1981a: 2-3)

He insists that the study of informal speech—lullabies, nursery rhymes, neighborly advice, a pointing towards the next house, gossiping neighbors—does not lead us towards the origin of language but to a late state, possible only after the accomplishment of formal speech. "The nursery and the parlor presuppose the meeting house and the court and the formal languages spoken there" (Rosenstock-Huessy 1981a: 7). Pre-formal speech on the other hand, may be explained as a variety of animal expression, a matter of natural history, biology and physiology. In a grammar of Latin written with his friend Ford Lewis Battles he provided an illustration of animal (pre-formal) and formal speech as they might occur in our everyday interaction:

> When you yell "iiiiiiiih" and your chum yells back "iiiiiih," you are two little animals making inarticulate noise. When you, however, say to him: "Now listen, Johnnie," and he says, "I listen, Billy," you are two people speaking to each other in articulated speech. What is the difference between the two cases? In articulated speech, the process of listening is clearly defined between another person and yourself. You summon him to act as a listener. The roles are distributed between you two, because one in the same act first is suggested as an order on your side; then, the same act is acknowledged as a voluntary reaction on his side. You and he enter in this specific relation. In answering you, "I listen," he partly identifies himself with you since he admits that he knows exactly what you mean. Furthermore he preserves his personality by adding "I." Speech is both identity with, and distinction between, people. It is like weaving a pattern out of several fibers. For his "I listen" is not the same sound as your "listen." It has passed through his conscience and consciousness and he had to reshape it before he passed it back to you. Now the sentence "I

> listen" carried back to you something quite different from the noise "iiiiiiiih." It was now a declaration of cooperation, of acknowledgement of his having heard you. A sentence is a personal relation between answerable people. Articulated speech is communication between responsible people. (Rosenstock-Huessy and Battles 1975: 14-15)

As human beings we speak sometimes as animals—and such language can be explained in the same manner as we explain the grunts, growls and songs of animals—sometimes informally (when we speak inconsequentially), and sometimes we speak formally. In light of the absence of names in pre-formal animal speech and the prevalence of pronouns in informal speech, he renames these three varieties of language prenominal, nominal and pronominal, declaring that if we wish "to understand the origin of formal speech it must be from a man's work or an old man's deed" (Rosenstock-Huessy 1981a: 4). With these matters taken care of, he then declares that "we may well inquire when and where formal language is called forth, and what constitutes the contribution of language in a hitherto speechless community. The authentic place and the legitimate moment for the birth of language can now be explored" (Rosenstock-Huessy 1981a: 7).

And where does Rosenstock-Huessy look for this "authentic place" and "legitimate moment" for the origin of language?

> Until we have faced the situations of a human society when and where speech is lacking we cannot even understand the second question of why the instruments of language were cast in grammatical forms. The question of the origin of language makes sense as a sequence of two questions. First, when, in our own experience, is

> new speech indispensable? Second, when, then, did speech become indispensable? Without any present day experience of speech as originating anew under our noses, from necessity, we shall have no yardstick for the past. (Rosenstock-Huessy 1981a: 7-8)

Rosenstock-Huessy proposed that we look at our own experience of language in order to discover the origin of speech, and to look precisely at those situations in which we are unable or unwilling to say what we must say, prohibited from speaking or simply not listened to when we do speak. In this "hell of non-speech" we discover the social forces that provoke human beings to speak to each other and establish relationships of peace instead of isolation, war, tyranny and the anarchy of all against all.

> In plunging into the darkness in which man cannot yet speak or no longer does speak to his brother man today, we shall prepare ourselves best for the answer to the questions: what is speech?, how does it originate?, why do we speak?, which, of course, are one and the same question in its divers aspects.
> We are, then, going to inquire under what conditions modern man is not on speaking terms with his brother. This obviously is not a purely linguistic or philological question. If members of a family are not on speaking terms, something is wrong with the family. A moral question is implied. When nations are not on speaking terms, they are at war. (Rosenstock-Huessy 1981a: 9)

With this move, all questions regarding language and its origin, beginning with What is language? have been torn out of the linguist's familiar territorial grasp, and Rosenstock-Huessy is well aware of this:

> Our way of putting the question for the origin of language shifts the field of the question into the realm of politics and history. The question "when must man come to speak?" is disclosed as a question which must have been answered by other authorities than the teachers of English or Arabic or Sanscrit. They deal with languages as facts. Our question deals with languages as question marks of political history. (Rosenstock-Huessy 1981a: 9)

Because Rosenstock-Huessy chose to approach the origin of language as "our problem of understanding what happens when a language is not functioning," he offers us not a componential analysis of phonology, syntax or semantics, but a semiology of making meanings with others, a tentative, risky, dangerous and failure prone activity not produced like sweat or piss by bodily organs but produced moment by moment—if at all—by human beings who make each other into human beings through this semiosis.[12]

This point of departure for investigating the origin of language was neither arbitrary nor a purely theoretical necessity: his orientation arose out of his personal experience as a soldier in the First World War, and in his work with factory workers and industrial arbitration in Germany immediately after that war. His basic insights were first written down in the trenches as letters to Franz Rosenzweig in 1916, and can be clearly seen in his works on industrial law from the post-war period, such as this 1926 remark in *Vom Industrierecht*: "before two individuals may talk to each other in words about things they must be mutu-

---

[12] The important difference between language produced by natural processes and language as human activity was discussed briefly by Thomas Duncanson. He noted the "drastic, unfamiliar *naturalism* in his thinking about speech" but argued that "Rosenstock-Huessy saw speech as natural, not in some uninteresting biological or even psychological sense, but in the grand phylogenic sense that in speaking human beings realize their deepest and most complete well-being and advance their humanity" (Duncanson 2001: 14).

ally responsive, they must recognize each other as persons" (Rosenstock-Huessy 1926: 86).

Finding ourselves in a social disaster, we are compelled to establish relationships with others because the relationships are not given to us; if we wish to recognize and be recognized as a brother, sister, friend or coworker in situations of social disorder, we must establish those relationships with our own acts. "Speech is the political constitution of a group beyond the life time and living space of any individual, beyond common sense and physical sense" (Rosenstock-Huessy 1981a: 31). In an essay first written in 1939 and revised in 1955 ("In defense of the grammatical method"), Rosenstock-Huessy argued that this is what his method of research reveals: social disorder is the condition in which language originates.[13]

> What is wrong with society? That there is war, revolution, crisis, and decadence in it. Without these evils, we should live in the Garden of Eden, and that means, without self-conscious reflection on our social situation. Social disintegration is a blessing in disguise since it compels us to wake up. The grammatical method insists that the negative aspects of society compel us to think, to speak, to write, to study, and nothing else makes us think really. (Rosenstock-Huessy 1970a: 11-12)

The four evils that are the primary focus of Rosenstock-Huessy's sociological and historical writings are presented in

---

[13] Much later Baudrillard would make a remarkably similar suggestion: "John grows up normally, but doesn't talk, and this drives his parents to distraction. When he is about 16, at last, one teatime, he says: 'I'd like a little sugar.' His mother is staggered and asks, 'But John, why have you never said anything up to now?' 'Up to now, everything was perfect.'
If everything is perfect, language is useless. This is true for animals. If animals don't speak, it's because everything's perfect for them. If one day they start to speak, it will be because the world has lost a certain sort of perfection." (Baudrillard 1990: 83-84)

that same essay in terms of social relations across times and spaces:

> "*anarchy* prevents translocal units from cooperating" (ibid.: 12)
>
> "'Decadence' means to be unable to reach the future" (ibid.)
>
> "In *revolutions*, the new men, the future generation does violence to the existing order and to the people formed in and by the past" (ibid.: 13)
>
> "Wars disregard *extraterritoriality*." (ibid.)

All four evils Rosenstock-Huessy diagnoses as diseases of speech for they each emphasize one aspect of social life while neglecting or suppressing another. In respect of the aspects of social life that each evil neglects, we could say that each evil is a speech defect since it prevents the expression of a necessary aspect of social life. In the face of these four evils language appears not as a fact of nature but as a social miracle.

> The cry for peace and order is a desperate cry. Shouting for freedom and for regeneration of the good old days is of the utmost violence. The lullabies and sugar coating of common sense are not acceptable to crying, weeping, shouting, raging people. They must experience the miracle of seeing the dead come to life again, and foes become friends, and dissent become agreement, and shouts become new words. ... Formal speech produces exactly these miracles. (Rosenstock-Huessy 1981a: 31)

That speech is a social miracle occurring in the face of these four evils points to the fragility and temporal nature of language, new speech being "created under the pressure from graves in back of us and cradles ahead of us, from foes in front of us and dissension within our own ranks" (Rosenstock-Huessy 1970a: 30). The failures of speech to set the world aright indicate that language is not a perfect machine for the production of social order any more than it is a mere reflection of an existing order.

> If it had not failed time and again, we might think speech to be infallible. As a natural process, speech would be infallible. Most anthropologists are convinced of the natural character of speech. They never ask under what conditions it must function. In all their research, they naively presuppose that man first can speak and then goes into politics and "organizes" society. The opposite is true. Man must speak if he wishes to have a society; but very often he cannot speak and then his society breaks down. ... Shall we be able to articulate our chaos into order once more? There is no guarantee for success since at no time has every tongue or every speaking group succeeded in provoking men to trust and freedom – some have, some have not. All speech must take the risk of being misunderstood by common sense. (Rosenstock-Huessy 1981a: 31-32)

The four evils that Rosenstock-Huessy identifies are related to our basic orientations in life, "the two axes of time and space, with their fronts backward, forward, inward, outward," these being not arbitrary "verbal definitions of the social order" but rather "open to a unanimous experience and an identical consciousness of all human beings" (Rosenstock-Huessy 1970a: 13-14). The task of speech is "the perpetual conquest" of the four diseases of speech.

To the four diseases, four different styles of speech bring relief. Men reason, men pass laws, men tell stories, men sing. The external world is reasoned out, the future is ruled, the past is told, the unanimity of the inner circle is expressed in song. People speak together in articulated language because they fear decay, anarchy, war, and revolution. The energies of social life are compressed into words. The circulation of articulated speech is the lifeblood of society. Through speech, society sustains its time and space axes. These time and space axes give direction and orientation to all members of society. Without articulated speech, man has neither direction nor orientation in time or space. Without the signposts of speech, the social beehive would disintegrate immediately." (Rosenstock-Huessy 1970a: 16)

We speak in order "to unify, to simplify, to integrate life" across these four fronts in time and space. "Without this effort, we would go to pieces by either too much inner, unuttered desire, or too many impressions made upon us by our environment, too many petrified formulas fettering us from the past, or too much restless curiosity for the future." (Rosenstock-Huessy 1970a: 18). Every living being as well as every social group "has to defend a present under the simultaneous stress from past and future. To live means to look backward as well as forward, and to decide, in every moment, between continuity and change" (Rosenstock-Huessy 1970a: 17-18). The struggle for existence "is implied by every word we speak" (Rosenstock-Huessy 1970a: 10).

The origin of the first word and the origin of the next word is the same in kind, for language is always a new origin. Grammar arises with our decisions as to how to order our world, how to integrate ourselves into it. The language maker is placed at the center and at the origin:

> [W]e sustain the time and space axes of our civilization by speaking, because we take our place in the center of this civilization, confronted as we are with its four aspects: its future, its past, its inner solidarity, its external struggle. And in this delicate and dangerous exposure to the four fronts of life, to the inner, the outer, the backward, and the forward front, our words must strike a balance; language distributes and organizes the universe, in every moment, anew. It is we who decide what belongs to the past and what shall be part of the future. ... Whether I say, in our days "Europe was a great civilization," or "Europe is a great civilization," passes judgment on the life and death of Europe. I either relegate it to the past or I credit it with a future. And whether I say: we all should have peace on earth, or: these dictators should keep quiet, proves where I draw the line of inclusiveness or exclusivity, respectively, between myself and the people whom I consider "we," on one side and some unspeakable people, somewhere in the outside world. (Rosenstock-Huessy 1970a: 19-20)

Yet this speaking I is, for Rosenstock-Huessy, not an autonomous ego bursting forth in speech: we all speak first in response to having been spoken to and in expectation of being heard and responded to in turn.

> We speak in our anguish or in our curiosity to minds whom we try to make into our listeners, readers, students. This is the intellectual responsibility shouldered by the most skeptical and most uncommunicative thinker. Even Sorel, who shouts for violence, in his doctrine, actually, and first of all, shouts for readers for his treatise. The first outcry of human self-consciousness about society is the word: Listen! (Rosenstock-Huessy 1970a: 23)

With "the 'you' that is expected to listen ... the dualistic concept of a world of subjects and objects is abandoned" (Rosenstock-Huessy 1970a: 24) and language is seen to be necessarily and always a Zweistromland in time rather than a cognitive system in no need of a respondent. However, having posited a language which is always "originating anew under our noses" yet which is always in the first instance a gift from without and entails the articulation and transmission of grammatical forms to our neighbors and descendants, we are faced with the objection noted at the beginning of this paper: both the use of language that one finds (or is given) and the transmission of forms certainly seems to imply the preexistence of a language ready-made rather than the origin of language in every speech act. The objection registered by Roy Harris seems appropriate:

> Language-use is presented as a matter of stringing units together, the allowable units and their combinations as being already available in advance for that operation, the combined whole then being slotted into some external environment or situation. This...is language 'as we know it'. *But it isn't*. It is an analysis imposed on language by adopting one narrow and rather questionable perspective. (Roy Harris 1998: 6)

Can this apparent contradiction in Rosenstock-Huessy's understanding of language be comprehended? How might Rosenstock-Huessy have responded to Roy Harris in the above quotation or to the axioms of Integrational linguistics?

3. Space, Time and Grammar: The Logics of Experience and of Writing

> No child founds communities properly speaking. It learns languages which exist and operate. (Rosenstock-Huessy 1970a: 9-10).

This statement taken by itself seems to contradict the basic ideas of Integrational linguistics. It would be easy to interpret this as a blunt statement of what Harris calls 'The Language Myth', i.e. that language is an autonomous system not made by human beings and that language is what makes communication possible.[14] We may juxtapose to this a statement written in 1912 about the role of language in the making of law in medieval Germany which Rosenstock-Huessy reaffirmed decades later as the key to his thinking:

> The intellectual conduct of the age was maintained only by the unifying influence of the Latin hieratic language, because the living vernacular always overpowers the thinking of individual man who assumes that he could master it; it is wiser than the thinker who assumes that he thinks, whereas he only speaks and in so doing faithfully trusts the material of language; it guides his concepts unconsciously, towards an unknown future.
> (Rosenstock-Huessy 1912: 144)

Here again language seems to be some *thing* acting on us, a thing which we must "faithfully trust". These statements—and many like them throughout Rosenstock-Huessy's writings—present the reader with the most significant difficulty in understanding his thought, for in his writing *Sprache* (German writings), *speech* and *language* (English works and translations) appear to refer in one sentence to the act of people speaking to one another and in the next to what Harris would refer to as the products of communicative activity. The principal theoretical question for the integrationist is how Rosenstock-Huessy understood the relationship between language as action and language as something which exists and operates "out there" in our world. If he ever saw a theoretical difficulty in writing *Sprache-speech-*

---

[14] See especially Harris's 1981 book *The Language Myth*.

language and meaning sometimes action, sometimes object in the world, it is not something he ever addressed directly.

If these same statements are read in light of Rosenstock-Huessy's insistence that language is in its origin and always the call of one to another, then rather than referring to language as a thing out there he is always referring to a community of speakers teaching us their language that we might make it our own, voices not within our brain but from the world around us who guide us into the world we make together "towards an unknown future."[15] It is the speaking community, not a linguistic system, that teaches us and guides us. This reading of Rosenstock-Huessy reveals a marked contrast with Saussure:

> The first thing which strikes one on studying linguistic facts is that the language user is unaware of their succession in time: he is dealing with a state. Hence the linguist who wishes to understand this state must rule out of consideration everything which brought that state about, and pay no attention to diachrony. Only by suppressing the past can he enter into the state of mind of the language user. (Saussure 1922: 117; quoted in Harris 2005: 90)

For Rosenstock-Huessy, our language is always a response to a prior call from another: we listen to the past and speak now towards the future. His understanding is also in marked contrast with the "scientific" linguistics of Max Müller who argued that "Languages can be analyzed and classified on their own evidence ... without any reference to the individuals, families, clans, tribes, nations or races by whom they are or have

---

[15] Bernard Charbonneau would later cry "No, I am not alone, I speak, I write the same language as generations of men. ... The meaning of my words goes beyond my individual self." (Charbonneau 2013: 359).

been spoken" (Müller 1861: 76; quoted in Harris 2005: 86). Harris noted that this assumption leads Müller

> to treat the viewpoint of the language user as totally irrelevant to the scientific investigation of language. The language user knows little or nothing of the past history of the linguistic forms currently in use, nor of their relationships to forms in other languages; and moreover does not need to possess any such knowledge for everyday communicational purposes. ... The scientific method that Müller espouses requires the linguist to abstract from the speakers altogether, to ignore the communicational activity of the language community and to treat 'the language' simply as a set of forms and combinations of forms. (Harris 2005: 88)

The integrationist insists that the products of communicative activity become meaningful signs *only* when they are *made* signs in communicative activity by the speaker/writer and the hearer/reader, but Rosenstock-Huessy saw our entire experience of the world as constituted by meaning making together with others, an orientation of thought that makes his ideas difficult for anyone accustomed to ignoring the role of the speaker/writer/listener/reader in the spoken/written.[16] This is not the same as saying that the not-I or the world is a linguistic fiction of the I, but rather an acknowledgment that the only world we know is one which is already saturated with language when we encounter it. This holds not only for the human community of speakers and hearers, writers and readers, but of our entire physical and social environment. Whereas for Saussure "the physic-

---

[16] Hahn (2011) notes that Rosenstock-Huessy's remarks on law as a world born of language (see the quote above, Rosenstock-Huessy 1912: 144) marked him as an "academic eccentric" among the legal scholars of the time.

al world lies outside the language system as such" (Harris 2005: 93) Rosenstock-Huessy argued on the contrary that

> "Nature" is an abstraction from the saturated-with-language-world, the world minus speech. "Nature" is the result of a subtraction. It is a misleading word, because it seems innocent, a primordial sound, an "a priori." Yet this is to get everything upside-down for in our actual experience voices call us into life first of all, and water, earth, and wind may concern us only after membership in society and participation in language securely lash us above the abyss of nature. (Rosenstock-Huessy 1962: 43-44)[17]

We are born into a world that precedes us and continues on after us. In that world are innumerable objects and events that we may perceive as meaningful or meaningless, related or unrelated to us or to anyone else, and language is a part of that experience from the womb. We may theoretically understand our interaction with the world in what is often called "objective" fashion, seeing and hearing only isolated objects, movements and sounds; in this manner of interacting with the world, nothing can mean anything for meanings are not perceptible things: there can be no signs.[18] Nor is there space and time, nor even nature, since these are also not perceptible things but abstractions, interpretations of the world of experience. However if we

---

[17] Rosenstock-Huessy is here following Max Scheler. See the latter's review of Fritz Mauthner's *Beiträge zu einer Kritik der Sprache. 3. Band. Zur Grammatik und Logik* where he reproaches Mauthner for his nihilism: "Hier ist überall purer Nihilismus, dem Sprache allmächtig ist und der sie zugleich verachtet, das letzte Wort—und ein "artikuliertes Lachen" über das große "Nichts", das bei der Subtraktion Welt minus Sprache—gemäß dieser Lehre—übrig bleibt, die letzte Geste. [etc.]" (Scheler 1914: 119).

[18] Perhaps this way of experiencing the world as not addressed *to me* lies at the origin of autism?

abandon the need to insist upon this (impossibly) objective relationship to a world which is not altered by our own existence, our interest in it, and our naming it, we may consider our relationship to the world around us as we indeed experience it: a world in which we and all those around us interact motivated according to our needs, desires, discomforts, fears, loves and hatreds. To be born into a human world is to be born into a world with language. To join the human race is not merely a consequence of our biological birth; to become human is to answer, to become a language-maker ourselves, an activity that presupposes an interlocutor.

The language that is given to us, the language that we find in the world around us, is a language, a world of signs—books, newspapers, sound recordings, road signs, price tags, gestures, handshakes—made by others to mean something to others in their world. That it means something to the original makers is a result of their making it mean something in a particular situation at a particular time; that it should mean something to us or to anyone else requires our making it mean something to ourselves in our situation and in our time.[19]

> When we answer, we neither repeat merely what the first speaker has said nor do we start in our own language. ... To articulate, then, is a highly complicated act that implies both: identity and variation. Without identifying ourselves with the language as it stands, and as we find it, we cannot say our word, and without varying and deflecting this material in a specific direction that is con-

---

[19] This responding act of sign- and meaning-making is never guaranteed: "If no one understands me, at least, beyond myself, these signs are there, black on white. Perhaps... No, I have not been dreaming, I have spoken, I have written; the work of an entire life is there, abandoned, like a fruit fallen from the tree. I had to speak, but for that reason, in the absence of a yes I have received this no that no one even spoke. I remain alone, rendered mute by my speech, for no neighbor, no public recognizes it." (Charbonneau 2012: 359).

stituting a new situation created by our own choosing, our entering the ring of the speaking folks would be useless. ... the irresponsible way of using ready-made slogans and judgments in mere repetition without making them ourselves here and now, under our own name, is a vilification of language. (Rosenstock-Huessy 1970a: 49)

Repetition as a vilification of language in Rosenstock-Huessy's understanding contrasts sharply with contemporary semiotic theory from Pierce's types and tokens to Derrida's iteration.[20] While Rosenstock-Huessy insisted that articulation is an *act* that implies identity and variation, Derrida insisted that the sign/mark contains in itself both identity and difference apart from any relation to iterator, reiterator, hearers/readers and contexts:

This iterability, as Sari concedes, is indispensable to the functioning of all language, written or spoken (in the standard sense), and I would add, to that of every mark. Iterability supposes a minimal remainder (as well as a minimum of idealization) in order that the identity of the selfsame be repeatable and identifiable in, through, and even in view of its alteration. For the structure of iteration—and this is another of its decisive traits—implies both identity and difference. (Derrida 1988: 53)

The integrationist would object that one can only regard these as repetitions/reiterations if one ignores (as Derrida does) the listener/reader, the difference that time makes and the situation of the "repetition", an objection that Rosenstock-Huessy would no doubt have appreciated. Whether Barthes considered "official

---

[20] Although Rosenstock-Huessy never responded to either Pierce or Derrida, Harris and other integrationists have. See especially Hutton (1990) on Pierce and Harris (2003) on Derrida.

institutions of language" as vilifications of or typical of language is not as clear: "All official institutions of language are repeating machines: school, sports, advertising, popular songs, news, all continually repeat the same structure, the same meaning, often the same words: the stereotype is a political fact, the major figure of ideology." (Barthes 1975: 40). Barthes, Harris and Rosenstock-Huessy might all have agreed that the unsponsored language of slogans was politically irresponsible and destructive of human relationships, but Rosenstock-Huessy went so far as to insist that in authentic speech there are not only no repetitions but "Es gibt keine Synonyme. [There are no synonyms.]" (Rosenstock-Huessy 1956-1958: II, 77).

For Rosenstock-Huessy, we orient ourselves in that world into which we are born through naming the elements in our inner experience, external encounters, past experience and desired future worlds. What does it mean to name?

> The name is the right address of a person under which he or she will respond. ... Names give orientation. ... All superstitions arose because religions wanted eternal recipes for giving names. The true life of human speech defies all recipes. The names under which the parts of the world must be made to move change with the times. (Rosenstock-Huessy 1970b: 42-43)

Time and space are not themselves objective material realities but linguistic creations of everyday experience, and upon these the scientific notions of space and time are dependent:

> To speak has to do with time and space. Without speech, the phenomena of time and space cannot be interpreted. Only when we speak to others (or, for that matter, to ourselves), do we delineate an inner space or circle in which we speak, from the outer world about which we speak. ...

But the truly human phenomenon of space is found in the astounding fact that grammar unites people within one common inner space. Wherever people articulate and vary one theme, they move in an inner room or community as against the world outside.
And the same is true about the phenomenon of time. Only because we speak, are we able to establish a present moment between past and future. Because I am telling you all this here and am waiting for your answer, is it possible for you and me to forget past and future, and to call this hour an hour, this paper a unity, this time one moment, one time span. By human speech, space and time are created. The scientific notions of time and space are secondary abstractions of the reality of grammatical time and space. Grammatical time and space precede the scientific notions of an outer space or of a directed time. For they presuppose an inner space between the scientists and some contemporaneity between them, too. Without the pre-establishment of one inner space of "science," no scientific analysis of time and space holds water, or even can take place at all. (Rosenstock-Huessy 1970a: 20-21)

Here Rosenstock-Huessy is making an argument similar to those put forth by Roy Harris in *The Semantics of Science* and elsewhere. Harris criticized Holt-Jensen's account of the language of science with the remark that it offers us "the comforting reassurance that the language of the natural sciences is scientific because it is the only language in which scientists can get answers to scientific questions" (Harris 2005: 160). Harris himself insisted that the language of science projects

> back upon Nature the assumptions built into an ancient philosophy of language, ... Those tacit linguistic assump-

tions were responsible for building up the traditional picture of a universe filled with discrete objects of various sizes, each equipped with its own battery of properties and having its own unique position in space and time. Similarly, the binary distinctions between possibility and impossibility, truth and falsehood, observer and observed, were anchored in the linguistic operations of verbal description, not in the structure of the universe allegedly described. The discoveries of science are reflections in a linguistic mirror. With the assistance of language, scientists extrapolate from their instruments to the universe, from the part to the whole. Without that help, they would be stranded in a linguistic no-man's-land. (Harris 2005: 187-188)

Neither for Harris nor for Rosenstock-Huessy does this recognition invalidate or diminish the accomplishments of science. What it does do is force us to notice and account for both the social and the linguistic dimensions of science and our claims to knowledge, for once we have named our experiences, speaking puts us into a second order of experience: "never does a listener, a jury or a judge hear reality itself; they always hear people telling them about reality. And the reflecting mind is in no better position than the judge" (Rosenstock-Huessy 1981a: 44). Following this recognition, it is but one short step for Rosenstock-Huessy to see in the verb forms of human speech the social markers of time which will vary from one community's form of social organization of time to another's, and thus from one formal grammar to another.

In *Magna Carta Latina*, written after he learned that his son was failing Latin in school, Rosenstock-Huessy complained that "Latin is taught after the Alexandrian method, as though sounds make a word, and words a sentence" (Rosenstock-Huessy and Battles 1975: ii). In writing a new grammar as a response to his son's failure, he wanted to write a textbook that offered not a dead language made of sounds, words and sentences, but the language he knew and loved, hence the title *Magna Carta Latina: the privilege of singing, articulating and reading a language and of keeping it alive*. The Latin declensions remained the same as in any Latin textbook, but the manner and order of presentation were intended to correct a failure of speaking across the generations.

> "His Father's Latin" would not be true to the father's faith if it treated language as a mere tool or, as people are impudent enough to style it, as a means to an end. ... We would, then, commit the sin of sins, the sin against vivification, if we treated language as material, as a mere vehicle for ideas. (Rosenstock-Huessy and Battles 1975: vii)

Since language for Rosenstock-Huessy was not the concatenation of sounds and sentences nor simply a vehicle for the transportation of ideas and information but the making of social relations, the grammatical forms labeled and tabled by grammarians—indicative, imperative, subjunctive, nominative, accusative, dative etc.—all exist as the results of processes of forming and reforming, creating and recreating relationships across times and spaces, and thus they take on a wholly different character in his thinking about language than one finds in traditional grammars and modern linguistics. Under Rosenstock-Huessy's examination all of the formal distinctions found in traditional grammars, the mental structures that linguists "find" in the language organ and trace out in theoretical notations reveal their political origins:

> We draw the conclusion that language serves the purposes of peace, order, representation and credit. The eternal

origin of new speech is based on man's mortal danger from war, crisis, decay and revolution. ... If our diagnosis is correct, the structure of language should bear witness to its political purposes. (Rosenstock-Huessy 1981a: 17).

His discussion of the imperative in *The Origin of Speech* will suffice as an example of how he treats these traditional categories:

> The logic of an imperative and its corresponding report demands that a supertime be established which neglects the separation of two bodies and their biological times. The order given by one person and the other's reporting back correspond so much to each other that they beget one common time. ... What we find between people who trust one another in commands given and fulfilled is not a frame of reference but a field of correspondence. The distinction is fundamental. A "frame" seems to exist outside our sayings or acts. This field of correspondence, however, comes into being by sayings and by acts, and does not exist outside of them. ... After this [the order fulfilled], the field collapses and disappears. (Rosenstock-Huessy 1981a: 47)

Continuing his discussion of the imperative as the establishment and acting out of a time-bound social relation he argues that what all linguists and formal logicians have assumed — "that sentences are the independent elements of speech" (Rosenstock-Huessy 1981a: 48) — is untenable. He does so on the basis that in social life, the command "March into Germany" makes no sense without a response (such as "We have marched into Germany") for the logic of speech demands that the imperative sentence "does not end until he [the original speaker] hears that it is fulfilled" (Rosenstock-Huessy 1981a: 48). Our "stubborn forgetfulness of the obvious ... that the logic of the sentences of language is based on responses between people" (Rosenstock-Huessy 1981a: 62) leads linguists to base their analysis on an inadequate appreciation of the temporal and social dimensions of language, a theoretical blindness that he attributes to literacy: "The abstract sentence, we may venture to suggest, is conditioned by its literary character. Speech, in its origins, was unwilling and incapable of formulating sentences into which speaker and listener did not enter" (Rosenstock-Huessy 1981a: 42). The trouble with linguists, he complains, is that

> they always stopped at the analysis of the "completed" sentence. In so doing, the reason for grammar remains invisible. "March" and "we have marched" are not two different tools such as a hammer and a wrench I may have in my tool chest. "March" and "we have marched," correspond to each other as aspects of one process... (Rosenstock-Huessy 1981a: 48)

Rosenstock-Huessy then describes the three features that distinguish authentic speech "from all texts analyzed by the tradition of linguistics":

> First, speaker and listener exchange places. The speaker becomes listener; the listener becomes speaker. Second, this changes the style of the sentences spoken. In advance, the imperative puts a burden on the listener. Afterwards the narrative unburdens this listener who reports back and quite literally carries back the burden put on him before the act. Third, sentences are the beginnings and endings of actual changes in the physical world. They are not "mental" or "intellectual."
> (Rosenstock-Huessy 1981a: 49)

The constant references to language throughout Rosenstock-Huessy's writings are characterized by an insistence upon the material consequences of language: language is the human-creating, time-creating, space-creating, world-creating, world-altering and self-changing action of one who cannot refrain from speaking, which is to say, from responding. Language is not an abstract system in the brain or in the heavens but a maker and changer of brains and heavens as well as futures and pasts, self and other:

> All speech rides the future of a new heaven and a new earth. All speech draws out the speaker from behind his isolation into a realm of communality with the person or persons who listen. This realm is not a mere fantasy; some material partition in space and some historical bridge through time must result from speech when it is in full force. (Rosenstock-Huessy 1970b: 60)

4. The power that makes us speak: gods and the politics of language

At this point we may touch upon the central and most difficult point in Rosenstock-Huessy's theory of language as maker of social relations. We have already seen that in his view it is language that makes us human beings above and beyond our animal existence by integrating our determined bodily nature with our undetermined temporal nature. And we do this in large part by creating times and spaces though our linguistic activity. Language comes to us from outside—father, mother, neighbor —through our experiences of being spoken to, being named and placed in life through ritual, incorporated into the social life of family, neighborhood, church, school, work and play, and called to political speech in times of social crisis. It comes to us not as a biological inheritance (although of course our anatomical and physiological capacities for speaking or writing are biologically determined and inherited), nor as a socially imprinted system (a "prison-house of language") over which we have no control. The nature of language is that it comes to us as a call from a world woven entirely of language, and we make it "our" language with our response; yet it is our response alone that makes language possible: without it there is no language, only a solitary cry in the wilderness of nature.

What is language, that it creates times, spaces, men and women, and the relationships amongst all these? First of all it is not an autonomous system but the establishment of and invitation to a relationship into which we may enter, and with our entry we cooperate in the making, maintaining and changing of that relationship. The speaker's proposed reality is answered through affirmation, negation, counterproposal or silence, and in the latter case language and social life remain unfinished and in expectation of response or fear of social disintegration. The voice that gives us our name articulates an entire world of relationships and invites our participation. This leads Rosenstock-Huessy to describe the driving force in the creation of language thus: "The power who puts questions into our mouth and makes us answer them, is our God" (Rosenstock-Huessy 1993: 725). He elaborates this point a bit in a 1954 lecture: "God is the power that makes us speak things for the first time in our life. Therefore the parents are gods for the child inasfar as they enable the child for the first time to speak" (Rosenstock-Huessy 1992/1997: 8, lecture 3 (September 30 1954), 16). The college boy abandons the god of his fathers — "parents, teachers, dear God with his white beard" (Rosenstock-Huessy 1988: 26) — and begins to listen to the voices of other gods:

> the voices of politics (i.e., of the times), of the people, of faith, of philosophy, of love, as invisible voices within him. By making demands, they begin to urge him toward a new self-chosen position in life, toward his vocation. (Rosenstock-Huessy 1988: 26)

Here we find gods, creatures rarely encountered in twentieth century linguistics treatises, but in Rosenstock-Huessy's thought we are not dealing with the orthodox gods of theology for in his understanding "gods are not primarily metaphysical powers divorced from life, but first and foremost experiential powers with names" (Cristaudo, 2017). However we name them —if we are aware enough of them to do so—our gods are our "highest sources of appeal," the desires, loves, hatreds, or other "real powers we serve through our daily choices" (ibid.). It is these gods—social forces, drives, demands—that push us towards each other and language. Language is neither instrument nor a means for transmission, but a power that transforms us and our social realities.[21] When our gods die, our language changes: "Catastrophes are the collapse of worlds and the language that has woven them—the sources of appeal and authority" (Cristaudo 2012:73). Which of these commands from without we respond to, which commands orient us towards the world beyond ourselves, this is what determines the world in which we live, the nature of our social relations, and the forms of our languages.

Thus it is our hearing ourselves addressed by name and called out by a name and as "you" that introduces us to a world that desires our participation, and as Rosentock-Huessy's friend Franz Rosenzweig noted "Only an 'I' not a 'he,' can pronounce the imperative of love" (Rosenzweig 1972: 178). This is the world of the lover and the beloved, the world of proper names, the "individual without category ... it carries its here and now with it" (Rosenzweig 1972: 186-187). Fear and the desire for power reduce the world to an 'it,' a world that can neither call to us nor respond. The demand for a third person objective lang-

---

[21] On this see Hasselaar (1973: 237 and following) and especially Cristaudo (2012: 78-80) where Rosenstock-Huessy and Rosenzweig's conception of language as a power is contrasted with Saussure's understanding as indicated in the famous diagram in the *Cours de linguistique générale*.

uage in which world and others all become '*it*'s reveals a political orientation of an I, solitary, unnamed and hidden from itself, dominating and controlling a world of objects, a world of exploitation, slavery, and rape, a language in which both You and I are prohibited, each for different reasons.[22] In a world of 'it's there can be no language and there can be no meaning for there is no one to make anything mean anything to anyone else; to speak presupposes the recognition of you and I as persons (Rosenstock-Huessy 1926: 86). For Rosenstock-Huessy, a language limited to the third person (e.g. the language of science) reveals a political crisis, a disease of language, for authentic speech requires the full range of persons, and not only You and I and It, but of singulars, duals and plurals as well, and the continual circulation of all of these voices through call and response, name and answer. Without that integration of a multiplicity of voices establishing themselves in a variety of relations with each other and those relations changing according to times and places, we slip back into the "hell of non-speech," a condition of inhumanity in which there is no peace for no one makes peace in word and deed.

Rosenstock-Huessy's references to God and gods making us speak may lead (and often has lead) his readers to interpret the political dimensions of his thought in terms of religious conservatism or even fascism, and a reading which understands his "Sprache" as a system that controls us without our free participation only strengthens that political interpretation. Yet in order to interpret him in this way it is necessary to ignore not only everything he wrote about the role of the respondent in making and fulfilling his relationships with the past and future, but everything he wrote about the political origins of speech and the role of time in the making of all social relationships.

---

[22] For more on this in relation to Rosenstock-Huessy's "dative thinking," Bakhtin's "absolute need of love" and Fromm's analysis of the necrophilia of western culture, see Pigalev (1997).

Voorsluis (1984: 311) noted that in Rosenstock-Huessy's understanding of freedom, it is the freedom to *say* 'yes' or 'no' that forms the very basis of our freedom, and this is only possible as a response to words addressed to us by another. As for time, the role of time in political life is evident in the very language in which politics is discussed—conservative, progressive, revolutionary, reactionary—but Rosenstock-Huessy's thinking on time and the making of times cannot be grasped at all in these terms. Rather he viewed political life as connecting past and future as well as here and there through speaking new conditions of peace into existence. His insistence upon the impossibility of repetition is rooted in this understanding of time, as is his insistence that the future determines the past: we understand our past and the past of others in terms of the future we hope and strive for. Instead of pitting past against future as conservative and revolutionary theories do, Rosenstock-Huessy speaks of teachers and students and "the creation of a body of time":

> The pupil, then, is not compelled to go beyond his death but he wants to get before his birth. ... a young man who learns, penetrates into the before-himself time, by backwardizing. He holds out a feeler into the past. ... Before him, men lived already. Whether he likes them or disapproves of them, they have formed all the matters and objects and words and laws and habits and rituals which he may conform with or reform. His freedom depends on his getting back of these forms into the time when they were still in process. To learn means to go before the forms into their formative moment. Because then, the past and my background cease to be rigid determinants of my own form and habit. In backwardizing, we reenter the ranks of those who determined the past. The parallel to the teacher, then, is quite literal. The man who teaches determines the future by his experiences. The man who

> learns determines the past instead of being merely determined by it. ...
> Now, how to get teacher and student together? One holds out his feeler into and "after-me" time; the other feels his way into a "before-me" time. In the hour in which they communicate, they build out of these two elements a common present. (Rosenstock-Huessy 1981b: 31-32)

The present is that "body of time" that young and old create together out of their experiences (pasts), hopes (futures) and love—or hatred—for each other.[23] "Without Engels, no Marx" (Rosenstock-Huessy 1956-1958: I, 12) is a splendidly succinct expression of Rosenstock-Huessy's theory of language as arising out of social crisis and creating new social relations. When language is understood to be the co-creation of social relationships by persons all of whom are freely engaged in that creation and responding to each other, the traditional labels of conservative and progressive, revolutionary and reactionary simply do not apply. For Rosenstock-Huessy, political life is a new creation with every act, and each act may lead us towards heaven or it may plunge us all into hell.

---

[23] Kroesen discusses the implications of this particular aspect of Rosenstock-Huessy's theory of language in relation to technology and the language of socio-technical relations. He remarks that "If our language no longer brings us into a common understanding, it entails also a loss of historical memory" (Kroesen 1995: 59). On this topic readers may also be interested in a blog post by Nicholas Carr "Conversation points" (http://www.roughtype.com/?p=3110) and the a remark made by Ta-Nehisi Coates in his article about cell phone use on public transportation: "I think what we have here is a working definition of an asshole –a person who demands that all social interaction happen on their terms."
http://www.theatlantic.com/national/archive/2013/03/how-the-quiet-car-explains-the-world/273885/

5. Conclusion: The Language Maker as Peace Maker

In 1973 Roy Harris published his first book *Synonymy and Linguistic Analysis*. In his concluding remarks he wrote

> Within the context of any inquiry which treats linguistic knowledge only in terms of complex pairings of 'forms' with 'meanings', the problem of validating synonymity statements is—and must remain—insoluble. But on the basis of a more detailed analysis of communicational relevance it will become possible to state more accurately the conditions of communicational equivalence with respect to which natural languages are structured. Discussion of the kind which has been presented in the preceding chapters may be regarded as merely preliminary to an investigation which opens up the possibility of replacing 'synonymy' by a more precisely defined set of equivalences, and thus providing a more adequate conceptual framework for the analysis of natural languages (Harris 1973: 159).

Harris's criticism of any approach to language which isolated *forms* and *meanings* from the situations of their actual occurrence in communicational exchanges led him to a critique of the foundations of linguistic theory (including his own reference above to "natural languages") and philosophy of language that he has been elaborating for the past forty years. His understanding of signs as things made within a social situation of communication between interlocutors and sign makers/interpreters of all sorts has focused on the signs made and the theoretical issues that arise when taking time and circumstance into account. Rosenstock-Huessy died in 1973 after spending the last 70 years of his life developing a theory of social relations based upon linguistic interactions. Both Harris and Rosenstock-Huessy rejected the study of language as a natural object and both insisted that language only exists as social activity: when we wait for the last living speaker to study a language, Harris insisted, it is already too late, for it takes at least two to make language. The phenomena which Harris and Rosenstock-Huessy investigated and discussed overlapped in many ways: gesture and action as responses to speech, the importance of writing for linguistic theory, the marriage ceremony, the lay perspective, and most of all their insistence on the temporal and political dimensions of language.

By insisting that the study of language must be pursued within its natural setting of human communication, Harris approached language in the same context within which Rosenstock-Huessy had studied law and revolution, church and state, command and obedience, slavery and freedom, calendars and religions, art and song, marriage and meals, history and prophecy, creation and revelation: the social life of speaking human beings. While Harris focused on analyzing what he called the "products of communication," Rosenstock-Huessy focused on the social forces that compel us to communicate with each other. The difference in their respective approaches invites an attempt to put them together, as does the refusal of both of them to enclose their thinking within a disciplinary boundary.

Some of those who have written about Rosenstock-Huessy have interpreted his ideas about language as closely to the idea of language as a pre-existing system or ready-made tool as they can,[24] and Rosenstock-Huessy has given them plenty of

---

[24] For a particularly clear example see Maurin (2003), where Rosenstock-Huessy's remarks on nominating (as well as remarks by Otto Bollnow, Martin Heidegger, Carl Jung, F. Nietzsche, Walter Otto, Karl Rahner, Max Scheler and Benjamin Lee Whorf) are offered in support of the mathematician Erich Kähler's views on language and reality. In Maurin's argument "Language is not only an organ (for cognition) available to be used or not: *language is control over man.*" (Maurin 2003: 961). Rohrbach (1973), Hasselaar (1973), Kroesen (1995), Jakubowski (2011b) and Cristaudo (2012) do make the case for a social understanding of language but none of them

reasons to do so: his language often appears to contradict what he is at other times stating clearly. If one reads "Language establishes relationships" according to traditional, structural, Chomskyan or cognitive theories of language as "Language as a system (whether a gift of god or product of biological evolution) establishes relationships" then it is inevitable that language will be understood as something preexisting and external to those relationships. It is, as Harris remarked of Chomsky's theories, "a fascist concept of language if ever there was one" (Harris 1983: 119). Reading Rosenstock-Huessy as if he were reproducing Harris's "Language Myth" renders his works incomprehensible, incoherent, a mass of contradictions while at the same time forcing a radically conservative or even fascist political interpretation of his remarks on the relation between individual and society, individual and state. Should that same statement (and many other statements of his) be read according to an integrationist understanding of language, understanding it as something like "The language we make together establishes us in our relationships" we have not an external system forcibly and inexorably shaping human lives in accordance with its structures and strictures, but human beings making our worlds together through speaking (writing, signing) to each other, through making language together.

To the reader not blinded by the "language myth" it is overwhelmingly obvious throughout Rosenstock-Huessy's work that his "grammatical method" is not an attempt to analyze autonomous linguistic structures but an attempt to indicate the social function of grammatical forms in organizing the world and allowing us to integrate our life with past generations and future generations, both here and across the border, by attending to those socially created and maintained forms from the past and

---

discuss Rosenstock-Huessy from the perspective of linguistic theory, and apart from a brief note on Saussure in Cristaudo's book, there are no references to the literature of linguistics in any of their works.

teaching them to the following generation. The grammar of creation is the grammar of language makers and not at all a grammar of "natural language." Grammatical forms follow from and are determined by the situation in which the need to communicate arises, and those situations are embedded in our experiences with others and the times and spaces we create together.

Although reading Rosenstock-Huessy in light of integrationist theory reveals a coherent and comprehensive theory of language as a social activity, any semiology that one might hope to derive from his writings will be sketchy at best. He was interested in language as a social activity, but appears to have had no interest in a theory of signs and sign making of any kind. Aside from a few profound but scattered remarks, writing is always assumed under the larger concept of Sprache/speech/language or simply ignored. In like manner his numerous discussions of marriage ceremonies, law, eating and drinking customs, games, clothing and dress, liturgical objects and rites are all pursued as though these are matters of speech without any attempt to indicate why he regarded these as part of the world of speech, nor what theoretical implications might arise if these varied phenomena are regarded as varieties of speech. Using his own terms, we can say that in spite of the many pages he devoted to arguing against that view of language which he rejected, he did not name it. Roy Harris did. Against what Harris named *The Language Myth*, Integrationist semiology took up many of the questions that occupied Rosenstock-Huessy and takes up many more that he did not ask.

While Rosenstock-Huessy did not work out a semiology, he did what Roy Harris as a linguist did not do: he worked out a sociology appropriate for a world experienced as saturated with language, a theory of the establishment of social relations through linguistic activity, of the articulation of perceived social evils and the means for correcting and improving them. It is a social science of the making of peace, of integrating then and there with here and now for you and I through grammatical agreement, a peace and an agreement that is either made anew with every act of authentic speech or else it collapses in silence or scream.

In keeping with his understanding of the origin of language as arising out of political crisis, he described his politics in terms of translation in one of his early works—*Angewandte Seelenkunde* (1924; English translation: *Practical Knowledge of the Soul* (1988))—and of border-defying piracy in his last, *Dienst auf dem Planeten* (1965; English abridgement: *Planetary Service* (1978)):

> *Crossing over to another shore: that is the risk of politics.* People have to change into new people, their sentences into new sentences. So the study of any grammatical method can't itself be a logical or mathematical theory. It has to be a courageous translation, a venture and an advance into unseen territory. (Rosenstock-Huessy 1988: 6)

> Peace is always something explicit. It has to be concluded in an area where no common language existed before. So this last chapter is going to concern itself with the coming language of the pirate's peaceful country. Our Esperanto won't be seeking words for bread and wine and money. It must proclaim a calendar of our tears and laughter common to all of us. People who keep peace among themselves share joy and sorrow. If they don't weep and joke together they certainly aren't at peace with one another. Pirates' Esperanto must fill the gaps left by the silencing of each group destroyed by technological progress. (Rosenstock-Huessy 1978: 97)

He imagined or perhaps hoped that one day his thinking would be understood not as linguistic science, but as a search for peace. And for Rosenstock-Huessy, the path of the peace maker was the path of the language maker, even though not every language maker sets out to be a peace maker.

> And my own direction of thought, probably, will have to be listed as the meta-ethical search for a synchronization of mutually exclusive social patterns of behaviour, as "the metanomics of the great society" which must contain contradictory ways of life. My grammar of assent, my grammatical organon, is devoted to the task of supplementing the statute law of any given society with the metanomics that explain and satisfy our enthusiasm for the synchronization of the distemporary, of old and young, black, brown and white, government and anarchy, primitive and refined, highbrow and lowbrow, innocence and sophistication, all at peace, in one human society. (Rosenstock-Huessy 1970a: 41)

This is certainly not the linguistics you studied in school, and in light of Rosenstock-Huessy's self-perception it is small wonder that linguists have ignored him.

Acknowledgements
I am grateful for nearly twenty years of conversation and correspondence with Paul Mendes-Flohr and Wayne Cristaudo concerning E. Rosenstock-Huessy and F. Rosenzweig. Without Paul and Wayne, no David Bade.

A revised and abridged version of this paper was published as "*Respondeo etsi mutabor*: Eugen Rosenstock Huessy's semiological *Zweistromland*" in *Culture, Theory and Critique*, 2015 v.56 issue 1 pages 87-100.

References

Barthes, Roland (1975). *The Pleasure of the Text.* New York: Hill & Wang.

Baudrillard, Jean (1990). *Cool Memories.* London: Verso.

Carr, Nicholas (2013). "Conversation points" posted on his blog *Rough Type* March 28, 2013 (viewed 22 January 2014) http://www.roughtype.com/?p=3110

Charbonneau, Bernard (2012). *Une seconde nature: l'homme, la société, la liberté.* Paris: Sang de la Terre : Médial.

Chomsky, Noam (1965). *Aspects of the Theory of Syntax.* Cambridge: MIT Press.

Chomsky, Noam (2009). *Noam Chomsky on Language and Cognition.* Muenchen: Lincom.

Chomsky, Noam; Berwick, Robert C. (2011). "The biolinguistic program: the current state of its development" pp. 19-41 in Anna Maria di Sciullo and Cedric Boeckx (eds.), *The Biolingusitic Enterprise: New Perspectives on the Evolution and Nature of the Human Language Faculty.* Oxford: Oxford University Press.

Coates, Ta-Nehisi (2013). "How the Quiet Car Explains the World" *The Atlantic* March 11, 2013 http://www.theatlantic.com/national/archive/2013/03/how-the-quiet-car-explains-the-world/273885/ (Accessed 22 January 2014)

Cristaudo, Wayne (2012). *Religion, Redemption, and Revolution: The New Speech Thinking of Franz Rosenzweig and Eugen Rosenstock-Huessy.* Toronto: University of Toronto Press.

Cristaudo, Wayne (2017). 'Introduction.' In Eugen Rosenstock-Huessy. *In the Cross of Reality. Volume 1: The Hegemony of Spaces.* Translated by Jurgen Lawrenz. New York: Transaction Publishers, pp. xv-xxxii.

D'Antuono, Emilia (1999). *Ebraismo e filosofia: saggio su Franz Rosenzweig.* Napoli: Guida. (Judaica ; 2)

Derrida, Jacques (1988). *Limited Inc*. Evanston: Northwestern University Press.

Duncanson, Thomas (2001). *Never One Thing: Philosophical Anthropology in the Speech Thought of Eugen Rosenstock-Huessy*. Thesis (PhD), University of Iowa.

Hahn, Hans-Joachim (2011). "Akademischer Exzentriker, häretischer Christ oder 'nichtjüdischer Jude': Aspekte des Sprachdenkens bei Eugen Rosenstock-Huessy" *Jahrbuch des Simon-Dubnow-Instituts* X, 39-87.

Hall, Christopher J. (2005): *An Introduction to Language and Linguistics: Breaking the Language Spell*. London: Continuum.

Harpham, Geoffrey Galt (2013). *Language Alone: The Critical Fetish of Modernity*. London: Routledge.

Harris, Roy (1973). *Synonymy and Linguistic Analysis*. Toronto: University of Toronto Press.

Harris, Roy (1981). *The Language Myth*. New York: St. Martin's Press.

Harris, Roy (1983). "Theoretical ideas." *Times Literary Supplement*, no. 4202 (14 October 1983), 119.

Harris, Roy (1998). *Introduction to Integrational Linguistics*. Oxford: Pergamon (Language & Communication Library, Vol.17)

Harris, Roy (2003). *Saussure and His Interpreters*. 2nd ed. Edinburgh: Edinburgh University Press.

Harris, Roy (2005). *The Semantics of Science*. London: Continuum.

Harris, Roy; Taylor, Talbot J. (1997). *Landmarks in Linguistic Thought. I, The Western Tradition from Socrates to Saussure*. 2nd. ed. London: Routledge.

Hasselaar, J.M. (1973). *Inleiding tot het denken van E. Rosenstock-Huessy*. Baarn: Uitgeverij Ten Have.

Hutton, Christopher (1990). *Abstraction and Instance*: The

Type-Token Relation in Linguistic Theory. Oxford: Pergamon Press.
Jakubowski, Zbigniew (2011a). "Eugen Rosenstock-Huessy i jego myśl" *Argument* 1:1, 103-114.
Jakubowski, Zbigniew (2011b). "Myślenie mowy w dążeniu do osiągnięcia ładu i tożsamości społecznej według Eugena Rosenstocka-Huessy." In Ryszard Żelichowski (ed.), *Ideologie - Państwa – Społeczeństwa*. Warszawa: Instytut Studiów Politycznych Polskiej Akademii Nauk, Collegium Civitas, 19-38.
Jespersen, Otto (1992). *The Philosophy of Grammar*. Chicago: University of Chicago Press.
Kroesen, Otto (1995). *Tegenwoordigheid van Geest in het tijdperk van de techniek: een inleiding in het werk van Eugen Rosenstock-Huessy*. Zoetermeer: Meinema.
Maurin, Krzystof (2003). "An approach to the philosophy of Erich Kähler." In Erich Kähler, *Mathematische Werke = Mathematical Works*. Berlin: Walter de Gruyter, 960-963.
Müller, Friedrich Max (1861). *Lectures on the Science of Language*. London, Longman, Green, Longman, Roberts & Green
Pigalev, Aleksandr (1997). "Bakhtin and Rosenstock-Huessy: 'absolute need of love' versus 'dative thinking'" In: Carol Adlam et al (eds.), *Face to Face: Bakhtin in Russia and the West*. Sheffield, England: Sheffield Academic Press, 118-128.
Rorty, Richard (2007). "Pragmatism and romanticism." In his *Philosophy as Cultural Politics (Philosophical Papers*, volume 4). Cambridge: Cambridge University Press, 105-119.
Rosenstock-Huessy, Eugen (1924). *Angewandte Seelenkunde: eine programmatische Übersetzung*. Darmstadt: Roetherverlag. English translation by Mark Huessy and

Freya von Moltke: *Practical Knowledge of the Soul.* Norwich, Vermont: Argo Books, 1988.

Rosenstock-Huessy, Eugen (1925). *Soziologie. Band I. Die Kräfte der Gemeinschaft.* Berlin & Leipzig: W. de Gruyter & Company.

Rosenstock-Huessy, Eugen (1926). *Vom Industrierecht. Rechtssystematische Fragen. Festgabe für Xaver Gretener.* Berlin: H. Sack.

Rosenstock-Huessy, Eugen (1946). *The Christian Future, or, The Modern Mind Outrun.* New York: Charles Scribner's Sons.

Rosenstock-Huessy, Eugen (1947). "Rückblick auf 'Die Kreatur'" *Deutsche Beiträge: Zur Geistigen Überlieferung* 1947: 208-216.

Rosenstock-Huessy, Eugen (1956-1958). *Soziologie.* Stuttgart: Kohlhammer. [While pagination refers to the original edition, I quoted from a draft version of the English translation by Jurgen Lawrenz that had not been edited or published at the time of writing. That translation, edited by W. Cristaudo and F. Huessy has since been published as *In the Cross of Reality, Volume 1: The Hegemony of Spaces.* New York: Transaction, 2017.]

Rosenstock-Huessy, Eugen (1962). "'Es regnet' oder die Sprache steht auf dem Kopf." In his *Die Sprache des Menschengeschlechts: eine leibhaftige Grammatik in vier Teilen.* Heidelberg: Verlag Lambert Schneider, Band I, 35-85.

Rosenstock-Huessy, Eugen (1963-1964). *Die Sprache des Menschengeschlechts: eine leibhaftige Grammatik in vier Teilen.* Heidelberg: Verlag Lambert Schneider.

Rosenstock-Huessy, Eugen (1964). "Im Prägstock eines Menschenschlags oder der tägliche Ursprung der Sprache." In his *Die Sprache des Menschengeschlechts:*

eine leibhaftige Grammatik in vier Teilen. Heidelberg: Verlag Lambert Schneider, Band II, 451-594.

Rosenstock-Huessy, Eugen (1970a). *Speech and Reality.* Norwich, Vermont: Argo Books.

Rosenstock-Huessy, Eugen (1970b). *I am an Impure Thinker.* Norwich, Vermont: Argo Books.

Rosenstock-Huessy, Eugen (1978). *Planetary Service: A Way into the Third Millennium.* Norwich, Vermont: Argo Books.

Rosenstock-Huessy, Eugen (1981a). *The Origin of Speech.* Norwich, Vermont: Argo Books.

Rosenstock-Huessy, Eugen (1981b). "Man must teach" In his *Rosenstock-Huessy Papers. Volume 1.* Norwich, Vermont: Argo Books, chapter 3.

Rosenstock-Huessy, Eugen (1988). *Practical Knowledge of the Soul.* Norwich, Vermont: Argo Books.

Rosenstock-Huessy, Eugen (1992/1997). *Comparative Religion, 1954.* Jericho, Vermont: Argo Books. (*The Eugen Rosenstock-Huessy Lectures*, v 8)

Rosenstock-Huessy, Eugen (1993). *Out of Revolution: Autobiography of Western Man.* 2 ed. Providence and Oxford: Berg Publishers, Inc.

Rosenstock-Huessy, Eugen (1997). *Lingo of Linguistics – 1966.* Norwich, VT: Argo Books. (*The Eugen Rosenstock-Huessy Lectures* v. 29)

Rosenstock-Huessy, Eugen and Ford Lewis Battles (1975, orig. ed.: 1937). *Magna Carta Latina: the Privilege of Singing, Articulating and Reading a Language and of Keeping it Alive.* 2nd. ed. Pittsburgh: Pickwick Press. (Pittsburgh reprint series, number 1)

Rosenzweig, Franz (1972). *The Star of Redemption.* Translated from the Second Edition of 1930 by William W. Hallo. Boston: Beacon Press.

Saussure, Ferdinand de (2013). *Course in General Linguistics.*

Translated, edited and annotated by Roy Harris. London: Bloomsbury Academic.

Scheler, Max (1914). "Fritz Mauthner. *Beiträge zu einer Kritik der Sprache. 3. Band. Zur Grammatik und Logik. 2. Auflage.* Stuttgart: Cotta" *Die weissen Blätter*, 1:VI (Februar): 118-119.

Stahmer, Harold (1968). *"Speak that I may see Thee!" The Religious Significance of Language.* New York: The Macmillan Company.

Toolan, Michael (1996). *Total Speech: An Integrational Linguistic Approach to Language.* Durham and London: Duke University Press.

Voorsluis, B. (1984). "Subject en vrijheid volgens Eugen Rosenstock-Huessy (1888-1973)." In B. Voorsluis et al. (eds.), *Vrijheid: een onderzoek naar de betekenis van vrijheid voor de methodologie van de menswetenschappen.* Amsterdam: VU Uitgeverij, 291-328.

II

Signs Unfounded and Confounded. A reply to Søren Lund.
(with Adrian Pablé)

Abstract
This paper responds to Søren Lund's critique of Roy Harris and integrational linguistics published in this issue. We demonstrate that Lund's characterization of Harris as an armchair linguist and integrational linguistics as merely a development of ideas found in his predecessors is based on ignorance of Harris's writings. We argue that the integrational conception of signs was developed by Harris as a response to his personal linguistic experiences as both a student in post-war England and later as a Romance philologist and dialectologist, which so obviously clashed with the linguistic theories of his days. Furthermore, the paper refutes Lund's views of (i) natural signs as 'found' (not made), (ii) the indeterminacy of the sign, and (iii) integrationism as a form of radical relativism, and attempts to give the reader what the authors think is a more accurate understanding of a Harrisean semiology.

1. On armchairs and other chairs.

In his paper, Søren Lund offers 'refutations' of three theses of integrational linguistics. He begins his discussion by characterizing Roy Harris as an 'armchair linguist', and integrational linguistics as an elaboration of the positions of earlier linguists. We shall begin our response to his article with Lund's introductory remarks on Harris and his predecessors, and then attempt to point out why we think his refutations of integrationism are unconvincing. We shall begin each discussion point by citing Lund in order to make our responses relevant to the article under scrutiny.

Lund (2012: 5) claims that Harris is "an essential armchair linguist" and adds in a footnote

> Harris reports (1990:18) from fieldwork he apparently conducted in dialectology, and he cites as evidence a reply from an informant. But, curiously, the paper from which this alleged evidence comes from does not appear in the references to the 1990 paper in question. (Lund 2012: 38)

Lund has not done his homework here, for prior to being the first appointee to the Chair of General Linguistics in Oxford, Roy Harris sat briefly in "the only established Chair of the Romance Languages in Britain, inaugurated in 1909" http://www.ling-phil.ox.ac.uk/romance-linguistics). While both chairs may have been armchairs before or after Harris occupied them, they were hardly that while Harris rocked them. Furthermore, between 1966 and 1974—before he even had a chair to sit upon—Roy Harris published eight papers: on Gallo-Romance morphology (Harris, 1966), paradigms in vulgar Latin (Harris, 1968), Franco-Provençal historical morphology (Harris, 1968a), Italian dialectology (Harris, 1967 and 1969), medieval French orthography (Harris, 1970), French lexicology (Harris, 1972) and French phonology (Harris and Love, 1974), as well as fifteen reviews of books on romance linguistics, nine papers on theoretical linguistics and reviews of the same. And those publications followed a decade of earlier publications on medieval French literature. One can find in those early publications abundant evidence that Roy Harris the Romance linguist had a prodigious appetite for the investigation of language in medieval manuscripts and published texts as well as in Alpine villages. The transcriptions and maps in the papers on dialects demonstrate that Harris could hold his own against any traditional linguist—indeed, enough to be appointed to a professorship at Oxford.

At the same time that Harris was doing linguistics in the spirit of the prevailing view, he was making observations that escaped other contemporary linguists, and was considering their theoretical implications. The fact that Harris refers back to an incident from that period in the 1990 passage Lund mentions demonstrates that Harris continues to return to his own linguistic experience in order to better understand both the original experience and the theoretical positions he developed later. Perhaps more interestingly in light of Lund's claim regarding Harris 'the armchair linguist' is that in the passage mentioned Harris draws on that personal experience to evaluate the existing literature on the topic. The passage is worth quoting in full here:

> In a paper published in 1962 Ivić (p. 34) wrote: 'For decades the classic and most controversial question of dialectology has been: 'Do dialects ... actually exist?'. Many years before, Schuchardt—perhaps the most brilliant linguistic scholar of his day—had given an emphatically negative answer to that question. From my own experience of fieldwork in dialectology, the best evidence I can cite in support of Schuchardt's answer was given to me by an old man whom I asked whether

the patois of his Alpine village was the same as that of another locality a few miles distant. I here translate his reply, given in (what I at that time called) 'Valdôtain':

> Is it the same? I would not know how to answer you. Even in this village the younger people speak differently from my generation. And in the next valley perhaps they use words we don't use here. But, for all that, everyone understands everyone else well enough. Is that the same?

By turning my own question back on me, he had made me understand that the mistake lay in the question. What I was asking corresponded to nothing in his own linguistic experience which could provide a determinate answer. When theorists begin to ask unanswerable questions about language (or—which amounts to the same thing—questions which can be answered 'yes' or 'no' as you please) that is the surest indication that in their investigations linguistic myth has taken over from linguistic reality. (Harris, 1990a, p.18)

Lund appears to reject this anecdote on the grounds that Harris does not cite the paper in which the research was published. The incident concerning the villager did not appear in those papers published in the 1960s; is there something wrong with recounting an incident dating back to one's early days as a fieldworker many years later after one has finally understood what it meant? Harris undertook the fieldwork "in August 1966 […] at twenty-five localities in the Aosta valley" (Harris, 1969, p.133) and his published papers on the language of that region (what he then called the Valdôtain dialect) were written before he had integrated that experience into his theoretical understanding of language. Yet by his own account the encounter with the old man during his fieldwork did lead Harris to subsequent theoretical reflection and a new understanding of language.

Even though the issues discussed in Harris (1990a) did not arise in the papers of 1967 and 1969, there are other early papers—both in linguistics and in literature—in which one can find not only evidence of Roy Harris the competent but orthodox data-collecting linguist, but also, and more importantly, Roy Harris the data-questioning linguist, and Roy Harris the probing critical philosopher of language and linguistics. One can even find some of the original questions that would eventually lead to the development of integrational linguistics. As one example, in a 1967 review of *Latino "circa romançum" e "rustica romana lingua"*, a collection of 7-9th century texts, Harris comments:

> one is surprised to find that the discussion of scriptae is conducted without any reference to the complex problems of correspondence beteen written and spoken languages. The subject is touched upon only in the appendix, and there only in connection with phonetics. One would like to have seen in the preface a reminder of the variety of types of relation which may obtain between spoken and written discourse. For it is doubtful whether the beginner can make much of the notion of the development of a scripta at all, unless he is given some idea of the level or levels of abstraction involved. Without such guidance, he tends to be left with the impression that at one time (in some idealized Classical period) Latin was "written as it was spoken", and that gradually the spoken language changed while the written language remained static, or lagged far behind, until the post-Carolingian period when the new vernaculars were again "written as they were spoken". ... Thus the fact that there is any linguistic problem as regards how changes in a

spoken language may be expected to give rise to changes in a corresponding written language becomes obscured. It is of course true that at present general linguistics offers no satisfactory theoretical framework for the treatment of such problems, but this is no reason for ignoring their existence. Indeed, one might have hoped that precisely in such a field as this traditional philology would have been able to make some distinctive contribution to modern linguistic theory. (Harris, 1967a, p. 29)

When it does not simply make do with the (armchair) linguist's logic and intuitions, linguistic theory has been and remains largely dependent upon written records as its empirical basis, yet linguists even today assume that the oral and the written are related directly and unproblematically in some manner that is theoretically insignificant. Harris alone pursued the theoretical implications of this problem, and by doing so identified a crucial problem in linguistic methodology. Harris noted these problems precisely because he was not an 'armchair linguist' but one who already in 1967 had been deeply involved in the linguistic study of historical texts for more than a decade.

In a paper published a few years later Harris investigated word criteria in French, and in the process questioned both criteria proposed by earlier linguists and the universality of "word" as a unit of linguistic analysis. On "potential pause" as a criteria for identifying words, Harris wrote: "all it is is a misguided attempt to transfer into the analysis of speech the traditional 'word-divider' of writing, namely the space" (Harris 1972, p.121-122). In the conclusion they remarked "The 'something' about French which the investigation of word criteria shows up is the fact that French has no unit which corresponds exactly to the 'word' of Latin (or of English)" (Harris 1972, p. 133). Here we see not 'armchair linguistics' but the probing questions of a linguist intimately acquainted with the facts of spoken and written French (and Latin and English) drawing out the theoretical implications of that problem noted in the paper of 1967.

In one of Harris's last writings on Medieval French, a 1976 review of *L'expression de l'affectivité dans la poésie lyrique française du moyen âge (XIIe-XIIIe s.): étude sémantique et stylistique du réseau lexical 'joie'-'dolor'*, he noted the possibility of alternate interpretations:

> By means of a liberal treatment of other words as mere 'substitutes' for *joie* and *dolor*, it is possible to make the thesis look plausible. But then is the 'réseau lexical joie-dolor' anything more than a construct imposed upon the language of the trouvères by its investigator? (Harris, 1976, p. 94)

It was Harris's knowledge of the language of the troubadours—not a theory, integrationist or otherwise—that allowed him to see that the "linguistic facts" of a "reseau lexicale" are in fact a linguist's fiction. Far from a simple dissolution of linguistic facts conceived as eternal objects waiting for the linguist to observe, Harris recognized that this constructive activity was essential not only for understanding the limits of theory but for understanding language *tout court*. And this recognition arose not from the daydreams of an armchair linguist but as an unavoidable conclusion in the face of conflicting interpretations of apparently identical linguistic "facts" known to Harris and the linguists and literary scholars with whom he found himself in disagreement.

2. Whence the fundamental ideas of integrationism?

Lund next characterizes integrational linguistics as a set of ideas taken from others, something that he claims Harris himself acknowledges:

> According to Harris, the integrational school's fundamental ideas are already present to a certain extent in the thinking of John Firth, Bronislaw Manlinowski, Kenneth Pike and Edward Sapir (Harris 1998:10). (Lund 2012: 6)

This (apparently innocuous) statement reveals a problematic failure on the part of the author, Søren Lund, to come to grips with integrational linguistics. For Lund, integrational semiology is merely a continuation of what was already clear to other pragmatically-oriented linguistic thinkers before Harris. Lund believes that Harris takes from Saussure the conception of linguistics "as an essentially lay-oriented discipline" (Lund 2012: 6) as well as an anti-epistemological position, and from Wittgenstein the view "that (integrational) linguistic theory should be a kind of lay therapy" (Lund 2012: 7). It seems to us, in fact, that Lund envisages as an alternative to integrational linguistics, a linguistic theory that complements 'segregational' insights with 'integrational' ones. He even claims that if his "radical reading" is incorrect and "integrationism should be interpreted in a more charitable way" (Lund 2012: 29), then we are all already integrationists. However, what did Harris *actually* write about his predecessors and whether they qualify as proto-integrationists?

> Although there are significant strands of integrationist thinking in the linguistics of Sapir, Malinowski, Pike and Firth (Harris, 1998a), in none of these cases did this develop into anything more than a cautious modification of the prevailing segregationist programme. It always stopped short of calling in question whether the linguist is in a position to do what segregationists have claimed, on behalf of linguistics, to be able to do; namely, to identify by the application of objective criteria a determinate

> system of signs that constitutes 'the language' of a given community or a given individual. (Harris, 1998, p. 10)

On the following pages Harris continues by identifying six segregational assumptions coupled with their corresponding integrational counterproposals. But contrary to Lund's assertion, Harris does not identify integrationist ideas *avant la lettre*. For a fuller discussion of Harris's understanding of the relation between the fundamental ideas of integrationism and the ideas of Firth and others, we turn to an earlier paper (Harris 1987) in which the linguistics of Firth, Pike, Sapir and Malinowski are discussed.

In that paper Harris provided a brief note on Sapir's recognition of the social function of language:

> An interesting case is that of Sapir, who acknowledges that the normal function of language is to articulate many and varied patterns of social behaviour. Sapir's example is borrowing money. "If one says to me 'Lend me a dollar,' I may hand over the money without a word or I may give it with an accompanying 'Here it is' or I may say 'I haven't got it' or 'I'll give it to you tomorrow.' "Each of these responses," says Sapir, "is structurally equivalent, if one thinks of the larger behavior pattern" (Sapir 1933: 12). Yet although Sapir realized this, he does not seem to have realized its theoretical significance, or at least not bothered to analyse the theoretical implications. The integrationalist insight is glimpsed, but then not followed through. Sapir apparently fails to see that this kind of structural equivalence is not something outside language, but something without which what is said would be outside language - that is to say, would be meaningless. (Harris 1987: 135)

There is a world of difference between having a glimpse of something and pursuing the theoretical implications of that insight. "Recognizing a truth is not to be equated with realizing its theoretical implications" Harris would later write in regard to Firth (Harris, 1990, p.42). Malinowski similarly falls short of developing an integrationist position in spite of his remark regarding language as a "mode of action":

> It is not surprising that the clearest expression of an integrational perspective on language should have come from one of the leading figures in social anthropology of the interwar period, Malinowski. But Malinowski's most famous dictum, that language is "a mode of action, rather than a countersign of thought," when watered down into such statements as "the context of situation is indispensable for the understanding of the words" (Malinowski 1923: 307), or "the utterance has no meaning except in the context of situation" (Malinowski, loc. cit.) appears to reduce readily to truisms with which nobody would disagree. As interpreted by J. R. Firth, Malinowski's claim emerges in the sadly emasculated guise of recognizing an 'outer' layer of contextualization statements which the descriptive linguist is obligated to undertake in order to 'complete' the description of a language. It is like giving a final road-test to the already assembled car. Thus viewed, what Malinowski says is drained of its most radical theoretical content. (Harris, 1987: 135-136)

Harris then identifies the theoretical failures of Pike and Firth:

> In America, the attempt to integrate linguistics into the general study of communicative behaviour was pursued most systematically by Kenneth Pike, while in England a

> similar emphasis emerged in the work of Firth, for whom "the central concept of the whole of semantics..., is the context of situation. In that context are the human participant or participants, what they say, and what is going on" (Firth 1957: 27). In both Pike and Firth, however, one sees a further consequence of the compromise between the segregationalist and integrationalist positions. Although Firth uses the term integration, for him the analysis of that wider integration begins "when phonetician, grammarian and lexicographer have finished." In other words, Firth works from utterances 'outwards,' and not from the total context 'inwards.' Like Pike, he seems to have conceived of the nonverbal part of communicative behaviour essentially as language carried on by other means. This is evident even terminologically in the case of Pike, who introduced such units as the "behavioreme" (a term clearly modelled on phoneme and morpheme). Thus, in both cases, the approach eventually adopted envisaged an extension of the analysis of language systems to embrace a certain range of related social facts, rather than any rethinking of the basic assumptions underlying the postulation of language systems in the first place. (Harris 1987: 136)

In conclusion Harris articulates why integrationism is not a development on the basis of these eminent predecessors, but a rejection of the main principle upon which their science of linguistics rested, i.e. the autonomy of language as a system of signs:

> These cases are instructive because they enable us to pinpoint a deeper reason why segregationalism has dominated modern linguistics for so long. It is simply this: that even those linguists most sympathetic to an inte-

grationalist approach to language on the theoretical level were in teaching methodologically committed to segregationalist practices. There was a failure, in short, to come to terms with the fact that a thorough-going integrationalism requires us to recognize a principle which may be called the 'non-compartmentalization principle' (Harris 1981: 165). Whatever name we choose to give it, this is the principle that as human beings, whose humanity depends on social interaction, we do not inhabit a communicational space which Nature has already divided for us between language and the nonlinguistic. Or, to put it another way, language is not an autonomous mode of communication and languages are not autonomous systems of signs. (Harris 1987: 136)

Only on one occasion does Harris allude to another linguistic school espousing a 'non-segregational' theory, namely the Italian 'neolinguistic' school inspired by Benedetto Croce (Harris 1996: 7, fn 9). However, this does not mean for Harris that Croce, or any of the Neolinguists, would qualify as proto-integrationists.

Lund's characterizations of Harris and integrationism, as discussed in this section, are intimately related; an understanding of Harris that labels him an armchair linguist is one that also finds nothing new in his linguistics. According to Lund (and other critics), Harris is guilty of recycling ideas that were not only not his own, but which are relics of a theoretical past beyond which modern linguistics has progressed. Pace Lund, what we find is that the principles of integrationism arose not from a development of earlier theories—whether those of Saussure, Sapir, Malinowski, Pike or Firth—nor from the armchair linguist's native speaker intuitions, but from attention to *actual linguistic experience*. This, however, is not tantamount to claiming that integrational linguistics took shape in a historicodiscursive vacuum – obviously it did not. In describing his student days Harris himself wrote of the linguistic situation in which he and his fellow students found themselves and how that shaped their theorizing:

> As students of language and languages, we were taught a linguistic orthodoxy which manifestly conflicted with our own linguistic experience. The war was a time when innovations of all kinds abounded in spoken usage and could not be ignored. The conflict between what we were taught and what we could observe for ourselves was blatant and pervasive [...] Wartime English was clearly *not* the English described and exemplified in our school books [...] It was a time when familiar expressions abruptly and inexplicably acquired new and sometime contradictory meanings (*You've had it*.). [...] The upheavals of evacuation had long since taught us that speech went around with people: it was not mysteriously anchored to places. And sound laws were hard to reconcile with the inconsistencies of pronunciation that could be heard within the walls of a single wartime classroom. At no level did one ever feel convinced that the orthodox story actually made explanatory sense of one's own linguistic environment or the linguistic activities in which one was daily engaged. [...] Given the manifest disparity between our first-hand linguistic experience and what we were taught about language in school and at university, we were faced with an awkward choice. Some of us, not unreasonably, decided that the linguistic orthodoxy was antiquated rubbish [...] Others, more cautiously, decided that the experts must have got it right after all [...] and consequently wrote off the perceived disparity between linguistic orthodoxy and linguistic experience [...] Only a very small minority, of

which I was one, opted for neither of the aforementioned solutions, but treated the disparity itself as a major source of linguistic interest. [...] *Why isn't language as they say it is?* This, in retrospect, seems to me the most obvious, the most basic, the most inevitable question that was bound to emerge from the educational experience of my generation. (Harris 1997: 238-239).

As the above passage demonstrates, the principles of integrationism were developed upon the basis of attention to primary experiences of language rather than on the basis of an analysis of linguistic data that is a theory-laden abstraction from the moment it is recorded. It took years of experience followed by reflection upon that experience to arrive at the principle tenets of integrationism, but it is from that experience and Harris's reflection upon it that integrationism developed. In a letter to David Bade, Harris himself identified the original situation which eventually led to his realizing that the belief in languages as 'fixed codes' could not yield satisfactory answers to his questions arising from primary linguistic experience:

> The first time I began to have doubts about the concept 'a language' was on one occasion years ago during my period as a research student when I had to plough through at some speed a great number of medieval texts, manuscripts and anthologies of various provenances, looking for 'examples'. One evening I found myself reading a poem and realized, to my surprise, that although I could understand it well enough, I had no idea where it originated, what date it was, or what language it was written in, except that—I presumed—it must be some variety of Romance.
> At the time I explained this experience to myself as being due to the fact that my (imperfect) acquaintance

> with Old French, Old Provençal, Old Spanish, Catalan and various Italian dialects was sufficient to enable me unconsciously to construct a kind of hypothetical protolingua that approximated to whatever language the poet had been using. But later I came to realize that this 'explanation' was even more difficult to understand than the facts it was supposed to 'explain'. (Roy Harris, letter to David Bade, 18 February 2006)

Harris originally interpreted his experience—understanding a text without previously having encountered the language in which it was written—according to the prevailing psycholinguistic theories, attributing his understanding of the text to the unconcious construction of a hypothetical protolingua. Yet that original experience was a matter to which he returned and continued to question, developing from that experience—not from his original theoretical explanation of it—his critiques of his predecessors. Eventually Harris concluded that the Saussurean notion that 'there is no linguistic sign outside the context of its language' was wrong. The armchair linguist, like the linguist who takes his ideas from other theorists, never returns to contemplate the original experience but only attends to "data" that has been prepared according to theoretical dictates. In developing the principles of integrational linguistics Harris discarded existing theories and pursued the theoretical implications of what he would call 'first order' linguistic experience. We shall now turn our attention to the three integrational theses at which Harris eventually arrived and which Lund rejects.

3. Three integrational theses.
3.1. Thesis 1: On the integrational sign.

> The second axiom ... seems fairly controversial. It purports that the value of a sign is a property of the act

of the 'proficient integrator' rather than of the sign itself. (Lund 2012: 10).

Lund begins the section entitled "The inadequate character of the Integrational sign" with a serious misreading. Harris did not claim that the value of a sign is *a property of an act*: he wrote that "The value of a sign is a function of the integrational proficiency which its identification and interpretation presupposes" (Harris 1993: 321). Of this distinction Harris wrote "A proficiency is not an act. If it were, the world would be a quite different place. Proficiency is a potential" (email to the authors 26 October 2011). In integrationism, a sign is the product of creative and purposive activity and does not preexist that activity as something one finds, takes and interprets. The writer of Lund's paper must mean something by the marks which he makes on the page or those marks are not signs at all, and the first act that a potential reader of Lund's paper must perform is to identify those marks on paper as having been the product of Lund's (or someone's) sign making activity, i.e. *to make them signs again as a reader.* Without those two acts of sign making there is no sign, only ink on paper. In the case of Lund's paper, it is only when two signs have been made, one by the writer and one by the reader, that communication or miscommunication may take place. Perception reveals only a black and white object. It is an act of intelligence based upon past learning that identifies that object as (electronic) paper with (electronic) ink, and the ink as purposely applied in order to communicate; in that act of identification we make the ink-marks-on-paper a sign of a particular kind, namely an academic paper which we may or may not understand and to which we may or may not wish to respond. Further examination allows us to identify (identification being an act of the reader) the various ink marks as signs written in accordance with that social practice called 'Standard English'; what Lund meant by his signs is not so easy to identify and interpret. Our response to Lund may in fact be one more example of the failure of communication due to the *indeterminacy of linguistic signs*.

The issue of making a sign versus finding one is crucial in arguments about construing or understanding natural objects and events as signs, as well as misunderstanding any and all signs. Harris (1997: 49) noted that when Robinson Crusoe found a footprint it did not matter whether anyone intentionally made a footprint as a sign; all he found was a footprint. Crusoe himself made it into a sign, namely a sign that someone besides Crusoe must be on the island. In similar fashion the present authors found something in their email inboxes; we have both actively attributed to that something a significance, namely that Søren Lund is trying to communicate with us rather than identifying that email as spam. That attribution and all that has followed from it may be *mistaken attributions of significance*. We begin with Lund's remarks on the latter.

3.1.1. Mistakes

Lund argues against the integrationist understanding of signs by claiming that mistaken attributions of significance prove that the meaning of a sign is independent of anyone's attribution of meaning:

> In addition, I would take exception to Harris's idea that significance is constituted solely by attribution. It is true that we attribute significance to things, but sometimes we do so mistakenly. Given that mistaken attribution is possible, it follows that significance is not constituted by attribution. (Lund 2012: 16)

What 'follows' is not *that significance is not constituted by attribution* but precisely that the meaning of a sign is the product of an activity of the one attributing significance, for without that active sign-making there could be no mistaken signs. The activity of the sign maker as interpreter is just as important as the activity of the one who made the original sign with the intention of communicating something to someone. In integrationist theory, "signs are not prerequisites of communication, but its products" (Harris 2005: 110), and "there is no 'linguistic message itself'. Or rather, the "linguistic message itself" is an artifact of the theoretical perspective and the analytic methods adopted by linguists" (Harris 1997: 267). When Lund misunderstands Harris, what is demonstrated is that Lund has made Harris's language mean something that Harris did not mean, and this is something Lund did, not something which the ink on the paper tried to communicate to him. And if Lund wishes to understand what Harris wrote, no interrogation of the ink on paper in the books by Harris will clear up this mistake since the written sign did not write itself in order to mean something: Harris wrote something and one must ask Harris what he meant by what he wrote, for the problem (we do not say mistake) may be resolved by negotiation involving both persons in communication. The significance of the sign according to integrationist theory is always constituted by both the writer and the reader, the speaker and the hearer; we speak of miscommunication when one of the persons communicating believes that something went wrong. What follows a perception of misunderstanding (or in Lund's terminology, mistaken attribution) may be restatement, elaboration, discussion, negotiation, appeal to an authority (such as a dictionary), irritation and insult, a parting of ways, fighting, warfare, nuclear meltdown or some other disaster that makes further efforts at communication or other alternatives impossible. The stakes in mistaken communication can be extremely high; hence the insistence within integrationism on the fundamental importance of the lay person's perspective and on taking responsibility for one's language as speaker and hearer, writer and reader.

Lund assumes that signs have an 'inherent' significance: thus, one can attribute significance 'mistakenly', that is, make a sign mean something other than what it means all by itself apart from any person and independent of space and time. On what basis do we judge attribution of significance as 'mistaken' or not? Take the case of visual experience. Presumably one would judge such an experience as 'mistaken' or not on the basis of verbal evidence. Suppose a philosopher-turned-neuroscientist invents an illustrative story for his/her students (or readers) involving two hypothetical individuals, A and B, in which B, standing at the window in A's house, tells A: "There's a *rat* in your garden". *A* walks to the window himself, looks down into the garden and says "No, that's my *hamster*!". The scientist is likely to make the following claim at this point, namely that B has made a 'mistaken attribution', i.e. 'what B sees' and 'what he says he sees' do not match, and the proof of it is provided by B's statement concerning the animal in the garden. Yet, as the integrationist would point out, the communicational exchange in this anecdote is an exchange between two anonymous interactants. The anecdote tells us that B is in A's house, but it says nothing about whether A and B are old friends, or mere acquaintances, or perhaps perfect strangers? What is more, B may always refer to rodents as 'rats', but that is a bad habit of his which the scientist's illustrative story is likely to be silent about. What this example illustrates, we believe, is that the whole semiotic discourse of 'mistaken attribution' is the result of an abstraction – here of envisaging communication as an act (performed by an anonymous stand-in) of attaching the wrong linguistic label to a referent. Or let us imagine another (personalized) scenario: for Adrian Pablé to remain seated and pontificate about the 'proper' name of an insect while my wife is running around the house panic-stricken, telling me to 'kill *that bug* on the wall!' is either to fail completely to integrate the present communicational activity or to be deliberately cruel. In both cases described above, an appeal to 'reality' is of little help for the simple reason that what is at issue is not reality, but why someone said what he/she said in a particular situation (to a particular individual). The meaning of what that person said is whatever was meant, not what the dictionary (or encyclopedia) tells us it means. Interpreting what was said 'correctly' is a matter of integration, and the problem of whether or not what the hearer (reader) construes the speaker (writer) as having meant is 'the same' as what the speaker (writer) intended cannot be resolved by any recourse to the notion of 'codes' serving as a guarantor of mutual understanding.

Nor will an appeal to science solve the matter of attributing the right (inherent) names to objects or the proper significance to scientific terms if that was what was at issue, not even if it is the case that the interlocutors agree on the authority of science to interpret the universe and legislate names. Why? Because descriptions, explanations and the terminology in which these matters are discussed are all continuously debated, geographically differentiated and change over time. Lunds' semiology fails to take time into account, as it fails to address the multiple issues related to synonymy, i.e. are *mouse, ratón, khul'gan, siçan, Maus, ratolí, topo, sorcio, muis, hiiri, pelė*, etc. synonyms or do they differ in meaning, and in either case what does this mean? Science is in large part a history of contested attributions of significance to natural, indeterminate and non-existent objects like mouse, human error, missing links, light, life, race, *the* English language, intelligence, quarks, MERGE, cold fusion, the primitive mind, the real number of planets, phlogiston and memes of all sorts. If the history of science is any indication of the nature of the linguistic sign, then we must conclude that if the indeterminacy of a sign renders it incomprehensible, the history of science is nothing but a perpetual history of mistaken attributions and incomprehension.

Whether one calls it attribution of significance or sign-making, a sign misunderstood is precisely a making of the wrong sign from a given material, and the only one in a position to call a mistake a mistake is the person who meant what he or she said or the person who for whatever reason comes to believe that he or she has been mistaken. In order for someone not to be mistaken the sign need not do anything—how could it? Why would it? The *sign-maker* must make the right sign, and the right sign will be simply that sign which will lead him/her to do the one thing necessary (to quote a great Danish writer).

But what constitutes the right sign as opposed to the wrong sign? Lund writes of mistakes as though one can identify a mistake simply on the basis of the inherent meaning of the sign without any reference to the persons engaged in communication via signs. A look at the mathematical theory of error reveals the interesting (to the integrationist) identification of measurement error with necessary uncertainty and variation:

> Strictly speaking, we ought, in the expression of our general idea, to use the word "uncertainty" instead of "error." For we cannot at any time assert positively that our estimate or measure, though fallible, is not perfectly correct; and therefore it may happen that there is no "error" in the ordinary sense of the word. And, in like manner, when from the general or abstract idea we proceed to concrete numerical evaluations, we ought, instead of "error," to say "uncertain error"; including, among the uncertainties of value, the possible case that the uncertain error may = 0. (Airy 1861: 4)

Measurement *presupposes* the correct identification of the objects to be counted, the units of measure, and the validity of the purpose for measurement. With those matters assumed to be correct, the inevitable phenomena of error, variation or uncertainty—"no measurement can ever be exact" (Zebrowski, 1979: 22)—can be dealt with mathematically to the degree required by the results desired, for "The acceptable error in a measurement will depend on the reason the measurement is made" (Zebrowski 1979: 22). In contrast to measurement error, no mistake in identification or classification much less a confusion of purpose can be identified or rectified by any mathematical treatment because such mistakes can only be identified by reference to purpose and corrected on that basis. The only way to identify a mistaken attribution of significance in any particular case is through an appeal to the sign-maker, an appeal that Lund refuses to allow.

Rather than pursuing the matter of errors further, we recommend a reading of two other of Lund's fellow Danes— Jens Rasmussen (1990, and other papers) and Erik Hollnagel (especially Hollnagel 1983, Hollnagel and Amalberti 2001, and Hollnagel and Woods 2005)—not as integrationists *sans la lettre*, but as the best means for countering Lund's inadequate understanding of the phenomena of errors and mistakes. We turn instead to his argument regarding 'natural signs' where the issue at stake is whether nature is trying to tell us something or not.

3.1.2 Natural signs

> Signs are sometimes made, but sometimes – as in the case of medical symptoms and other natural signs, *pace* Umberto Eco – they are discovered. Harris is simply wrong when he likens all signs to language, in the sense of having to be constantly remade, on the penalty of dying. On the contrary, we need to distinguish between signs made and signs found. Falling air pressure will still be a sign of a developing storm, even if human beings lose all knowledge of meteorology and no longer possess barometers, etc. That is not to say that such signs are,

> using Harris's phrase, simply 'given' to us. Besides, there is a false dichotomy here between what is given and what is made. Signs not yet made still have to be discovered; they are not obvious. (Lund 2012: 16-17)

Lund's understanding of the significance of nature is as old as the Biblical narrative of creation:

> And God said, Let there be lights in the firmament of the heaven to divide the day from the night; and let them be for signs, and for seasons, and for days, and years. (Genesis 1:14)

The Gospel of Matthew provides a different situation, for in this passage every natural sign is attributed to something that "ye say" or that "ye can discern" (we will not argue that Jesus was an integrationist *avant la lettre* on the basis of this passage):

> The Pharisees also with the Sadducees came, and tempting desired him that he would shew them a sign from heaven. He answered and said unto them, when it is evening, ye say, it will be fair weather: for the sky is red. And in the morning, it will be foul weather to day: for the sky is red and lowering. O ye hypocrites, ye can discern the face of the sky; but can ye not discern the signs of the times? A wicked and adulterous generation seeketh after a sign; and there shall no sign be given unto it, but the sign of the prophet Jonas. And he left them, and departed. (Matthew 16:1-4)

According to Lund's doctrine of natural signs, red sky in the morning means foul weather, red sky in the evening means fair weather, clouds mean rain, high bodily temperature means illness, and smoke means fire whether or not the Sadducees say or discern anything and whether or not it actually does rain, etc. Nature speaks loud and clear everywhere and always, independently of all human knowledge and experience, and with no intention of communicating anything to anyone. Lund goes further than Jesus by insisting that the meaning of natural signs is not in any way determined by our living engagement with the world but may be read directly from the sign itself. Lund does not consider *recognition* to be a matter of human activity upon which signhood depends – and for this reason, when Harris writes of 'recognizing' signs, he accuses Harris of contradicting his own semiology:

> Furthermore, Harris writes: "I recognize and contextualize it [the tree] in a certain way in relation to certain activities", isn't that "recognizing its sign value"? But if that value is a matter of sheer making, thenn we are back at egocentrism: the only thing that the sign is *qua sign*, is what *I* make it to be. And what could that be other than a pure figment of my imagination, having nothing to do with the tree itself since the tree's spatial property is impertinent to the sign of that particular tree *as a sign*? Why does Harris even mention 'recognizing' when his recognition has nothing to do with his view of the sign... (Lund 2012: 16)

Integrationism acknowledges that it is the task of every human being to interpret objects and events as meaningful or not in our living engagement with the world. Natural objects and events may have no significance for us here and now and in such situations may be ignored; under other conditions we may indeed interpret similar objects and events as relevant and therefore significant. We may make a connection between smoke and fire (for instance) and thus interpret, understand or recognize smoke as signifying fire. What do recognition, interpretation and understanding all entail? Human activity, and in integrationial semiology 'recognising' a sign is 'making' a sign! It implies that I integrate my present visual experience with a past one, and thus identify something as something I have already encountered in the past (or as belonging to the same type). That identification and classification are creative acts involving memory. Similarly in the case of 'making' signs as opposed to 'discovering/finding' signs: again, 'discovering' a sign is an activity which requires integration, e.g. of experience. Smoke / red spots are *not signs of anything* without the concrete, experiencing subject. No red sky, no cloud, no tree, no barometer has ever tried to tell anyone anything about the coming of dawn or dusk, sunshine or rain. Rather we inform ourselves of our situation by making signs of the world around us, and we as well as our friends, neighbors, family members and weathermen sometimes try to tell others something about the coming weather based upon our understanding and interpretation of meteorological phenomena. To speak of "signs not yet made" which "still have to be discovered", as Lund (2012: 17) does, is to render meaningless the notion of "human creativity": *either we are signmakers or we are not* – there is no middle-way.

Lund's semiology of natural signs appears to imply that everything *may* be a sign—an object meaningful in itself apart from all experiencing subjects—but leaves open the possibility that nothing at all *has* to be a sign. If so, the status of any object as a sign or not is unknown prior to the human act of deciding, discovering, finding or recognizing that something is or is not a sign, and this prior to any interpretation of the meaning of the sign once it has been recognized to be a sign (i.e. made into a sign). For Lund, apparently, some natural objects and events may mean something but there is no need to assume that all must mean something.

If it is accepted that some objects are signs and others are not, we must ask for whom are natural signs signs? And we respond: to *me* – or else it is not a sign for *me*. For what could and why would any particular cloud, grain of sand, finger, hair, insect mean exactly the same thing objectively and always to everyone everywhere and what would be the point of understanding everything as a sign of something? In real life—we are assuming that attention to the facts of experience are relevant to rational inquiry—we only seek to identify natural objects as signs and interpret them according to how we understand their relation to our activities as, say, scientists or living beings. This holds true not only for natural signs as Lund would have them, but of the data of scientific enquiry in general. What Hollnagel and Woods (2005) wrote of data collection is equally true of signs:

> In the words of Sherlock Holmes, "it is a capital mistake to theorize before one has data". Yet it is an even greater mistake to believe that data can be collected without some kind of theory or concept. Data exist only in relation to a set of concepts or a classification scheme and are not just waiting to be picked up by a meandering scientist. (Hollnagel and Woods 2005: 50)

If it is then admitted that the significance of signs depends upon the theories, concepts, circumstances, experience and activities of particular persons, this means for Lund that we have plunged into 'egocentrism'. So in order to avoid solipsism and egocentrism Lund himself must assume that *all* natural objects and events are signs independently of an observer, and construct a theory of signs accordingly, for the status of any object or event qua sign must be an eternal and inherent property of that object or event and must not be dependent upon individuals, time and circumstance.

Clouds mean 'rain', and behold, it rains. Voilà! We have correctly interpreted the inherent meaning of the sign, and that independently of our experience. If it does not rain, however, we are left with a dilemma: either clouds are signs or they are not. If they are signs but it does not rain then either clouds are not signs of rain or the clouds were lying, for if clouds sometimes mean 'rain' and sometimes mean 'no rain' then we hardly have a natural sign whose meaning can ever be known for certain. And we must ask: can natural signs lie, and if so, do they? Perhaps clouds really only mean there is precipitation in the atmosphere and maybe it will rain but maybe not? Whence this indeterminacy of the significance of clouds?

Analogously, where Harris's example of the landmark (discussed by Lund) is concerned:

> There is, indeed, a certain ambiguity in the way Harris presents the case. It can be argued that the sign's value *qua* a sign depends on the fact (if fact it is), that the tree stands in a certain spatial relationship to the house, to the road leading to it, etc. If the tree in question does not exhibit that factual relationship, then Harris is just mistaken in making it into a sign having that indexical function. [...] In case Harris is willing to admit that its spatial features are what causes the tree to be of some use or value as a sign, then I think he is wrong in not recognizing the potentialities of things to be signs; [...] In fact, though, Harris keeps insisting that the value of the tree as a sign has no basis in the vact that the tree has a certain *spatial relationship*; this value has nothing to do with the thing itself, nor with what anybody thinks it has – pure egocentrism, as far as I can see. [...] The potential impact of the sign's value is wholly a matter of the integrational proficiency of the driver, with due reference to the biomechanical and macrosocial parameters that shape the proficiency in question. It is curious, however, that the impact of the sign's spatial relationship to the

> house does not constitute a part of Harris's contextualized 'program of activities'. The driver, it seems, operates independently of the fact that there is a spatial relationship from the tree to the house. Therefore, he is not constrained by the possible influences other than the responses to his *own* activities. (Lund 2012: 15-16)

Lund thus insists that the tree functions as an index for Harris (indicating that soon he has to turn in order to get into the right road leading to his house) precisely because it has the *potential* of functioning as such a sign: in other words, Harris 'finds' (or 'discovers') the sign rather than 'making' it. The indexical potential inherent in the tree qua sign has to do with its spatial relationship to Harris's home, according to Lund, i.e. the tree must already be meaningful (its inherent spatial property) in order for Harris to attribute to it that particular indexical value at all. It is certainly true that Harris is unlikely to make the tree which stands just outside his working-place an indexical sign signaling to him that soon he will have to turn left to get to his house. His choice will be constrained in so far as presumably he will pick a tree that stands 'in some proximity' to the road which leads to his house. The constraints that Harris *qua* sign-maker is subject to are the same as for anybody else, namely biomechanical, circumstantial and macrosocial ones (Harris 1998: 29). To reiterate a point made previously: in order to distinguish between objects that have 'sign potential' and those that don't, we need to be able to *rule out categorically* that certain objects can be 'potential signs' of something (otherwise the phrase 'potential sign' is meaningless). What the integrationist claims here is that only the sign-makers themselves make something into a sign (or not) – the so-called observer-independent 'external world', with its objects and their 'inherent properties', cannot limit human creativity.

3.1.3 When is nature a sign?

Is the air pressure falling or is it rising? Just ask the barometer! Alas, last time we looked, it said nothing about falling or rising, it just sat there doing nothing discernible. Do those clouds mean rain, or only 'Do not bother sun bathing today'? We need only ask the clouds to be more specific in their messages. And does that tree mean 'My house is 8.2377 meters away on the left', or merely 'My house is nearby'? Can it possibly mean either of these things to anyone but me, and that while I am living there (I have not lived there always)? We need only ask the tree to be more definite in its meaning - right? If only natural signs, historical events, barometers, human speakers and writers would be more direct and to the point in their efforts to communicate! The world of our experience makes it rather difficult to accept Lund's semiology of an inherent and unchanging meaning in the world around us.

Just as the meaning of natural objects such as clouds when taken to be signs is dependent upon personal circumstances and both past and future events (i.e. does it rain or not? Was I going to go sun bathing or water the garden?), the meaning of past events can often only be argued (by someone) in the future—and we use the word 'argued' advisably in any discussion of the meaning of history—and that only by someone intent on making the past a sign of something. The remark found on the Internet "Please *let this be a sign* of a return to rationality in the Republican party. This would have been unthinkable a year ago" is indicative of the fact that we expect human actions to signify something, that from them we can discern human thought, feeling, intentions and possible futures, but that what we can learn from observable actions is knowable only in part—if at all—after the passage of time and further actions by the same (or by different) actors. We attribute meaning to—and argue about the meaning of—human actions based upon subsequent events.

As in the case of a return to rationality in the Republican Party, the meaning of natural signs are often taken to refer to future possibilities, whether hoped for or feared. Ed. R. Meelhuysen of the Bible Research Company has identified "Twelve signs that we are very near the end of the world":

> I strongly believe that we are very close to the beginning of the time of Tribulation and the sequence of Events of Revelation culminating with the "end of the world" as we know it! Here are twelve of the most evident signs that are being fulfilled. Most were prophesied by the Bible or other prophetic writers.
> (http://www.bibleplus.org/12signs.htm accessed 13 July 2011)

If these twelve signs are indeed signs, then is it possible for any science of linguistics, semiology or history to determine their meanings for the future? It is of course possible to investigate and argue about the possible meanings of signs such as "The near saturation of the gospel to every language tribe and people", "financial collapse in countries around the world", and the growth of knowledge, spiritualism, moral decline, ecumenism, governmental regulations and any of the other signs listed by Mr Meelhuysen, *and this is just what Meelhuysen and his readers and respondents do*. Who is to say whether these people have mistakenly attributed or correctly divined the meaning of these "natural" signs? In every case of signs of the end of the world, the final, definite and determinate proof of their being signs of the end of the world will entail the end of any possible interpreter, scientific or not. These events certainly are signs because people have made them signs of something, yet the meaning of these signs cannot be simply read off from the events and social situations Meelhuysen mentions no matter what scientific methodology we might employ, for the existence of such things as "growth of knowledge" and "moral decline" are themselves debatable, and that apart from any question of their being signs. Exactly the same considerations apply to landmarks, but Lund disagrees:

> Actually, it could be argued that the integrationist sign presupposes that very sign concept, namely the Saussurean bi-planar sign, which Harris finds inadequate. In the long passage quoted earlier, he speaks of a 'tree' serving as a 'landmark'. In the immediate surroundings, phenomena are often exposed to signification when a spatial-temporal object becomes provided with content. However, the important thing is that no *integrated activities* are involved in calling the phenomenon in question a 'landmark' or 'tree'. In other words, Harris seems to presuppose a signhood which appears not to be integrational in nature because the act or process of making something (e.g. an object) into a sign is not *per se* an integrational act of contextual activities. It is simply the irony of Harris's own example (which he claims is supported by our own experience) that it demonstrates the very existence of a social convention, which he wants to refute (Lund 2012: 17)

To call an object "tree" or to refer to something as "moral decline", are certainly integrational acts or processes. Moreover, in the example of the tree Lund conflates 'perceiving a tree as a tree' and 'telling somebody else that this is a tree'. *Pace* Saussure, the two integrational processes require different kinds of integrations and orders of knowledge (see Harris 2009: 166). The indeterminacy of the sign, the second thesis that Lund rejects, arises directly from the recognition that the sign is necessarily the product of communicational activity rather than something existing external to and independently of the sign-maker.

3.2 Thesis 2. On the indeterminacy of the sign.

> First, the integrationist doctrine assumes that *all* signs are indeterminate. What is the epistemological value of this assumption? In order to make sense, the tenet needs to be expressed in linguistic signs; otherwise it would not be understandable. Furthermore, in accordance with the integrationist claim, these linguistic signs are indeterminate. Take now the proposition 'p': "All linguistic signs are indeterminate", and apply it to itself. The integrationists must apply signs in order to make sense; but at the same time the signs which they apply are, according to their own claim, characterized by indeterminacy. Consequently, *ex hypothesi*, the propositions of integrationism are themselves indeterminate and thereby incomprehensible. In short: integrationists presuppose what they, in fact, deny. (Lund 2012: 19)

There can be no numerical identity of spoken or written signs for the simple yet profound reason that no two signs—whether utterances or texts—can be made of exactly the same physical materials. That in itself precludes the identity of any two signs, even without considering the temporal dimension of signs and communication. If sameness or similarity is to be declared, that must be an analytical act of some human being. Saussure understood this and proposed the rather unconvincing notion of 'approximate sameness' in his discussion of the intersubjectivity of mental concepts:

> All the individuals linguistically linked in this manner will establish among themselves a kind of mean; all of

> them will produce - doubtless not exactly, but approximately - the same signs linked to the same concepts...
> (Saussure, CLG, § 2, p. 13)

Linguistic variation is the only experience and the only data available to the linguist, yet from that world of singularities the linguist (e.g. Saussure) produces determinate signs. How? Harris argues:

> A classic example is Daniel Jones's account of 'the phoneme'. In his *Outline of English Phonetics* (1962) he states as a basic fact: 'No two persons of the same nationality pronounce their own language exactly alike' (§55). He goes on to mention various reasons why this is so, including regional provenance, 'educated' and 'uneducated' speech, and 'individual peculiarities for which is it is difficult or impossible to account'. His introduction of 'the phoneme' is intended to explain how, in spite of these many differences, they all manage to speak 'the same language'.
>
> In order to do this, Jones sets up two related theoretical manoeuvres. One is to postulate what he calls a system of 'cardinal' sounds, defined by reference to extreme positions of the organs of speech. In ordinary conversation, no one actually uses the system of cardinal sounds, but every sound a speaker utters can be measured, according to Jones, by approximation to one of the cardinals. (He gives them numbers, even while admitting that there are an infinite number.) For Jones, what makes phonemics a 'science' is this ultimate possibility of physiological measurement.

The other theoretical manoeuvre is to introduce the concept of positional variant, or 'allophone'. Certain allophones, he claims, are regularly substituted for others in certain phonetic environments. (Why this should happen is not explained.)

Between them, the phoneme and its allophones explain how all the different pronunciations we hear are actually pronunciations of sounds of 'the same language', in spite of not sounding alike. Nevertheless, Jones sacrifices consistency when he admits that there are cases where it is difficult to prove whether or not a phonetic distinction is phonemic (e.g. §466). (Roy Harris, email to David Bade, 13 September 2011)

"The view that 'everyone speaks differently but somehow they all manage to communicate'" Harris wrote in that same email, "sums up succinctly the problem encountered in orthodox linguistics". For Lund, semantic indeterminacy entails incomprehensibility and therefore "the propositions of integrationism are themselves indetermined and thereby incomprehensible" (Lund 2012: 19). Linguistic indeterminacy, however, does not mean that what is said/written by someone must hence be 'unintelligible' to someone else. Signs are *indeterminate* because there will be as many integrational processes involved as there are hearers/readers. What these people take an utterance/sentence to mean may well be very similar. No integrationist has ever said that what integrationists say/write will not be subject to sign-identification and sign-making on the part of their hearers/readers—quite the contrary.

The indeterminacy of the sign is nowhere more obvious than in scientific debates regarding terminology and nomenclature. In a recent study of terminology related to libraries and information science, Morales López (2008) provides page after page of definitions for various terms. He discusses dozens of definitions of "Information science" and "informatics", devoting 45 pages to a discussion of the history of the use of these two terms, concluding that there was never any consensus on the meaning of either term. He quotes an authority on the subject who declared in 1971 that both terms referred not to any determinate science but to a combination of different disciplines and that the meanings of the terms "varied according to the authors consulted" (175). Thirty years later, he declares, there is still no agreement on the meaning of these terms, yet their use continues unabated and everyone seems to think they know what they are talking about!

It is clear from the definitions that Morales López quotes that when each of the authors used the terms "informatics" or "information science" they each meant what they each meant and not what the other authors meant. The definitions Morales López discusses are in many ways similar, it is just that each of the information scientists quoted keep arguing about what is different—and therefore wrong—with other definitions. And this is the essence of the integrational understanding of the indeterminacy of the sign: when *I* say/write something *I* mean by *my* words what *I* mean, and it is that meaning that *I* wish the hearer/reader to understand and not someone else's or a dictionary's meaning. This is not egocentrism; *I* have something to say and *I* want *you* to understand *me*. *I* make linguistic signs, gestures, *I* use objects in the vicinity, *I* enact something, *I* restate *my* point in other words, *I* define *my* terms and *I* argue with my interlocutor when *I* believe that he/she has misunderstood what *I* mean. And all of those activities I engage in not because I am enclosed within my solipsistic (or 'egocentric') world but because I am trying to communicate with someone else.

With his insistence upon the inherent and objective meaning of the sign, Lund effectively banishes all persons involved in any communicative act as irrelevant. He misunderstands and misrepresents the integrationist position when he claims that the thesis that *signs are made* implies "egocentrism because the only thing the sign is *qua* sign is what *I* make it to be" (Lund 2012: 16). Not so, for integrationism insists that the communicational relationships among persons is the only reason for the existence of signs at all.

Lund (2012: 20) stresses the importance of 'unambiguous' communication and 'utterances [which] are completely understood'. However, is there ever a moment in our lives when we have the impression to have understood (or have been understood) 'completely'? We don't think so, but this does not mean that successful communication cannot be attained. Likewise, integrationists do not presume to communicate 'unambiguously' with one another. In fact, Adrian Pablé has had to read some passages in Harris' writings again and again (and still struggles with understanding some of them). By reading passages one finds difficult on various occasions one gets the impression of understanding something 'better' or 'more clearly' – hardly, however, 'completely'. The belief that certain communication situations are examples of 'unambiguous' communication stems from extrapolating seemingly unambiguous words and phrases from the continuum of activities in which uttering these words is embedded.

In the realm of language, does yes always mean 'yes'? Does no always mean 'no'? Obviously they do not, since in the preceding sentences both are used as metalinguistic notations. Since words do not always mean the same thing and, as our own experience with mass media and political discourse notoriously proves minute by minute, they (i.e. we) mean now one thing, now their opposites or nothing at all, it cannot be that the meaning of the sign be associated solely with the sign, excluding both sign-maker and sign-interpreter as well as time and circumstance. Every speaker/reader of any language knows that, but

Harris alone pursued the theoretical implications of that indeterminacy further than any other linguist or philosopher ever had.

The linguistic sign does not have an eternal meaning that forces itself equally upon speaker/writer and hearer/reader, for if it did I could never mean anything except what the sign imposes (as Whorf claimed). Nor would misunderstanding and mistaken attribution be possible: misunderstanding is a common phenomenon precisely because the act of interpretation—construing something as a sign and making it mean something—is involved in every act of hearing/reading. The sign itself – could it actually exist 'in itself'– could not care less whether the result is communication or miscommunication. Clouds, words in dictionaries, and all signs considered independently of communicating beings never attempt to communicate anything; weathermen, lexicographers and Italian peasants do attempt to communicate, and integrational semiology makes this cloudy issue perfectly clear.

3.3. Thesis 3. On epistemological relativism

> It is evident that this radical contextualist approach can be turned against itself. If it is the case, as Harris states in the proposition, that 'there is no universal dimension of rightness that applies to all statements alike ....' this must, according to Harris's own contextualism *stricto sensu*, mean that he is stating a particular truth which is only valid in the situational context, or which only applies in the context in which it is stated. Is this really Harris's intention because that would boil down to only a trivial statement? On the contrary, what he means is, of course, a generalized truth that not only applies in the situational context. But this goes against Harris's own doctrine in which all truth (even his own just stated) are context bound. And again: 'there are no statements about

> the past which must be regarded as true ....' What kind of status does this proposition have? Is it only true relative to the situation? If so it is uninteresting and idiosyncratic. If not, he has committed a blatant self-contradiction according to his own premises. Here we see Harris, the logician, at his worst. It does not seem as if he knows about a Cretan who said that all Cretans were liars: how about the permissive relativist who said that all forms of life are valid – including those which absolutise themselves and condemn relativism? (Lund 2012: 28)

Lund claims that Harris, when talking *qua* integrationist (discussing communication or, as it were, history), states 'generalised truths' which are context-independent. But this is to misinterpret the very idea of sense-making as integrationists understand it. To be sure, an individual may claim that something is an 'absolute truth', and he/she may refuse to discuss it with others: however, this certainly goes against the Socratic principle, dear to Harris (2009b), that everything needs to be subjected to critical scrutiny, including one's own beliefs. Every linguistic statement, in fact, is *sponsored*: for knowledge to exist there needs to be a *knower*, whose knowledge is the result of a context-bound integrational activity. 'What I believe/ know to be true' does therefore not have an atemporal status: rather my knowledge/belief is always contextualized and subjected to my integrational proficiency by those who stimulate my thoughts, whether in speech or writing. It is thus always possible for someone to disagree with what integrationists say or write: this in turn should not be taken as a warranty for absolute freedom of interpretation, the latter not being a corollary of freedom of speech (Harris 2009b: 115). Hence, neither is 'integration', which constitutes the bulwark of a Harrisean semiology, exempt from the biomechanical, macrosocial and circumstantial constraints on communication (and self-communication). Harris himself must have subjected the axioms of integrational semiology to critical scrutiny innumerable times (and still does), as any responsible language-maker (and language-master) ought to. This does not 'relativize' Harris's conviction that integrational linguistics constitutes the right (and perhaps only possible?) way of thinking about language and communication. But that conviction is not context-independent: it is 'made' every time Harris sits down 'in his armchair' and thinks about integrationism. Harris is not an absolutist – he is an intellectual waiting to be challenged by people asking intelligent questions about integrational semiology, able to prove his theory wrong – and hence his question at the end of the *Introduction to Integrational Linguistics*: "Does the orthodox position in turn provide a basis on which to subject the assumptions of integrationism to critical scrutiny?" (Harris 1998: 150). It seems that those who have tried so far have failed to convince him. It is likely that Lund's critique will not impress him either.

It is important to underline that Harris is not attempting to silence everyone else in linguistics; he is not desperate to convert unrepenting segregationists into integrationists, either. In fact, the present authors do not know of any case in which Harris pushed a non-integrationist to embrace integrationism – on the contrary: unlike many other founders of linguistic schools, Harris never was interested in recruiting followers to increase his integrational troops. Harris waits for people to approach him, as the present authors did. Integrationism is not something you embrace because it offers interesting prospective academic careers, or because it can be applied to so many domains of linguistics, or because it allows you to fully concentrate on data-collection and not bother about theory: one has to make integrationism one's own and take responsibility for that choice.

Charges of relativism and poor logic simply miss the whole point of what Harris is arguing about with his focus upon the 'lay speaker'. Returning to the encounter with the peasant in the Italian Alpine village that Lund dismissed at the beginning of his article: we suggest that what Harris realized as a consequence of this encounter was that there is no socially shared knowledge (made visible by being communicated) which supposedly transpires when dialectologists explore lay people's perceptions of varieties of language. Harris eventually realized, as he would later elaborate in his book *After Epistemology* (Harris 2009), that knowledge and beliefs never exist in any determinate (underlyingly given) state: being confronted with that question in that particular situation, the informant took Harris' question seriously by giving an honest answer: besides the fact that dialectal 'sameness' is not just a matter of geographical variation (but also a generational concern), more importantly, 'sameness' is not an issue as far as understanding (as part of first-order communication) goes. 'Sameness' and 'non-sameness' might be an issue in other communicational situations, such as when the natives of one locality, when amongst themselves, make fun of the speech of people from another locality. It might well be that jocular remarks about 'words they use in the next valley that we don't use here' were part of the old man's linguistic experience, but he may have felt that this was not what the dialectologist interviewing him (i.e. Harris) wanted to hear. At the level of communication, at any rate, the researcher's question did not seem to point to any real concern for the informant. What Harris must have realized at the time, therefore, was that linguistic inquiry *had to be* 'lay-oriented' in the sense that linguistic knowledge (including dialect perception) is not collective, i.e. existing as something extraneous which the individual has access to in virtue of being a member of a particular collectivity. Questions about language are highly personal, i.e. they should be asked – not to a *representative* of a group – but to a *person*, who has his/her own (i.e. unique) linguistic-communicational biography. Moreover, he may have realized that 'sameness' is not a semantically determinate concept, and therefore unsuitable for the purposes of a scientific metalinguistics.

If Lund wants to charge Harris with clinging to a form of *subjective relativism*, that is fine. What is important to understand, however, is that adopting a Harrisean stance does not lead to a solipsistic view of the individual: it is our responsibility as social beings to communicate with other individuals. Without language there is no hope for the individual to progress, advance his/her knowledge, understand his/her rights and responsibilities – we are social beings, and language is a social ability: we do not possess language in the first place to talk to ourselves, but to talk to our fellow-beings. It is correct that in *The Linguistics of History* (Harris 2004) Harris objects to the idea of linguistic absolutism in the sense that there are no linguistic statements (about the past) which are 'absolutely true'. But as he goes on to say:

> ...it does not follow from this that the truth is whatever we declare it to be. Playing off rigid absolutism against please-yourself relativism is the last thing that will help us make sense of history. (Harris 2004: 221)

Precisely because signs are *radically indeterminate* we are called to use language responsibly, which requires us to understand that our experiences are nobody else's experiences (and thus *they are relative*); but it does not follow from this that our experiences, being unique, are absolute (in the sense that they cannot, and should not, be subjected to further reflection, discussion, and possibly modification, rectification, etc.).

4. Concluding remarks

If we examine the three integrational theses in light of an informed view of Harris's chairs and predecessors, we can see both how and why Harris broke with all of his predecessors and arrived at the three theses that Lund rejects. All three theses are unacceptable for Lund because in Lund's semiology, no human beings ever mean anything—only sound waves, ink and other natural objects do.

The attraction of integrational linguistics for the authors of this article is precisely that it is the only linguistics, the only philosophy of language, the only semiology that we know of that had its origin in and has continued to develop on the basis of attention to the experience of the language-maker. *Signs are made to mean, not found ready-made*; language exists only because people want to communicate with someone. The origin of language is therefore not in the discovery of some objective meaning inherent in some arbitrary thing, but in making signs in order to communicate with others. That *signs are indeterminate* is a necessary consequence of understanding signs as the result of creative communicative activity. Every other linguistic theory that we know of begins with an abstraction and disregards all linguistic experience that has not been previously theoretically constructed. Among the many linguistic experiences that Harris has attended to are orthographic variations in manuscripts, public debates about brand names of toothpaste, public debates about good and bad English, terminological debates in the scientific literature, debates about the meaning of art, courtroom debates, historical debates, philosophical debates, linguistic debates, and the villager who claimed to be able to communicate with the inhabitants of his neighbour village despite all the linguistic variation that characterized his region. In all these cases and debates Harris has shown that *what is signified is what the participants construe as having been signified*. Precisely as a result of that orientation towards the world of our actual experience Harris has developed a linguistics appropriate for a world of facts that are debated because their existence is in fact debatable, a world not at all like a dictionary, nor like one in line with a Lundian semiology in which everything comes already made and provided with a definition that has nothing whatsoever to do with time and circumstance, and much less with you and me.

References

Airy, George Biddell. (1861). *On the Algebraical and Numerical Theory of Errors of Observations and the Combination of Observations.* Cambridge and London: Macmillan and Co.

Harris, Roy. (1966). "Gallo-Romance third declension plurals" *Revue de linguistique romane* v.30 nr.117-118, p.58-70.

Harris, Roy. (1967). "Piedmontese influence on Valdôtain syntax" *Revue de linguistique romane* v.31 nr.121-122 p.180-189.

Harris, Roy. (1967a). Review of D'A.S. Avalle, *Latino 'circum romançum' e 'rustica romana lingua'*. *Medium Aevum* v.36 nr.1 p.52-54.

Harris, Roy. (1968). "La structure des paradigmes en latin vulgaire" In: *Actas del XI Congreso Internacional de Lingüistica y Filologia Romanicas* (Madrid, *Revista de Filología Española*, Anejo LXXXVI), v.1, p. 391-398.

Harris, Roy. (1968a). "Notes on a problem of Franco-Provençal morphology" Zeitschrift für romanische Philologie v.84 nr.5-6 p.572-581.

Harris, Roy. (1969). "Pronominal postposition in Valdôtain" *Revue de linguistique romane* v.33 nr.129-130 p.133-143.

Harris, Roy. (1970). "The Strasburg Oaths: a problem of orthographic interpretation" *Revue de linguistique romane* v.34 nr.135-136 p.403-406.

Harris, Roy. (1972). "Words and word criteria in French" In: *History and Structure of French: Essays in Honour of Professor T.B.W. Reid*, ed. by F.J. Barnett, et al., (Oxford: Blackwell) p.117-133.

Harris, Roy. (1976). Review of G. Lavis, *L'expression de l'affectivité dans la poésie lyrique française du moyen âge (XIIe-XIIIe s.): étude sémantique et stylistique du réseau lexical 'joie'-'dolor'. Medium Aevum* v.45 nr.1 p.114-117.

Harris, Roy. (1987). "Language as social interaction: Integrationalism versus segregationalism" *Language Sciences* v. 9, nr 2, p. 131-143.

Harris, Roy. (1990). "Redefining linguistics" In: *Redefining Linguistics*, edited by Hayley G. Davis and Talbot J. Taylor. (London: Routledge), p. 18-52.

Harris, Roy. (1990a). "The dialect myth" In: *Development and Diversity: Language Variation Across Time and Space: a Festschrift for Charles-James N. Bailey* / edited by Jerold A. Edmondson, Crawford Feagin and Peter Mühlhäusler. (Dallas : Summer Institute of linguistics ; Arlington : Univ. of Texas. Summer Institute of Linguistics publications in linguistics, 93). pp. 3-19.

Harris, Roy. (1993). "Integrational linguistics" *Actes du XVe congrès international des linguistes*, ed. by A. Crochetière, J.-C. Boulanger, C. Ouellon, pp.321-323. Ste-Foy: Presses de l'Université Laval.

Harris, Roy. (1996). *Signs, Language and Communication*. London and New York: Routledge.

Harris, Roy. (1997). "From an integrational point of view" In: *Linguistics Inside Out: Roy Harris and His Critics*, edited by George Wolf and Nigel Love, p.229-310. Amsterdam: John Benjamins.

Harris, Roy. (1998). *Introduction to Integrational Linguistics*. Oxford: Pergamon.
Harris, Roy. (2004). *The Linguistics of History*. Edinburgh: Edinburgh University Press.
Harris, Roy. (2005). *The Semantics of Science*. London: Continuum.
Harris, Roy. (2009). *After Epistemology*. Gamlingay: Bright Pen.
Harris, Roy. (2009b). "Freedom of speech and philosophy of education". *British Journal of Educational Studies* v. 57 nr.2, p. 111-126.
Harris, Roy; Love, Nigel (1974). "A note on French nasal vowels" *Linguistics* nr.126 p.63-68.
Hollnagel, Erik. (1983). Human error: position paper for NATO Conference on Human Error, August 1983, Bellagio, Italy. Available on the author's website (viewed 11 October 2011): http://sites.google.com/site/erikhollnagel2/variouspapersandwritings
Hollnagel, Erik; Amalberti, Rene. (2001). The Emperor's new clothes, or, Whatever happened to "human error"? HESSD 2001 keynote address. Available on the author's website (viewed 11 October 2011): http://sites.google.com/site/erikhollnagel2/variouspapersandwritings
Hollnagel, Erik; Woods, David D. (2005). *Joint Cognitive Systems: Foundations of Cognitive Systems Engineering*. Boca Raton, Florida: CRC PRess.
Morales López, Valentino. (2008). *La Bibliotecología y Estudios de la Información: Análisis Histórico-conceptual*. México: El Colegio de México.
Rasmussen, Jens. (1990). "The role of error in organizing behavior" *Ergonomics*, v.33 p.1185-1199.
Saussure, Ferdinand De. 1983. *Course in General Linguistics*.

Translated into English by Roy Harris. Chicago and La Salle: Open Court Classics.

Zebrowski, Ernest. (1978). *Fundamentals of Physical Measurement*. North Scituate : Duxbury.

III

Language and Historiography[1]

Like many linguists, C. Behan McCullagh read Roy Harris and found nothing of interest, felt no challenge, and apparently came through the experience unchanged and unscathed. He offers the readers of his review of *The Linguistics of History* exactly the same story about the product of the historians efforts which he has been repeating for twenty years: the historian's history is a belief, arrived at solely on the rational basis of its explanatory power, with no personal, political or social factors involved.

> We believe descriptions of evidence to be true if the hypothesis that they are true best explains certain perceptual experiences, which we will then call perceptions of evidence. But if our explanations, even of perceptual ex-

---

[1] This response to McCullagh's review of *The Linguistics of History* in the journal *History and Theory* was written in 2005 for that journal but never submitted nor published elsewhere.

> periences, are fallible ... we cannot say for certain that they are true. ... I suggest that we would think them true if ... they remained the best explanation of our perception. ... Since we do not know, and for that matter never will know, such an ideal explanation, we judge explanations probably true when there is so much evidence in support of them that it seems reasonable to suppose that they would be part of an ideal explanation ... (McCullagh, p. 453-454)

But then, McCullagh claims, in order to act "in our own and other's interests" we decide what we shall (want?) to believe:

> In order to act in the world, in our own and other's interests, we must decide what the world is like, or to put it another way, which descriptions of the world to believe. ... When evidential reasons do not prove the truth of a belief beyond all possibility of error, pragmatic reasons can give us a good reason for believing it true nevertheless. (ibid., p. 454)

So historical beliefs are in fact personal and political through and through. Historians living under oppressive regimes are ever confronted with strong pragmatic reasons for believing whatever the state or the theocracy likes them to believe. In the absence of any "evidential reasons" as well in the their overabundance, historians, like religious fanatics, so often seem to prefer pragmatic reasons when justifying their beliefs. It comes as no small surprise then to find McCullagh criticising Harris for his "integrationist theory of truth" which McCullagh describes in the following words:

> If you observe the ways historians defend their accounts of the past, you will notice that they take some state-

> ments to be correct descriptions of what someone did or thought, and build on those. The statements they accept as true are statements that society generally agrees to be true. "Once a society has accepted the historification of a certain corpus of beliefs or assumptions about its past," writes Harris, "history has already been made" (201). ... When historians call their descriptions of the past "true," Harris observes that they want you to know that they have derived them by a process of integration from accepted beliefs about what happened in the past, and what people said and thought about past events, according to normal historical practice. To understand the truth of history, therefore, Harris says we should study very carefully "the mechanisms of historification," the process by which historians arrive at new historical beliefs (223-226). (ibid., p. 451).

A few paragraphs later McCullagh writes

> Having decided that descriptions of the world can tell us nothing about it he never takes their justificatory function seriously. He assumes their arguments have no real epistemic significance whatever. He thinks they are just moves historians make to extend their beliefs about what they regard as historical. (ibid., p. 453)

McCullagh criticises Harris for not considering "the logical structure of historical justifications" (p. 453) and states that Harris' "theory of truth leaves history open to manipulation by propaganda" (p. 442), a problem against which his own "beliefs" are apparently sufficient safeguards. Since the beliefs of McCullagh's historians are "justified" by evidence which can never be "beyond all possibility of error" he resorts to pragmatic reasons for believing "which descriptions of the world to believe." Are such beliefs not equally susceptible to propaganda?

Throughout McCullagh's review are significant misreadings, misinterpretations and misrepresentations. These are rather common and expected responses to Harris' writings, for Harris is, according to his own understanding as much as in the understandings of most of his readers, exposing and arguing against a myth. The very nature of that myth makes it difficult for those enthralled to this particular understanding of language to consider language from any other perspective. For Harris, the "language myth" underwrites the entire history of western ideas about language, and the evidences for it are nowhere more clearly evident than in McCullagh's review: if their were any measure of semantic determinism, none of McCullagh's or anyone else's misreadings and misunderstandings would be possible, not even in theory.

For many of Harris' readers, however, Harris has created "the language myth" himself, and it exists only in his mind and perhaps in the minds of his students and admirers. (See for example Joseph (1997)). The issue is, of course, both historical and semantic: is there a language myth and if there is, what is it and who invented it, Aristotle or Harris? For purely pragmatic reasons (e.g. academic politics and job security), most readers of Harris believe that the myth is a myth invented by Harris, not a justifiable historical fact. For Harris, on the other hand, I suppose that the "Language Myth" is an hypothesis to be investigated and argued, a means of understanding the perennial philosophical and political problems that beset any discussions of language. It is an orientation of thought, a way of speaking or writing about how we think about language, not a "thing" whose ontological status can be investigated in an abstract world of objective facts and disinterested persons without personal, social and political commitments. While I cannot speak for Harris, this seems to me to be an arguable statement of his position, which Harris and others are welcome to dispute.

My reason for writing is not to argue for or against McCullagh's views on writing or believing history, on his philosophy or politics of historiography. Rather as a reader and writer of histories, I found *The Linguistics of History* fascinating, challenging and changing me. I am well aware that Harris probably has far more critics than admirer's among linguists and philosophers, but I am not alone in finding his work of extraordinary value. I regret that I did not have the benefit of reading *The Linguistics of History* before publishing my own studies of the divergent historiographical traditions concerning the Mongol invasion of Java, and his book has been of immense value to me as I study Ramon Llull's political writings. Since McCullagh has given the readers of *History and Theory* no reason to pursue the study of Harris' extensive writings—quite the contrary—I would like to offer a counterpoint to his review.

Let me begin with some remarks by a linguist who has also found Harris' work stimulating, Deborah Cameron:

> One of the most important things I learned from Roy Harris was to read the texts of western linguistics as texts; to locate them in an intellectual tradition with a history, to pay attention to their rhetorical properties, to notice their discursive and ideological preconceptions. This is not to propound a postmodernist thesis that there is nothing "outside the text". Rather it is a corrective to the still-common idea that certain texts—scientific writings for example—can be read simply and straightforwardly for their content, treated as if they were not in any significant way historical, rhetorical or ideological productions. I find it more enlightening to assume that whatever kind of discourse one is dealing with, there is

something to be learned by considering not only what is said, but also how it is said. (Cameron 1997, p. 7)

There is nothing especially new about reading texts—historical documents or histori(ographi)cal writing—with a focus on the language itself, how it is written as much as what is written. The difference between Harris on history and other scholars who have focused on documents and historiography as texts, is the radically different perspectives on language which Harris has developed since the publication of his first book *Synonymy and Linguistic Analysis* in 1973. Five characteristic assumptions distinguishing his understanding of language from other theories, previous and current, are given in Harris (1990):

> An integrationalist redefinition of linguistics can dispense with at least the following theoretical assumptions: (i) that the linguistic sign is arbitrary; (ii) that the linguistic sign is linear; (iii) that words have meanings; (iv) that grammar has rules; and (v) that there are languages. (p. 45)

Harris' second book, *The Language Makers* (1980), focuses on a single point distinguishing Harris' integrational approach from all other philosophies of language: languages are made by people, they are not independently existing, autonomous biological (psychological, neurological) entities located somewhere in the brain. People mean something when they speak and write (sign, gesture, act in response to requests). Given this presupposition, history as an oral or written linguistic product of human cultural activity is necessarily and inextricably subject to all the limitations of language as a social activity.

One consequence of insisting that language is made by people and not some preformed, independently existing context free biological toolkit, is that texts and utterances do not "have" any meanings: people mean this or that and it is up to the hearer/reader to try to understand what the person meant—not what the text meant—and hence the radical indeterminacy of meaning. McCullagh completely distorts this point in his first paragraph:

> the meaning of a sentence is created anew every time the sentence is used, and depends upon many features of the particular context in which it is uttered or written. (McCullagh, p. 441)

For Harris and other integrationists sentences are not "used" nor are they uttered or written in any contexts: "sentences" are metalinguistic products of one kind of analysis of the linguistic products of a specific communicational event. There are no linguistic objects inserted into contexts, as though texts and contexts are independent.

> It is no part of the integrational sign's nature to stand in a correlational relationship with things which exist apart from it. The sign is created within a communicational context and is uniquely relevant to that context. It integrates, it does not correlate with. (Wolf, 1999, p. 27)

> In the integrational picture, there is not something called "language" and something called "reality" which need to stand in a correlative relationship. Rather, as individuals we live by integrating our world, and we do so by making signs in the contexts we actually are in. This is not to argue that we do or should live in nothing but an un-self-conscious present moment, unaware of past or future. It is merely to say that whatever the past, our science or our language has been, or will be, can only be established via the integration of a present moment, and can

only be operative when integrated into the here and now.
(Wolf, 1999, p.42-43)

Because every linguistic act is a singularity, language is always a new creative act, not the iteration of previously given linguistic material recycled from a storage bin in the mind.

This is not at all tantamount to saying that we can make a text mean whatever we want it to mean (we can, of course, but we will probably not be understood) but is simply to acknowledge that the facts as well as the interpretation of the *res gestae* are always contestable and usually contested. We do indeed make a text mean whatever it means to us, but we recognize (at least most of us) that an honest reading strives to determine the author's meaning. In *The Linguistics of History* Harris distinguishes between *res gestae* (what really happened), *historiae* (what historians say—or believe—really happened) and *opinio* (popular beliefs about what really happened). The historian who seeks evidences, proofs, documentation, has only *opinio* on which to draw, since the writings of eyewitnesses and other and earlier historians are not themselves *res gestae*, and as sources, the opinions of historians are not necessarily more valid than the testimonies of contemporaries and witnesses, even though we may judge or believe them to be. Unfortunately *res gestae* cannot be read as texts and the texts about the *res gestae* are texts and must be read as such and not as *res gestae*. Apart from any considerations of lies, fakes and frauds, the number of disagreements as to what happened in, say, Paris in May 1968, or Florida in November 2004 is probably equal to the number of persons involved. (Although I was alive during both of these events, I was not present in either case, my memory of what I saw on the television and read in the newspapers is hazy and probably conflicts with your memories, and therefore I (we?) can only rely on ... whose *opinio* and whose *historiae*?) That matters may sometimes seem more clearcut in the more distant past is primarily due to the lack of witnesses, viewpoints and interpretations, that is, the paucity or absence of any diversity of contemporary *opinio* and subsequent *historiae*. Wolf again:

> Both the past and the future are creations of the present. Their entire reality is dependent on their present construction. This is not to deny them reality. It is to endow them with reality. Otherwise, as Saussure suggested, the past would be as may be, we having forgotten it, and the future likewise, we not having lived it yet. The past and the future are modes of our present; they are part of the way we integrate things through signs. In order to 'emerge from' the past and to 'get to' the future, we integrate our world; we move on, not utterly passively, but through signs. (Wolf, 1999, p.28)

What happened, happened, whether we know about it or not (cf. the tree falling in the forest) and as historical fact "what happened" is entirely a matter of the past. What we know and how we express that linguistically are matters of the human activities of memory and telling or writing histories and thus entirely matters of the present.

For Harris, the possibility of interpreting any form of linguistic communication does not rest on the existence of shared mental codes (grammars and vocabularies) but on the world of earthly, human experience. But that world in which we all live and breathe, where the sun shines and grass grows or dies, where rain, wind, neighbor children and foreign armies assault us regularly, is known and experienced uniquely by each person, and therefore there can be no identity of meaning in language. Nevertheless, when someone says "The police are at the door" we can respond appropriately, since it really does not matter what exactly the speaker meant; what matters is whether the hearer can respond appropriately and in time. Unlike other theories of language, the role of the reader or hearer is central to integrational linguistics, and thus interpretation has as important a place as it does in historical research.

McCullagh's discussions of dictionaries, metaphor, irony and literal meaning reveal a total lack of awareness of the extraordinary diversity of opinions on these matters, not only within linguistics, but in information science, philosophy and literary theory as well. Literal meaning, Searle claimed, "is always relative to a set of contextual assumptions" (Searle, 1979, p. 120) and for many historical texts those contexts have to be reconstructed from hopelessly inadequate materials. The role of interpretation and the extent of indeterminacy and untranslatability, not to mention cultural and contextual resonance in the translation of any text are matters which McCullagh dismisses with an appeal to the "obvious":

> often it is possible to translate directly from one language into another, especially when the words refer to kinds of things and events that are common to both communities. (McCullagh, p. 449)

We would all probably agree that there are things and events common to both Americans and Australians, yet if we should attempt to list and describe those things and events, I suspect that the commonality would rapidly vanish for all things and events other than those which we mutually agreed were too trivial to quibble about. McCullagh's attitude towards problems of culture, register, politics and language in translation suggests that he relies on translations and has not attempted to work with documents arising beyond his native linguistic environment, while his bibliography is that of a monolingual reader of English. Even so, the problem is rooted much deeper. In an essay on Searle, Love argued that

> if all facts depend on language for their statement, then there is a sense in which all facts are institutional. This is not to deny that there is a state of affairs regarding the spatial relations between the earth and the sun, which is what it is irrespective of the existence of any institutions. But there is no saying what that state of affairs is (indeed no possibility of representing it to ourselves as a state of affairs at all) except via the medium of language. (Love, 1999, p.23)

Similarly in an essay on Austin, Love noted

> A language cannot be a nomenclature, for Austin any more than for the integrationalist. Words are not labels attached to, or names standing for, the components of a reality whose analysis into those components is manifest *in rerum natura*. We use language to paint a picture of the world, not to take its photograph: language does not have the kind of antecedently given capacity to reflect the true nature of things that we might ascribe to a camera. (Love, 1997, p. 64)

For McCullagh, as for many others, the primacy of literal meaning and the rules of the language provide a stability that guarantees the unproblematic production and interpretation of meanings to accompany each speech act. The world is given, language is given, and these need only be properly matched. For the integrationist, language is always problematic, there is no stability nor any guarantees: mutual trust among speakers is as good as we can achieve. Meaning is radically indeterminate in every speech act, not just in metaphor and translation.

For those unfamiliar with Harris' previously published writings, it should be noted that he is an award winning translator, and a large part of his editorial, translation and scholarly efforts have been focused on the history of linguistics: editing manuscript notebooks of Saussure, translating Saussure, the history of writing, and the history of linguistic ideas and philosophy of language from Aristotle to the latest work on the (non) implications of theories of distributed cognition for linguistic theory. Harris is not a linguist presumptously telling historians how to do/write history, nor is he, like McCullagh, a historian uncritically believing various received notions about language as though they are self-evident truths. Harris is a practicing historian, as well as a philosopher and a linguist, while McCullagh hits only one out of three.

Another significantly different characteristic of integrational linguistics is the role of lay understandings of language, and this has its exact counterpart in Harris' discussion of *opinio* in the making of history. Hutton suggested that Harris' remark that the "'language-user already has the only concept of a language worth having' ... implies that there is no such thing as a language expert. It seems there is a choice for the linguist: to shelter behind the technical discipline, or to participate in debates about language on the same level as the native speaker" (Hutton, 1997, p.53). Putting lay understandings of language at center stage is one of the most controversial aspects of integrational linguistics. It is therefore unsurprising to find McCullagh scoffing at Harris' corresponding move in *The Linguistics of History* to put *opinio* on a par with *historiae*, and even to suggest that Shakespeare was arguably the most important historian of his time.

The discussion of *opinio* was, for this writer, one of the most illuminating aspects of the book. My own interest during the past decade has focused on the vastly different historiographical traditions concerning the Mongols of the 13th century: official dynastic histories of China, chronicles, court poetry and romances of medieval Java, the brief and garbled accounts of the Javanese campaign in the Arab and Persian historical writings of the 14th century, and Ramon Llull's numerous references to the Mongols during the late 13th and early 14th centuries. In all of these there is nothing but *opinio* and conflicting *opinio* at that, yet these are the only sources for some episodes such as the Mongol expedition to Java. The choice of what sources to prefer, which variant to accept and which to reject, are all and always have been politically charged decisions. And what have historians done? Followed their national identities. And what have been the most debated issues? Matters of how to translate particular passages in particular versions.

> Once any reason has lapsed to give this word the special meaning which Berg wants to put in it, all traces of a consecration to Bhairawa-Buddha and of the proclamation of a political programme disappear from *Nagarakrtagama* 41:51. (Bosch, 1956, p.20)

Unfortunately—Bosch believes—the fictional political programme has become "fact" in most discussions of Javanese history.

Llull provides a different set of difficulties. The 1907 Gustau Gili edition of *Doctrina pueril* (edited by Obrador y Bennassar) "text original directament trelladat d'un m.s. quatrecentista" has the following passage on page 180:

> Mogels, tartres, bulgras, ongres d Ungría la menor, comans, nestorins, rosogs, genovins e molts d altres son gentils, e son homens qui no han lig

The standard edition edited by Gret Schib and published by Barcino gives the corresponding passage as

> Mogols, tàrtins, búlgars, ongres d'Ongria la menor, comans, nestorins, rosos, ginovins e molts d'altres són

gentils e són hòmens qui no han ley. (Llull, 1972, p.166-167)

What did Llull actually write? What does it mean to a historian that a text is directly transcribed from an old manuscript? Should the historian prefer the manuscript, its transcription by Obrador y Bennassar or the text critically established by Schib? Who were Llull's *genovins/ginovins*? They remain unidentified. Who is a *gentil*? What is the meaning of *no han lig/no han ley*? Not only the truth or falsity of Llull's statement, but any interpretation of it depends upon who the *ginovins* and the *gentils* were and how one translates that last key word. While no one knows who Llull was referring to with the word *ginovins*, Llull's use of the words *gentils* and *ley* is interesting: the Biblical meaning of *gentil* is "non-Jew" and this is the definition one may still find in dictionaries today. But this is not what Llull meant: for Llull, the *gentil* is one who is not a monotheist, i.e. one who is neither a Jew, nor a Christian, nor a Muslim, and who therefore has no *ley* or law. *Ley* in Llull's language means the revealed law of God or what we would call religion, and for Llull, only Judaism, Christianity (which does not include Nestorianism) and Islam are religions since only these have a law revealed by God. None of this is given "in the text"; the reader must already know these peculiarities of Llull's language in order to interpret it. And to this day no one can translate *ginovins* because no one knows who Llull meant.

The Mongolian translator of an essay of mine on Llull's references to the Mongols used an online dictionary to pinpoint the meaning of *gentil* and thus Llull's book *Libre del gentil e los tres savis* (a dialogue between a '*gentil*' and three wise men: a Jew, a Muslim and a Christian) became *The Book of the Christian and the three sages* since the online dictionary which he used identified non-Jews with Christians! In the study of Llull's works, as for all texts, popular notions of language and of history are inseparably linked to questions of scholarly language, terminology, analysis, periodization, metaphor, paleographical interpretation, textual criticism, translation and how all of these relate to "ordinary language", a problem specifically addressed by Harris in an earlier book, *History, Science and the Limits of Language*, and again in his most recent book *The Semantics of Science*.

Another word which appears frequently in Harris' writings is "indeterminacy" and this characteristic of language is, for Harris, not just a matter of indeterminacy in language:

> Integrationism is a philosophy of language which rejects fixed-code semantics lock, stock and barrel. Instead it adopts a different approach to communication altogether. In this approach, meaning is treated as being radically indeterminate, whether expressed by words or by non-verbal signs. But integrationism is not just a philosophy of language. The indeterminacy of meaning is, for integrationists, one of the basic features of the human condition, and is intrinsic not only to language but to the development of all human institutions, social and political. (Harris, 2005, p.109)

While much nonsense has been written about Heisenberg's *Ungenauigkeit* (Indeterminacy) and *Unsicherheit* (Uncertainty) Principle (Heisenberg used both words at different times; the difference in English translation, as in French, has considerable ramifications for theory), the meaning of indeterminacy which develops in Harris's discussion of the indeterminacy of meaning is very close to that which Jean-Marc Lévy-Leblond discusses in a number of publications on the philosophy of science and measurement (see e.g. Lévy-Leblond, 1996). One similarity between the two is that the efficacy and correctness of language and measurement are both inseparably bound up with the contexts of language and measurement respectively. Effective linguistic action in a wide range of activities neither requires nor implies identical shared meanings, obedience to rules of grammar, pronunciation and so on. Similarly, neither when measuring the distance from Paris to London nor in measuring the length of a glycerine molecule does one measure in millimeters. Furthermore, in measurement, there must always be an assumption of error, and therefore error is considered to be equivalent to variation. Hence, in measurement as in language, there are only variations in contexts and the significance of the variation depends entirely upon the context of communication, the reasons why one measures and speaks.

Daniel Davis suggested that one of the models for integrational linguistics and the notion of the three-dimensional sign is the study of history. He offered four comparisons between integrational linguistics and the study of history. The first concerns the issue of contextual communicational relevance.

> [H]istory does not define in advance the locus of the values it is concerned with. The 'value' it is engaged in studying is not to be found a priori in, for example, a linguistic system, or a culture, or an economy, though these may be seen as relevant to an attempt to reconstruct or represent the values which explain behaviour in any relevant situation. This corresponds closely to the issues involved in the three-dimensional sign, that it is the communicational context which determines which aspects of behaviour are communicationally relevant. (Davis, 1997, p. 26)

The second point concerns the reliance upon narrative. Davis suggested that "narrative can be said to be the kind of bridge between the importance of experience, and the relevance to communicational context, which is required in the foundation of the three-dimensional sign." (Davis, 1997, p. 27) The third point is that history is "concerned with politics in its most general sense":

> A history is a political claim; it is subject to political interpretation, evaluation, and contradiction; it is set within a political context. On the one hand, this acts as a check on the validity of the historical interpretation; on the other, it liberates the historical interpretation from almost any form of determinism, be it social, cultural, economic, or linguistic. That is, history makes claims about the nature of experience and values vis-à-vis an individual or group, but these claims are limited to a particular context. Furthermore, both claims and contexts are subject to debate. This is precisely comparable to the contingent melding of context and experience brought about by the three-dimensional sign. (Davis, 1997, p.27)

His final point is that history is "contingent on the political position of the historian. The first act of a writer or reader of history is to assess this position, as it is crucial to determining the rhetorical purpose of the interpretative act. It is the same with the integrational linguist." (Davis, 1997, p. 27)

For Harris, all human activities are necessarily moral and political engagements, whether responsibly or irresponsibly so. This is why language matters, and this is why history matters, and this is why science, art, religion, education and a zillion other human endeavors matter. Because meanings are radically indeterminate, all of these activities are, exactly as McCullagh insists, matters of belief and pragmatic choice, for better or for worse, sometimes good and sometimes evil. Whether one's actions and beliefs are regarded as justified or not, true or false, depends on who is doing the judging. Institutional authorities—historians and linguists no less than dictators and priests—resist such a fall from the pedestals of science and religion and the democratic leveling of the playing field, and it is perhaps in this political orientation that one can find the chief reason that Harris' writings are so frequently ignored or rejected. Should there be readers of this journal for whom such a political engagement is seen as a necessary concomitant of historical writing—and I think there are—*The Linguistics of History* should be the next book to read.

References
Bosch, F.D.K.. (1956). "C.C. Berg and ancient Javanese history" *Bijdragen tot de taal-, land- en volkenkunde* d.112, 1e afl, p.1-24.
Cameron, Deborah.(1997). "When worlds collide: expert and popular discourse on language" *Language Sciences*, v.19 no.1 p.7-13.
Davis, Daniel. (1997). "The three-dimensional sign" *Language Sciences* v.19 nr.1 p.23-31.
Harris, Roy, 1980. *The Language Makers*. Ithaca: Cornell University Press.
Harris, Roy. (1990). "On redefining linguistics." In Davis H. and Taylor T. (eds.), *Redefining Linguistics*. London: Routledge, p.18-52.
Harris, Roy. (2003). *History, Science and the Limits of Language: An Integrational Approach*. Shimla: Indian Institute of Advanced Study.
Harris, Roy. (2004). *The Linguistics of History*. Edinburgh: Edinburgh University Press.
Harris, Roy, 2005. *The Semantics of Science*. London: Continuum.
Hutton, Christopher. (1997). "The 'dictator of taste': rules, regularities and responsibilities." *Language Sciences*, v.19 no.1 pp. 47-55.

Joseph, John E. (1997). "The 'Language Myth' myth: or, Roy Harris's red herrings". In: Wolf and Love (eds.), *Linguistics inside out: Roy Harris and his critics*. Amsterdam: John Benjamins, p.9-41.

Lévy-Leblond, Jean-Marc. (1996). *Aux Contraires: L'Exercice de la Pensée et la Pratique de la Science*. Paris: Gallimard.

Llull, Ramon. (1907). *Libre de Doctrina Pueril del B. Mestre Ramon Lull*. Text original directament trelladat d'un m.s. quatrecentista ab proemi, illustracions y notes den M. Obrador y Bennassar. Barcelona: Gustau Gili.

Llull, Ramon. (1972). *Doctrina pueril*. A cura de Gret Schib. Barcelona: Barcino. (Els Nostres Clàssics A, 104)

Love, Nigel. (1997). "Integrating Austin" *Language Sciences* v.19 nr.1 p.57-65.

Love, Nigel. (1999). "Searle on language" *Language & Communication* v. 19 p.9-25.

McCullagh, C. Behan. (2005). "Language and the truth of history" *History and Theory* v.44 (October) p.441-455.

Searle, J.R. (1979). *Expression and Meaning: Studies in the Theory of Speech Acts*. Cambridge: Cambridge University Press.

Wolf, George. (1999). "Quine and the segregational sign" *Language & Communication* v.19 p.27-43.

IV

How Not to Study Swahili
Hannah Arendt, the Encyclopædia Britannica and the Violence of Authority

Kwa kumbukumbu ya mwalimu Albert Scheven:
Ajifunzaye haachi kujua.

Abstract
Hannah Arendt described Swahili as a "kind of no-language" and argued that its study was detrimental to the education of African Americans. The presuppositions which determined how Arendt read and interpreted the article on Swahili in the *Encyclopaedia. Britannica* (the source she cited) are examined, as are the linguistic ideas revealed in similar articles in other editions of that encyclopaedia. Arendt's views on Swahili are then related to her understanding of the role of speech in political life in order to draw out the political implications of her understanding of Swahili.

1. *Swahili: "A kind of no-language"*

In her famous essay "On violence" Hannah Arendt infamously wrote

> it seems that the academic establishment, in its curious tendency to yield more to Negro demands, even if they are clearly silly and outrageous, ... feels more comfortable when confronted with interests plus violence than when it is a matter of nonviolent "participatory democracy." (Arendt, 1973, p. 121)

To that remark she added an even more infamous footnote, beginning that footnote with remarks by "Bayard Rustin, the Negro civil-rights leader" which she quoted from a newspaper, setting his remarks within her own. Her brief account of his remarks concludes with the following comment

> what Negro students need is "remedial training" so that they "can do mathematics and write a correct sentence," not "soul courses." (Arendt, 1973, p. 191)

in which the words within quotation marks are apparently those of Rustin. She then continues with remarks on Swahili and other "nonexistent subjects", using as her reference the 1961 edition of the *Encyclopædia Britannica.*:

> What a reflection on the moral and intellectual state of society that much courage was required to talk common sense in these matters! Even more frightening is the all too likely prospect that, in about five or ten years, this "education" in Swahili (a nineteenth-century kind of no-language spoken by the Arab ivory and slave caravans, a hybrid mixture of a Bantu dialect with an enormous vocabulary of Arab borrowings; see the Encyclopaedia

Britannica, 1961), African literature, and other nonexistent subjects will be interpreted as another trap of the white man to prevent Negroes from acquiring an adequate education. (Arendt, 1973, pp. 191-192)

These remarks have drawn a great deal of attention to her attitudes towards race and education, particularly from African Americans, but their interest for me lies in how her ideas about language were connected to those of race, education, violence and above all politics. What I wish to focus on here is her description of Swahili, how she arrived at the understanding of Swahili that is evident in the footnote quoted above. How was it possible for her to write as she did based on what she found in the source she cited, the *Encyclopaedia Britannica*? Why was Arendt so vehemently opposed to the study of Swahili by African American students? What is the "intellectual state of society" that refers to an encyclopaedia—or any other information source—and stops with what is found there, no matter how well or how poorly that information was contextualized and understood?

2. *What was she thinking?*

Hannah Arendt is an author whom I have read, appreciated and loved for many years. Yet what she wrote of Africa, blacks and Swahili makes me cringe and we part ways. The question that has troubled me is how could she write as she did about African languages and literatures?

Her remarks on Swahili must be read within their immediate context—a debate on the education of African Americans in the 1960's—but also within the larger context of her understanding of Africa, slavery and the relation between speech and political life. Arendt was not passing judgement on Swahili out of the blue. Her comments were set within a broader argument concerning violence in American society, and within that argument she mentioned the discussion within universities about what subjects should be studied, who should determine the curriculum and how should students be involved in that decision. It is fairly easy to fill in the assumptions that underwrote her argument, making it a convincing argument for those who shared her assumptions. Her assumptions must have been something like the following:

> 1) European/Western civilization and science in particular is the origin and basis of the modern world, its political forms, economy and technology;
> 2) An education in European science and scholarship, European languages and literatures, is essential for social assimilation and employment in that European dominated world; therefore
> 3) The advancement of African Americans requires not just any piece of paper, but an education in the practices and methods of European science and scholarship, and furthermore,
> 4) The study of Swahili or any other African (Asian, indigenous American) language and literature is of no value towards attaining the goals expressly desired by members of the African American community.

The first part of that argument is a simple argument about education. Whether it is called education, socialization, cultural tranmission or reproduction, it is as much an argument about the relation between generations as it is about courses of study. Young-Bruehl described Arendt's views on education in her essay "Crisis in education" as "concerned with the relations of authority between adults and adults and adults and children" (Young Bruehl, 1982, p. 317). She noted that in Arendt's opinion "Educators should introduce children to the world, give them the tools for understanding it accurately and impartially, so that the children can, when they mature, act in the world intelligently" (ibid., p. 318). In Arendt's own words

> Our hope always hangs on the new which every generation brings; but precisely because we can base our hope only on this, we destroy everything if we so try to control the new that we, the old, can dictate how it will look. Exactly for the sake of what is new and revolutionary in every child, education must be conservative; it must preserve this newness and introduce it as a new thing into the old world. (Arendt, 1968, p. 192–3)

It is not a new argument, and a few years after Arendt wrote "Reflections on violence" a similar argument about education was eloquently expressed by Michael Oakeshott:

> Being human is recognizing oneself to be related to others, not as parts of an organism are related, nor as members of a single, all-inclusive "society," but in virtue of participation in multiple understood relationships and in the enjoyment of understood, historic languages of feelings, sentiments, imaginings, fancies, desires, recognitions, moral and religious beliefs, intellectual and practical enterprises, customs, conventions ... These languages are continuously invented by those who share them; using them is adding to their resources. They do not impose demands to think or to "behave" in a certain manner; they are not sets of ready-made formulae for self-disclosure and self-enactment; they reach those who share them as various invitations to understand, to admire, to approve or to disapprove; and they come only in being learned ...
> What is going on in this transaction, then, is not the transfer of the products of earlier generations to a new-

comer, nor is it a newcomer acquiring an aptitude for imitating current adult human performances; it is learning to perform humanly. Education is not acquiring a stock of ready-made ideas, images, sentiments, beliefs and so forth; it is learning to look, to listen, to think, to feel, to imagine, to believe, to understand, to choose and to wish. (Oakeshott (2001 [1972]), p.64-65, 67)

There is no question that Arendt was truly concerned about the state of education in the United States and the negative impact that she thought this would have on African Americans. If African Americans want to be doctors and lawyers, chemists and mathematicians, schoolteachers and librarians, then they need to study western medicine and western law, Boyle and Gauss, Pestalozzi and Dewey, and not waste their time on the poetry of Shaaban Robert or Tucker and Ashton's *Swahili phonetics*. If that were all there were to the issue, then the argument is irrefutable. Yet such considerations were not the only considerations in the thinking of the time. As one contemporary critic put it

> to ask the young to increase their technical knowledge in order to have good careers or serve the nation, to assure them a rise in that standard of living, to show them a reasonable course that will lead to the perfect society of tomorrow, to promise them comfort, plenty, institutional equality, and freedom of opportunity—all this is in the style of the old. (Ellul, 1968, p.285)

It is difficult to see how Arendt's (or Oakeshott's) view of education could be compatible with a view in which education is all about employment and career. If Arendt did not think of education as simply job training, then why such vehement objection to the study of Swahili and African literature? For

Arendt, it seems, learning Swahili was not "learning to perform humanly." The real basis of her objection to the study of Swahili arose from her understanding of how this was connected to the social and political motivations of the students, i.e. she objected to separatism and the politics of linguistic community. Young-Bruehl is undoubtedly correct when she suggests that it was because she connected the study of Swahili with the politics of racial identity, black nationalism and separatist ideology that Arendt denigrated the study of Swahili.

> When she wrote her "Reflections on Violence" in 1969, Arendt deplored the fact that black children who were not taught to do "mathematics and write a correct sentence" were encouraged to explore their identity as Afro-Americans. Though she agreed with Ralph Ellison that an ideal of sacrifice and heroism may be necessary for children who are victims of stark violence and hatred, who are homeless, she thought such an ideal quite different from the study of Swahilii and the cultivation of a separatist ideology. (Young-Bruehl, 1982, p. 318)

Before considering the political and social dimensions of the study of Swahili for African American students it will be of considerable interest to examine how Arendt herself studied Swahili. For even if it were true that what African Americans wanted was simply a better education and access to better jobs and careers, it would still not be the case that Swahili is "a kind of no-language" and the study of the languages and literatures of Africa would still not be "non-existent subjects." It is clear that they have only become this because of the context within which Arendt read what little she read about Swahili, i.e. an article in the *Encyclopædia Britannica* and her ideas about language and Africa.

3. *Swahili in the Encyclopaedia Britannica*

What is Swahili? The first edition of the *Encyclopaedia Britannica* (1771) has no entry for Swahili. The entry for Swahili makes its first appearance in volume 22 of the 9th edition of 1887. The unsigned article contains the following information:

> A term now commonly applied to the inhabitants of Zanzibar and of the opposite mainland ... who are subjects of the sultan of Zanzibar, and whose mother-tongue is the Ki-Swahili language. ... The Swahili are essentially a mixed people, in whom the Bantu and Arab elements are mingled in the proportion of about three to one; and the same is true of their speech, which of all the Bantu dialects has been most affected by Arab and other influences. The interest attaching to the Swahili people, who have figured so largely in the history of African enterprise during the last half century, is thus of a social rather than of a strictly scientific character. The energy and intelligence derived from a large infusion of Semitic blood has enabled them to take a leading part in the development of trade and the industries, as shown in the wide diffusion of their language, which like the Hindustani in India and the Guarani in South America, has become the principal medium of intercommunication throughout most of the continent south of the equator. During his journey from the indian Ocean to the Atlantic Commander Cameron found that a knowledge of this language enabled him everywhere to dispense with the aid of an interpreter, as it was understood by one or more persons in all the tribes along the route. Owing to this circumstance the intelligent and enterprising natives of Zanzibar have been found indispensable assistants in every expedition penetrating from the eastern seaboard

> to the interior since they began to be employed by Speke and Burton as porters and escorts. (p. 729)

Arendt, however, used neither the 9th nor the famous 11th edition, but the 1961 revision of the 14th edition. The original entry for Swahili Language in the 14th edition was written by Alice Werner, Professor of Swahili and Bantu Languages at the School of Oriental Studies in London, but the article in the 1961 revision was written by Archibald Norman Tucker, Professor of East African Languages, School of Oriental and African Studies, University of London. (The reader is encouraged to read Tucker's article in its entirety.) In Tucker's article we read that

> Swahili (Kiswahili) is a Bantu language spoken primarily on the east coast and islands of Africa between Lamu Island in the north and the mouth of the Ruvuma river in the south. It is spoken sporadically as far north as Mogadishu and there appear to be Swahili-speaking enclaves in Somaliland; it has also been heard as far south as Mozambique. A form of Swahili is also spoken on the west coast of Madagascar. ... There are about 15 main Swahili dialects as well as several pidgin forms in use.

So, *pace* Arendt, we learn that Swahili is indeed a language and that it has several dialects and pidgin forms, much like English. Tucker continues:

> Swahili as a lingua franca is current in: (1) Tanganyika, where it is the language of administration and primary education; (2) Kenya, where it is also the main language of administration and primary education, though alternative languages have been recognized in certain parts of the colony; (3) Uganda, where it is in competition with local languages; (4) Republic of the (former Belgian)

Congo, where a form of Swahili (sometimes called Kingwana) is one of the four permitted languages of administration..

In addition to being spoken in Somalia, Madagascar and Mozambique, we learn that it is the language of admimnistration and education in Tanzania, Kenya, Uganda and the Congo. Then in Tucker's next paragraph we learn that Swahili, like English, has borrowed extensively from other world languages:

> Although modern Swahili contains an enormous vocabulary of Arabic borrowings (as well as borrowings from Persian, Hindi, Portuguese and English), in its grammatical behaviour it is characteristically Bantu

Next, in his remarks on the history of Swahili we read that Swahili arose within the social world of Arab-Bantu contact in Arab settlements on the eastern coast of Africa at least since the founding of Pate (in A.D. 689):

> During the next 600 years other cities such as Lamu, Malindi, Mombasa and Kilwa were founded and reached a high level of civilization, until eclipsed by the Portuguese conquests in the early 16th century,. After the Arabs had returned and ousted the Portuguese in the early 18th century and transferred their court from Oman to Zanzibar in 1832, Swahili came into its own, enhanced by the intermarriage of the Arab overlords with the coastal people.

At this point Tucker mentions trade and slavery:

> During the early 19th century the spread of Swahili inland received a great impetus through its being the lang-

uage of the Arab ivory and slave caravans, which penetrated as far north as Uganda and as far west as the upper reaches of the Congo (Lualaba) river. It was later adopted by Europeans. It has been challenged by local vernaculars in certain regions and there has also been a tendency among some Africans to prefer the metropolitan language as lingua franca. Others, however, look to Swahili as the future national language of East Africa.

And lastly Tucker comments on Swahili literature:

> The earliest literature in Swahili was written in the Arabic script and a certain amount still exists in manuscript. ... the first complete Bible was produced by 1891 in the Mvita (Mombasa) dialect. For several years there was strong rivalry between this dialect and that of Zanzibar (Unguja), until the latter obtained official recognition as "standard" in the 1920s. Afterward, the written language progressed apace, under the encouragement of the Interterritorial Language (Swahili) Committee—later the East African Swahili Committee—and the years after World War II saw an enormous development. ... and a spate of government-inspired textbooks for schools and adult literacy campaigns, there are about 60 Swahili newspapers and broadsheets in East Africa and a dozen in the Congo area.

    For the reader who has read my account of Tucker's article the question of how Arendt came to her understanding of Swahili as "a kind of no-language" is unavoidable. Between Tucker and Arendt something happened: how did Arendt arrive at her understanding?
    Arendt's ignorance of African affairs is well known. Dossa (1980: 321) wrote "Her ignorance of African culture and lite-

rature was truly astonishing" and her reliance on an encyclopaedia underscores that ignorance: no one goes to an encyclopaedia to read about matters that they already know. The use of an encyclopaedia is an admission of ignorance: that is the first matter to consider.

> The organization provided by a dictionary or an encyclopedia is not designed for learning but for the rapid discovery of items of information in response to a recognition of specific ignorance. And the organization of information in terms of the modes of thought, or languages, which are the greatest achievements of civilization, is much too sophisticated for the beginner. (Michael Oakeshott (2001 [1965]), p.55)

Needing or wanting to know something about Swahili, Arendt resorted to a trusted source of information in the expectation of acquiring the knowledge she desired. Yet having read that article, how could she have understood the Swahili language to be a "no-language" and the study of Swahili language and literature to be "non-existent subjects"? In order to come to that conclusion it would be necessary to read the article with a certain set of preconceptions concerning the nature of language, dialect, lingua franca and literature, as well as notions about slaves, traders, Arabs and Africa in general. That is the second matter to note: everyone necessarily reads everything in light of an enormous background of previous reading, assumptions, prejudices, knowledge and ignorance, and the inerpretation of any text involves the integration of the new information with that prior experience. From her remarks we must additionally assume that she read the article selectively and uncritically, apparently paying attention to just those statements which she could readily fit into her prior understanding of the African world, its languages and literatures and their (non)importance for an education in the United States in the 1960's. And finally, perhaps most important of all, is the lack of evidence of any further reading: She accepted what she found, at least the part that interested her, interpreted it as it suited her and on that basis made her judgements concerning the nature and value of Swahili language and literature. No matter how hard the Britannica editors tried, "there's no way to defend yourself against a shallow reader" (Berry and Smith, 2007, p.102)

How did Swahili become a "kind of no-language"? What Tucker actually wrote in the 1961 *Encyclopædia Britannica* was that Swahili was a Bantu language with 15 main dialects and several pidgin forms, that it was "the language of the Arab ivory and slave caravans", that it was a lingua franca as well as a language of education and administration, that a standard form of the language was adopted in the 1920's, that some hoped that it would be "the future national language of East Africa" and that an indigenous literature was developing, including the publication of newspapers. Perhaps Arendt thought that lingua francas, dialects and pidgins were less than "real" languages? According to one of her biographers this was not her attitude towards Yiddish "which she, unlike many well-educated, assimilated German Jews, did not look down upon" (Young-Bruehl, 1982, p. 119). Perhaps the recent date of adoption of a standard language and literary production led her to conclude that the language and literature were not yet "mature" enough to warrant study by anyone other than missionaries, linguists and anthropologists? Was it Tucker's comment about its possibly becoming the national language of eastern Africa that made it a no-language, at least for now? Or was it his remark that it was the language of Arab traders and slaves? In the context of a debate about the future of education for African Americans the connection with slavery may have been at the forefront of her mind. If slavery reduced the enslaved to a subhuman condition, would that not make the language of slaves something less than a human language, a kind of no-language? She did not pursue that line of thinking, and may well have repudiated it had she been confronted with it; nevertheless, a negative valuation of dialects, pidgins, lingua francas and the language of slaves must have colored her reading of the article in the encyclopaedia.

On African civilization in general consider her remarks in *The origins of totalitarianism*: "it was tempting indeed [for the European] to simply declare that these [Africans] were not human beings" (Arendt, 1958a, p. 195; for more discussion see Dossa, 1980 and Budil, 2008). In *The human condition* Arendt noted that in Greek and Roman times

> A man who lived only a private life, who like the slave was not permitted to enter the public realm, or like the barbarian had chosen not to establish such a realm, was not fully human. (Arendt, 1958b, p. 38)

And further on "to have no private place of one's own (like a slave) meant to be no longer human." (ibid. p. 64). And in a later footnote we read

> The two qualities that the slave, according to Aristotle, lacks—and it is because of these defects that he is not human—are the faculty to deliberate and decide (*to bouleutikon*) and to foresee and to choose (*proairesis*). This is but a more explicit way of saying that the slave is subject to necessity. (ibid. p. 84)

In these passages Arendt was describing ancient ideas, but her ideas on freedom and necessity and their relation to the political sphere only modify some of those ancient ideas. For Arendt both those who are enslaved and excluded from the political realm and those who have "chosen not to establish such a realm" are admitted to be human in theory, but not in practice. Those students who chose to study Swahili were by that choice affirming both the full humanity of Swahili speakers and their own humanity as those having "the faculty to deliberate and decide (*to bouleutikon*) and to foresee and to choose (*proairesis*)."

The focus so far has been on what Arendt brought to the interpretation of what she found in the encyclopaedia, but the writer of an encyclopaedia article also brings a world of assumptions to bear on everything in the article. Those assumptions are evident in the language used as much as in the material selected for inclusion. In the unsigned (another significant matter) article on Swahili in the 9th edition the writer repeatedly commented on racial matters, describing the Swahili as a mixed people, whose "energy and intelligence derived from a large infusion of Semitic blood [that] has enabled them to take a leading part in the development of trade and the industries." This language is entirely absent from Tucker's article in which reference is made only to the prestige of Swahili being enhanced by intermarriage between the Arab rulers and the local population. The article in the intervening 11th and most famous edition is shorter than the articles in all other editions and is truly something to behold:

> A term commonly applied to the inhabitants of Zanzibar and of the opposite mainland ... who speak the Ki-Swahili language. The Swahili are essentially a mixed people, the result of long crossing between the negroes of the coast and the Arabs, with an ad-mixture of slave blood from nearly all the East African tribes. Among Swahili are found every shade of colour and every type of physique from the full-blooded negro to the pure Semite. Usually they are a powerfully built, handsome people, inclined to stoutness and with Semitic features.

They number about a million. They figured largely in the history of African enterprise during the 19th century. The energy and intelligence derived from their Semitic blood have enabled them to take a leading part in the development of trade and the industries, as shown in the wide diffusion of their language, which, like the Hindustani in India and the Guarani in South America, has become the principal medium of intercommunication in a large area of Africa south of the equator. During his journey from the Indian Ocean to the Atlantic (1873-1874) Commander V. Lovett Cameron found that a knowledge of this language enabled him everywhere to dispense with the aid of an interpreter, as it was understood by one or more persons in all the tribes along the route. (v. 26, p. 178)

Alice Werner's article "Swahili language" in the first printing of the 14th edition (1929) presents an interesting contrast not only with the articles of the earlier editions, but also with the later article by Tucker. Werner notes that europeans were ignorant of Swahili until it was first described—in a "very imperfect" manner—in a european publication by Henry Salt in 1814. It is a Bantu language that has "obtained wide currency as a trade language" and includes Arabic words although "Its grammatical structure has been little affected by Arabic influence." Contact with other languages has led to "an extensive use of borrowed prepositions and adverbs, which gives it greater elasticity and increasees its possibilities as a literary language." It is the official language in Kenya and Tanganyika, "indispensable to all civil servants, to settlers, missionaries and businessmen." Swahili speakers, she notes, "have the same facility of improvisation as the Italian peasants", a comment which puts Swahili speakers and their language on a par with European peoples and their languages. Her article is completely different in language, tone and attitude than the brief unsigned entry for "Swahili" which immediately precedes her article:

> Swahili (Wa-Swahili, i.e. coast people...), a term commonly applied to the inhabitants of Zanzibar ... who speak the Ki-Swahili language. The Swahili are derived from the negroes of the coast and the Arabs, with a varied admixture of slave blood. Colour and physique thus range from the full-blooded negro to the pure Semite... (*Encyclopaedia Britannica*, 14th ed., 1929, v. 21, p. 629)

In Werner's article we learn instead that "Swahili is not the language of any particular tribe; it grew up among the descendents of the Arab settlers on the coast, who intermarried with native women—usually Bantu." Race and slavery are absent from her description. Why? Because they were irrelevant for an accurate description.

Compare the articles from the 9th, 11th and 14th editions with the unsigned article in the current edition of the *Encyclopaedia Britannica online* (accessed December 2007). In this version we read that Swahili is a "Bantu language spoken either as a mother tongue or as a fluent second language on the east coast of Africa in an area extending from Lamu Island, Kenya, in the north to the southern border of Tanzania in the south" and that the name Swahili "refers to their language only and does not denote any particular ethnic or tribal unit." Swahili is

> a lingua franca in: (1) Tanzania, where it is the language of administration and primary education; (2) Kenya, where it is, after English, the main language for these purposes; (3) Congo (Kinshasa), where a form of Swahili is one of the four languages of administration,

the main language for this purpose being French; and (4) Uganda, where the main language is again English.

We also learn that "Swahili has been greatly influenced by Arabic" and that it "dates from the contacts of Arabian traders with the inhabitants of the east coast of Africa over many centuries." The language spread inland not only because it was used as "the language of the Arab ivory and slave caravans, which penetrated as far north as Uganda and as far west as Congo" but also because it was "adopted by European colonialists, especially the Germans, who used it extensively as the language of administration in Tanganyika, thus laying the foundation for its adoption as a national language of independent Tanzania."

In this description we no longer have mixed people nor infusions of blood, and in fact language is no longer associated with race, ethnicity, blood or tribe at all. Instead of borrowings we have loanwords, and instead of intermarriage we have "contact."

The reader who examines the various unsigned articles and the Werner and Tucker articles from the 14th edition will notice how the "same" facts about the people and their language provide very different texts and contexts for the readers' interpretation. Among the questions these articles leave for all readers to ask, linguists and non-linguists alike, are: Is it Bantu languages or Bantu dialects? What is the difference between a language and a dialect? What is a lingua franca? A national language? A standard language? What does it mean to be the language of traders and/or slaves? What is a mixed people? And most of all, what did the authors of these articles mean by these statements? It is not as simple as going to other volumes of the encyclopaedia and looking up language, dialect etc., for those other entries were written by other authors. The encyclopaedia is in fact a grab bag of new ideas and material recycled from past editions, absences and incompatible entries, and the biases, prejudices and assumptions of a variety of times and places.

In order to understand how Arendt came to her understanding of Swahili as a kind of no-language it may be helpful to consider the term *Lingua franca*. The current *Britannica Online* article *Lingua franca* by Salikoko Mufwene notes that the term is Italian for "Frankish language" and describes a lingua franca as a

> language used as a means of communication between populations speaking vernaculars that are not mutually intelligible. The term was first used during the Middle Ages to describe a French- and Italian-based jargon, or pidgin, that was developed by Crusaders and traders in the eastern Mediterranean (viewed 24 June 2008).

Entries for *Lingua franca* in the 1929 and 1961 versions of the 14th edition of the *Encyclopædia Britannica* are as different from this description as they are from each other, and the differences are instructive. In the 1929 version we read:

> **Lingua franca**, a term used in different parts of the world of languages used over wide areas as secondary to the indigenous forms of speech, thus enabling intercourse to be developed. English is frequently called the lingua franca of the whole world as, at one time, French was the lingua franca of diplomacy. English, in various degrees of distortion, is spoken all over the world, but in special areas are found examples of a lingua franca such as (1) the so-called mandarin Chinese, (2) Malay, (3) Hindustani, and (4) Swahili. ...
> **Swahili** (q.v.).—This important Bantu language has spread widely and is the lingua franca of Bantu Africa. (v.14, p.163)

Arendt referred the reader to the 1961—not the 1929—version and if she herself acquired her understanding of *lingua franca* from that edition, then that article provides us with some clear insight into her understanding of Swahili. From the 1961 version:

> **Lingua franca** is an auxiliary or compromise language used between peoples speaking mutually incomprehensible vernaculars. It may be one of a number of native languages like Swahili in east Africa, Hausa in west Africa and Hindustani in India; or it may be a mixed jargon like the pidgin English of the western Pacific. ...
> The term lingua franca was perhaps first applied to a jargon based on southern French and Italian which crusaders and traders developed ... Extension of trade routes, overseas colonization and slavery ... gave rise to a number of mixed contact jargons...
> Origin. —Such jargons generally begin as a compromise between two groups, each desiring to communicate, but unwilling or unable to learn the language of the other. The European may try to make himself understood by imitating the native's effort to speak the European language. The native, taking this imperfect imitation as a model, tries to reproduce it as best he can ... In plantations, slaves from mutually unintelligible tribes got their model from infrequent contacts with European masters and used their vague impressions of their masters' language as a basis of a lingua franca for communication among themselves. [etc.]. (v.14, p.163)

Linguistic science progresses, a fact both evident and deplorable in the changing entries in the *Encyclopædia Britannica*, but the differences between these entries are truly astounding. The primary examples in the 1929 entry are English, French and Chinese as well as Swahili. A lingua franca appears to have high status, as world languages "enabling discourse" and as the language of diplomacy. Swahili is characterized simply as an "important Bantu language", with no association with trade or slavery.

In contrast, William Francis Mackey's entry in the 1961 version begins by defining a lingua franca as an "auxiliary or compromise" language and a "jargon." The situation in which they arise is one of "mutually incomprehensible vernaculars" and a specifically oral context. Note in particular the the terms *vernacular* and *jargon*, as these terms appear also in the current *Britannica Online*. A connection is often made between vernacular language and the language of slaves. The entry in the 1911 edition of the *Encyclopaedia Britannica* (there is no entry in later editions) has the following definition:

> **Vernacular** (Lat. verna, dim. vernaculus, a slave born in his master's house), a term meaning native or indigenous, belonging to the country where a person is born. The word is practically confined in English usage to language, whether of the country as a whole or of particular dialects or idioms. (*Encyclopaedia Britannica*, 11th ed.)

Jargon does have an entry in the current *Encyclopaedia Britannica* online, also written by Salikoko Mufwene, and there we read that during colonial times *jargon* meant

> an unstable rudimentary hybrid language used as a means of communication between persons having no other language in common. ... Nonlinguists more commonly define jargon as the technical or specialized parlance of a specific social or occupational group such as physicians or lawyers. Jargon has also historically

been defined as gibberish or as an outlandish, unintelligible, barbarous, debased language; in this meaning it is similar to patois and carries negative connotations.

The examples of lingua francas that Mackey gives are first of all Swahili and other African and Asian languages and only secondarily "a mixed jargon like the pidgin English" of the Pacific region. Unlike the author of the 1929 version, Mackey denies the status of lingua franca to English, limiting the scope of lingua franca to pidgin English. A lingua franca originates when the interlocutors are "unwilling or unable to learn the language of the other." The "native ... tries to reproduce" the European's imitation of the native learner's English "as best he can." Instead of focusing on the role of lingua francas in enabling communication, they are persistently linked to situations of compromise, mutual incomprehensibility, mutual unintelligibility and the unwillingness or inability to learn. And instead of associating lingua francas with world languages and languages of diplomacy, they are characterized as "jargons", the product of the "vague impressions" of slaves and traders.

Any readers who consulted the *Encyclopædia Britannica* for the terms *Swahili* and *Lingua franca* would come to very different understandings of Swahili depending upon which version they used. Those who consulted the 1929 version for Werner's article and an understanding of lingua francas would understand Swahili to be an African equivalent of English, French and Chinese: a language used by many different linguistic communities to communicate in cross-cultural situations such as government, diplomacy, commerce and education, a language necessary for a multitude of professions from medicine to missions, civil service to international relations. On the other hand those who consulted the entries in the 1961 version—as perhaps Hannah Arendt did—might have come to the same conclusions as she did: Swahili is a kind of non-language for half-breeds, slaves and petty traders, and Swahili literature a non-existent subject. Yet whether or not Arendt referred to Mackey's article on lingua franca, she apparently understood Swahili to be a lingua franca in much the same sense as did Mackey.

The user of an encyclopedia has not only to navigate within the intellectual worlds of Werner, Tucker and Mackey, but within a universe of discourse that is not a closed, knowable system of semantic relationships such as Saussure and the structuralists imagined. From one article to the next the language and the theories found in an encyclopaedia are connected by little more than paper ... and the reader's assumptions. How then can and why should a scholar or anyone else use an encyclopaedia?

> When we are consumed with a greed for information, philosophy appears as universal knowledge. ... But this indiscriminate pursuit of universal knowledge is scarcely better than a romantic obsession. And it is foreign to the character of philosophy, because when we are intent upon what is a whole and complete we must resign what is merely encyclopaedic. ... It is only in the childhood of thought, when knowledge appears undifferentiated and each fresh piece of information seems significant just because it is fresh, that universal knowledge can appear to satisfy the philosophic passion. At all events, in these days when we are more conscious of the futility of knowledge than its blessing, it is not to be expected that an encyclopaedia will attract him who is looking for a philosophy. (Oakeshott (1933), p. 1-2)

Hannah Arendt used an encyclopaedia the same way many others use them. From her use we could identify four general characteristics of the use of an encyclopaedia:

1) encyclopaedias are used to find out what one does not already

know, i.e. their use is a tacit admission of ignorance;
2) the information found in an encyclopaedia requires interpretation and integration with what one already thinks and knows;
3) readers selectively attend to what they read and are rarely critical readers; and
4) encyclopaedias, as "authoritative" sources, are often the first *and* the last source, i.e the *only* source consulted.

Briefly put: the ignorant reader is often satisfied with an uncritical reading of an isolated bit of information from a source regarded as reputable. And of course, that is often all that is desired or needed. It is only in the case of those engaged in public political or academic debate that we demand more, as Hannah Arendt certainly demanded of herself in her other writings.

"The pursuit of learning," Oakeshott insisted, "is a conversation." (Oakeshott, 2001 [1950] p.109) To ask questions requires a critical reader; to answer them requires going beyond the encyclopaedia, something few users of encyclopaedias do. Why? The question needs to go deeper: Why do the same people who expect science to consist of evidence, interpretation, argument, counter-evidence, counter-argument and reinterpretation without end, expect of encyclopaedias the truth, enough of the truth, nothing but the truth, a truth that needs no interpretation and calls for no debate? More generally we might ask why, when scientists make their pronouncements, do people believe them?

Where would someone wanting to learn something about the Swahili language go to find out about Swahili? Readily available sources make vastly different claims about Swahili, as noted above. Consider the number of speakers of Swahili. There are reported to be around 85-90 million Swahili speakers in the world (5-10 million as first language) according to the *Wikipedia* entry (viewed 23 June 2008). The *Ethnologue* to which the *Wikipedia* entry refers the reader indicates that about 5 million speak Swahili as a first language with 30 million who speak Swahili as a second language, citing a 1989 publication by Holm as source of this information. An online article in 2004 noting the establishment of Swahili as the official language of the African Union states that there are 50 million Africans who speak Swahili as a first language and many more who speak it as a second language (Sebelebele, 2004).

What is the nature of this discrepancy between figures? What counts as Swahili? Are the criteria geographical, political or linguistic? There are web pages complaining that Kingwana speakers are not included in some counts of the number of Swahili speakers, and there are other web authors vehemently disputing the descriptions of certain dialects of Swahili as pidgins or degraded forms of the language. Do the different numbers reflect growth and spread of the language? Differing sampling methodologies or stastitical methods? Linguistic or nationalistic pride or prejudice? How does one find out? Indeed, is it possible to know the answer to this question at all? Can such questions even be asked without assuming certain linguistic ideas, namely the very ideas that such differences of opinion call into question?

To study Swahili requires a different approach than merely looking for an answer from an authority, a manner of inquiry completely different from "information seeking" as we call it. To study anything requires an engagement, not simply assent to the pronouncements of an "authority." Unfortunately, Arendt's study of Swahili is an example of how not to study Swahili, indeed, how not to study anything at all.

4. Why study Swahili? Freedom through linguistic marronage

> It's impossible to prefigure the salvation of the world in the same language by which the world has been dismembered and defaced. (Berry, 2000)

Hannah Arendt did not want to study Swahili. Nor did she think that African-American students ought to waste their time studying Swahili. Why study a language that is not a language? Why study a literature that does not exist? Arendt did not ask the students at Berkeley why they wished to study Swahili. Had she asked, the only acceptable answer would have had to convince her that Swahili was indeed a language, that there was in fact a literature in Swahili, and therefore the study of the language and literature of Swahili were not non-existent subjects. Yet this much she could have learned from the *Encyclopaedia Britannica*, had she read more carefully or followed up by consulting the references given in the articles.

Why did those students want to study Swahili? They did not want to study Swahili language and African literatures simply because these existed. They had other reasons, and it was her assumptions concerning (or knowledge of?) their reasons that disturbed Arendt.[1]

---

[1] A year prior to Arendt's essay Lyndon Harries, a teacher of Swahili at the University of Wisconsin, had written a short artice in *The Modern Language Journal* in response to the controversy generated by the offering of Swahili in the curriculum of the William Howard Taft High School in New York. In his article Harries remarked "It is doubtful if the general white community is sufficiently well informed about the status of Swahili in Africa to be objective in their understanding of this matter. More likely the desire of the black community is interpreted in a vague sort of way as another manifestation of black aggression in this country. There can be little doubt that some members of the black community do not themselves have an objective attitude in this respect, but for the majority the desire to learn an African language is the legitimate expression of their search for some kind of self-identity." (Harries, 1968, p. 146). Harries apparently felt that his students were on a search for

It is true that young people often do incredibly stupid, selfish, foolish, mean and contemptible things—just like the not-so-young—and some of those students studying Swahili may have desired to study Swahili for the worst of reasons, including racist animosity and a desire for an apartheid society. While I would condemn such motivations, there is no reason to assume that such were the only reasons for studying Swahili. Since I have no knowledge of the actual reasons in the cases to which Arendt was referring, I shall assume that at least some of the students wanted to study Swahili for more laudable reasons (see footnote 1 above for just such a defence). In the context of that time (1960's) and place (Berkeley), it is not at all difficult to imagine a few very good reasons for studying Swahili. Before pursuing that path, however, Arendt's ojections need a closer examination.

Arendt's argument was concerned with "acquiring an adequate education"; we must ask: An education for what? A job? Wendell Berry suggested that the "great and tragic mistake" of our educational system is that "We're teaching as if the purpose of knowledge is to help people have careers, or to make themselves better employees." (Berry and Smith, 2007, p. 101). In order to understand what motives—besides separatism—informed the students' desire to study Swahili, Berry's comments on education may lead us in the right direction. He argued that we should change the standard and focus on the community:

> I would make the standard that of comunity health rather than the career of the student. You see, if you make the

---

self-identity springing "from a sense of deprivation" and was "on the whole a good and worthy aspiration" (ibid.). Yet even Harries, the teacher of Swahili, could remark "If they were fully integrated citizens, the question of learning an African language would not arise for them" (ibid.). I can only say that if African Americans had been "fully integrated citizens" I *might* have had the wonderful but at the time undreamt of opportunity to study Swahili as a high school student.

> standard the health of the community, that would change everything. Once you begin to ask what would be the best thing for our community, what's the best thing that we can do here for our community, you can't rule out any kind of knowledge. (Berry and Smith, 2007, p. 100)

Arendt's objection to learning Swahili was a response to that shift of focus, from a eurocentric education for social assimilation under existing conditions to the creation of a local community neither dependent upon nor determined by the world within which Arendt herself had considerable status. The desire to study Swahili was surely related to the sense of community among African Americans, a community of which Hannah Arendt was not a member and about which she seemed to know very little. On at least some issues she was able and willing to learn from African Americans about their life, as her correspondence with Ralph Ellison demonstrated (see the discussion in Allen, 2001), but she did not pursue her inquiry in the case of studying Swahili. She considered the problems from the outside, not from the inside. And the only way out of the condition of outsider, Wendell Berry insists

> is for the teacher, the person of learning, the researcher, the intellectual, the artist, the scientist, to make common cause with a community. They must commit themselves to a community in such a way that they share the fate of that community—participate in its losses and trials and griefs and hardships and pleasures and joys and satisfactions—so that ... they'd begin to learn something. (Berry and Smith, 2007, p. 101)

That was a move that Arendt did not make, but it was a move that the students were making by their decision to study Swahili.

Arendt made her remarks in an article on violence, an article in which she condemned violence, in particular the violence advocated and carried out by African Americans. Her remarks reveal one of the contradictions throughout her work: an advocate for human rights, but were members of the black race really human? She decried the lack of education among African Americans, but denied that Swahili—spoken by 35 or 50 or 100 million people (see discussion above)—was a language. The desire to study Swahili, in and of itself, affirms both the language and the humanity of its speakers. Arendt believed that speech was one of the defining characteristics of humanity and along with action speech was one of the only two activities constituting the life of the polis "out of which rises the realm of human affairs ... from which everything merely necessary or useful is strictly excluded" (Arendt, 1958b, p. 25), i.e. the life of freedom. The denial of the status of language to Swahili was thus tantamount to a denial of the full humanity of Swahili speakers, a denial that they had a political life, an experience of freedom in addition to the common human experience of necessity. In *The human condition* Arendt discusses violence in relation to speech in Greek thought, stating that political action "in so far as it remains outside the sphere of violence is indeed transacted in words... Only sheer violence is mute" (ibid. p. 26). Commenting on Aristotle's definition of man as "a living being capable of speech" Arendt wrote

> Aristotle meant neither to define man in general nor to indicate man's highest capacity, which to him was not *logos*, that is not speech or reason, but *nous*, the capacity of contemplation, whose chief characteristic is that its content cannot be rendered in speech. In his two most famous definitions, Aristotle only formulated the current opinion of the polis about man and the political way of life, and according to this opinion, everybody outside the

> polis—slaves and barbarians—was *aneu logou,* deprived, of course, not of the faculty of speech, but of a way of life in which speech and only speech made sense and where the central concern of all citizens was to talk with each other. (ibid. p. 27)

If we read Arendt's comments on political life we can see how her views on the *polis* clashed with her understanding of what the students were attempting to do:

> The *polis,* properly speaking, is not the city-state in its physical location; it is the organization of the people as it arises out of acting and speaking together, and its true space lies between people living together for this purpose, no matter where they happen to be. "Wherever you go, you will be a *polis*": these famous words became not merely the watchword of Greek colonization, they expressed the conviction that action and speech create a space between the participants which can find its proper location almost any time and anywhere. (ibid., p. 198)

The destruction of political communities follows the loss of power, this latter being

> actualized only where word and deed have not parted company, where words are not empty and deeds not brutal, where words are not used to veil intentions but to disclose realities, and deeds are not used to violate and destroy but to establish relations and create new realities. (ibid. p. 200)

Violence is capable of destroying power Arendt claimed, but "it can never become a substitute for it" (ibid. p. 202). The combination of powerless and violence is tyranny, "an array of impotent forces that spend themselves ... in utter futility" (ibid.).

We can now see clearly Arendt's fear, her dilemma and her failure. For her, the study of a "kind of no-language" had to be a retreat from political life. The study of a language that she refused to study herself would "establish new relations and create new realities" and "create a space between the participants" that she could not enter into because she knew no Swahili. Because Arendt regarded Swahili as a no-language it followed from her way of thinking that the speakers of that no-language, whom she made it a point of describing as the descendents of slaves, were living outside the polis in a world entirely subjected to necessity, that they could only live in a social world of pre-political violence.

The students who wished to study Swahili had desires other than those Arendt assumed. They did not want what American education and Hannah Arendt offered them, for they did not wish to carry on in the old ways. They were, quite literally, looking "for another seat, another direction, another world" (Ellul, 1968, p. 286) by looking to another language. The students were creating a *polis*, but one in which Arendt did not want to participate, in which she could not participate unless she also studied Swahili, which she would not do because she thought it "a kind of no-language." For Arendt, the relation between Africa and the West was a one-way street: civilization, political life and freedom were found in the West, from which world the Africans must learn. For the African American students at Berkeley, the study of Swahili was analogous to the practice of marronage described by Roberts (2007). Marroon societies came into being exactly as Arendt described the origin of the *polis*, through the "organization of the people as it arises out of acting and speaking together, and its true space lies between people living together for this purpose." Yet Arendt could not accept that *polis*, nor even recognize it as such because she could not accept Swahili as a language.

Instead of recognizing, encouraging and celebrating the establishment of a political community, she insisted that the students submit to the existing political community, one which she very well knew continued to prevent and destroy whenever possible the power necessary for political life, especially as it arose among African Americans and the young. The ensuing violence that Arendt abhorred was predicted by her contemporary Jacques Ellul in terms that pointedly speak to the contradiction in Arendt's position on the study of Swahili:

> It never occurs to anyone that if the young are calling something into question, if they are beating desperately against our walls, it is they who may be right, and that what they are attacking may really deserve to be attacked. ... No reasonable person can conceive of the idea that the asocial teddy boy may be in the right, that what must be questioned is not he, but the society he opposes, and that the more we restrain the young, the more we cry, "Give youth some room!" But what we mean, of course, is room on *our* councils, on *our* committees, in *our* administrations... The cunning old man who detests you wins your support by offering you the back seat in a ready-made world that only needs to be developed in the direction he has established. But above all you must not look for another seat, another direction, another world, for then you would discover the implacability of the technical organization maintained by the serious people to whom you constitute a threat. (Ellul, 1968, p. 286-7).

The students at Berkeley were engaged in a linguistic marronage, securing for themselves a place beyond the world that only desired to fashion them to participate in "*our* councils, on *our* committees, in *our* administrations" (ibid.). Arendt's opposition to their decision and choice was perceived and understood by many as no less an act of violence than the physical violence which she condemned. The reversion to the pre-political social life of submission to necessity and the violence of tyranny would not be the consequences of students studying Swahili, but of the rejection of their choice of language and the political possibilities associated with that choice.

> O old men, of whom I am one—psychologists, sociologists, politicians, journalists, men of letters, all you who praise and charm the young—if you had the least semblance of honesty, you would have to shout: "Death to the young. Throw them all in jail!" For that, in the end, is exactly what you will do. (Ellul, 1968, p. 287).

And in words and indeed, the old men—and women—did.

Epilogue 2020

> *Wikipedia is a ubiquitous starting point for research. Students, librarians, even doctors check Wikipedia to begin their research, get an overview of a field, find relevant sources, and engage with the popular conception and summary of a subject.*
> *https://en.wikipedia.org/wiki/Wikipedia:The_Wikipedia_ Library/Cultural_Professionals*

This paper was originally written in 2007 in the context of calls within the world of computer programmers, librarians and others interested in the possibilities and problems of scholarly communication, for bringing the academic world into the wonderful new world of the Semantic Web, Web2.0 etc. These developments were themselves based upon the development of 'ontologies' in computer science and the promises made by the developers of those techniques. One of the proposals at that time was to link library databases to Wikipedia in order to improve the user experience for library patrons. The thought of grounding our databases and search engines, and thus our language, others' possible interpretations of our language, our searching possibilities within any given technical system the, intellectual relationships within our questions and the results of our research, all in one 'authoritative' source seemed to me a sign of a complete ignorance of what learning is all about. For me, learning is all about challenging what 'they say' and learning from reality; it is the antithesis of forcing all research and 'learning' to conform to an established consensus. Arendt's remarks on Swahili seemed to me then and now to reveal exactly where that form of mental slavery inflicted upon our children and ourselves will always and necessarily lead. 'Ontologies', whether based on a programmer's or scholar's assumptions, the Encyclopaedia Britannica or Wikipedia, cannot lead to 'an improvement in user experiences' but on the contrary forge the chains with which we shackle our future and enslave our descendents.

Bibliography

Allen, Danielle (2001). "Law's necessary forcefulness: Ralph Ellison vs. Hannah Arendt on the Battle of Little Rock" *Oklahoma City University Law Review* v.26 p. 857-895.

Arendt, Hannah (1958a). *The origins of totalitarianism.* Cleveland and New York: World Publishing Company.

Arendt, Hannah (1958b). *The human condition.* Chicago: University of Chicago Press.

Arendt, Hannah (1968). "The crisis in education." In: *Between Past and Future.* Rev. ed. New York: Viking Press.

Arendt, Hannah (1973). "On violence." In *The crisis of the Republic.* San Diego: Harcourt Brace Jovanovich, pp. 103-198. (Revised version of the essay originally entitled

"Reflections on violence" published in the *New York Review of Books* v.12, no.7, February 27, 1969)
Berry, Wendell (2000). *Life is a miracle: an essay against modern superstition.* Washington: Counterpoint.
Berry, Wendell and Jordan Fischer Smith (2007). "Field observations: an interview with Wendell Berry." In: Wendell Berry (Morris Allen Grubbs, editor), *Conversations with Wendell Berry.* Jackson, Mississippi: University of Mississippi Press, 2007, p. 86-102. Originally published in *Orion* Autumn 1993.
Budil, Ivo T. (2008). "Hannah Arendt and Africa." Paper presented at the 3rd International Conference on African Studies *Viva Africa*, 28 April 2008, Západočeská univerzita, Plzeň, Czech Republic.
Dossa, Shiraz (1980). "Human status and politics: Hannah Arendt on the Holocaust" *Canadian Journal of Political Science/Revuew canadienne de science politique*, v.13, nr.2 (June, 1980), pp. 309-323.
Ellul, Jacques (1968). *A critique of the new commonplaces.* New York: Knopf.
"Lingua franca." Article in *Encyclopædia Britannica*, 14th ed., 1929, v. 14, p.163.
Mackey, William Francis (1970). "Lingua franca." In: *Encyclopædia Britannica*, 14th ed., 1961, v.14, p.163.
Mufwene, Salikoko (2008). "Jargon" *Encyclopaedia Britannica Online*.
Mufwene, Salikoko (2008). "Lingua franca" *Encyclopaedia Britannica Online*.
Oakeshott, Michael (1933). *Experience and its modes.* Cambridge: Cambridge University Press.
Oakeshott, Michael (1950 [2001]). "The idea of a university" In his: *The voice of liberal learning.* Indianapolis: Liberty Fund, 2001. pp. 105-117. Originally published *in The Listener* v.XLIII.

Oakeshott, Michael (1965 [2001]). "Learning and teaching" In his: *The voice of liberal learning*. Indianapolis: Liberty Fund, 2001. pp. 35-61. Written in 1965 and originally published in 1967 in *The concept of education* edited by R.S. Peters (London: Routledge and Kegan Paul).

Oakeshott, Michael (1972 [2001]). "Education: the engagement and its frustration" In his: *The voice of liberal learning*. Indianapolis: Liberty Fund, 2001. pp. 1-34. Originally published 1972 in *Education and the development of reason*, edited by R.F. Dearden, P.H. Hearst a d R.S. Peters (London: Routledge and Kegan Paul).

Roberts, Neil (2007). *Freedom as marronage: the dialectic of slavery and freedom in Arendt, Pettit, Rousseau, Douglass, and the Haitian Revolution*. PhD dissertation, University of Chicago.

Sebelebele, Matome (2004). "Swahili: AU's official language." *BuaNews Online* 8 July 2004. Unable to locate in the original source. Cited from reprint viewed 24 June 2008 at: http://www.southafrica.info/ess_info/sa_glance/constituti on/ausummit04-swahili.htm

"Swahili." in *Encyclopædia Britannica*, 9th ed. 1887, v. 22, p. 729; 11th ed. v.26, p.178; 14th edition, v.21, p.629; 15th edition (accessed online December 2007)

Tucker, Archibald Norman (1961). "Swahili Language" in *Encyclopædia Britannica*, 14th ed., v. 21, p. 629.

Werner, Alice (1929). "Swahili Language" in *Encyclopædia Britannica*, 14th ed., v. 21, p.629.

Young-Bruehl, Elisabeth (1982). *Hannah Arendt: for love of the world*. New Haven: Yale University Press.

V

Signs, Language and Miscommunication
An Essay on Train Wrecks

Abstract
The movement of trains in the United States is coordinated by the use of a small number of standard codes of operating rules and variations upon them as well as various systems of signs, including railroad signs directed at railroad employees and highway signs directed at pedestrians and motorists. These signs, their intended meanings and the responses appropriate to them have been established by railroads and railroad associations, as well as federal, state and local agencies and laws. Nearly 200 years of accidents involving railroads has revealed that the interpretation of both train operating rules and signs associated with the railroad does not always follow the prescribed meanings. Understanding the reasons for these interpretations at variance with the prescribed meanings has been the object of considerable research over the past two decades and what has been learned has considerable importance for understanding all manner of sign systems, including linguistic signs.

1. A Train Wreck
Several years ago on a country road not far from my childhood home a friend of my family was killed along with his wife and three daughters when a train struck the van he was driving. The known facts concerning the accident are, according to my memory, that he drove around the lowered crossing gates after the passing of one train headed in one direction on his side of the tracks, and was then struck by another train travelling in the opposite direction on the far tracks. That particular crossing was marked by a standard railroad crossing sign in front of the tracks and equiped with crossing gates to prevent passage, flashing red lights and ringing bells. In addition, the oncoming train as well as the just past train were blowing their horns as they each approached their respective crossings.

With all these signs, how did the driver of the van fail to get the message? Did those signs communicate nothing to him? As far as I know there have been no attempts to ask railroad signs, warning lights and crossing barriers what they mean and for good reason: none of them mean anything for they have nothing to say. So what do we mean when we call them signs?

2. Railroads and Their Signs
> Because of the complexity and tempo of railroad operations, railroad traffic control systems exist to provide for the safe and efficient movement of rail equipment and goods. Over the years, the railroads have developed different systems for keeping their trains from running into each other. In the early days of railroading, there was no electricity and therefore there were no wayside signals in which to control train movements. Rather, train crews used timetables and train orders to operate. (Loumiet and Jungbauer, 2005, p. 31)

In the beginning there were no signs to inform anyone about the movements of trains, probably for the simple reason that there were no railroads, railroads themselves having appeared only in the 17th century (early 19th century if one dates railroads from the introduction of steam locomotives). Yet even after the invention of railroads some time elapsed before the first signs were erected by municipal or railroad officials in order to warn travelers of the dangers of loitering around or upon the rails.

> In response to a crossing accident in 1834, Massachusetts inaugurated the first safety legislation: in 1835 it required the carriers to mark all road crossings and the engineman to sound his bell as a warning. (Aldrich, p. 23)

Prior to the enacting of such legislation the situation in America shocked European visitors to the states. Aldrich records the remarks of one traveler who "marveled at unfenced lines and unguarded crossings. *"They* are not required to 'look out,' but *you* are," Bunn exclaimed" (Aldrich, p.21).

The purpose of those road crossing signs and the law requiring the engineman to sound a warning bell was to communicate to persons in the vicinity who were planning to cross the rails that there was potential or imminent danger in crossing. Neither the crossing markings nor the bell would be necessary were there no danger, and in the absence of that danger they do not in fact mean anything. Yet it was quickly discovered that neither the visible nor the audible signs were always successfull in communicating the intended message. Children, drunks, the blind, cattle, horses, and various other travellers consistently ignored written or other visual signs, as the deaf ignored the bells and whistles of approaching trains.

At night, on a sharp curve, walking into the wind, one might never hear a train approaching from behind. Of course, older or hearing-impaired individuals were at even greater risk and state reports contain depressingly large numbers of men and women described as deaf, insane, or aged, who were killed on the track. Rolland Stebbins was one such unfortunate. He was walking the track near Deerfield, Massachusetts, on August 7, 1848, when the Connecticut River Railroad ran him over. He was deaf and had not heard the bell or the whistle. (Aldrich, p. 21)

In certain circumstances company policies and municipal codes eventually required physical barriers to be erected in order to prevent such incidents as that in Deerfield, as well as others such as bulls entering the tracks, charging locomotives and derailing them (Aldrich, p. 21). In such cases an ounce of prevention is worth a ton of attempted communication.

The well documented history of the origin and development of railroad signs—both the standard codes of train rules and highway codes relating to railroad crossings for motorists, cyclists and pedestrians—means that two of the most common explanations for the operation of other kinds of signs—mainly divine origin and biological inheritance—have never been proposed as explanations for the universal grammar of railroad signs around the world, their symbiotic relationship with railroad tracks, grade crossings and driving manuals, and the generally high level of understanding that characterizes human responses to the presence of such signs. Nor are they in any sense "natural signs." By all accounts railroad signs worldwide have been constructed and installed in particular places as a consequence of citizen demands, governmental legislation and railroad company policies, all of those factors having been important in their origin. Clearly the study of the production and interpretation of railroad signs cannot be accomodated within the program of biolinguistics, nor to my knowledge have there been any attempts to do so.

Research on railroad communication and the role it plays in train wrecks has grown directly out of the recognition of the consequences of mixing living beings and locomotives, for in cases of physical interaction between those two classes of objects in motion the former almost always end up dead, creating in every case considerable problems for railroad companies. In the presence of railroads that cross human pathways, both railroad officials and public officials have realized the desirability of some means of warning those crossing the path of a train of the danger involved. The success of that public communication must be gauged in terms of personal injury and loss of life, and success has proven to be no simple task. Nor could the task simply be assigned to someone and thereby assumed to be taken care of.

> No doubt requiring that companies guard crossings and warn of trains was desirable, but at least in New York, fencing laws seem to have had little impact. Companies routinely contracted out the requirement to landowners, who just as regularly pocketed the money and did nothing. (Aldrich, p. 23)

Problems of misunderstanding and miscommunication have regularly dogged railroad companies, engineers and policy makers from the beginning (i.e. from the beginning of railroad communication systems). Unlike linguists for whom linguistic meaning is guaranteed by a biological inheritance (and, historically at least, by divine fiat), the very existence of railroad signs and therefore of their meanings have been the result of and have resulted in miscommunication, injury and death. The meaning of railroad signs appears to originate in a manner that differs from the genesis of meaning in everyday language—speech and writing—in significant ways, at least if we are to accept the accounts of the lexicon and semantic components in the standard theory. Far from being innate "organical structures" which have been accidentally put to use for communicational purposes with the evolution of railroad transportation systems, the forms and meanings of railroad signs are invented, argued and established by company policies, regulatory agencies and by lawmakers prior to their production and public installation. Rule books and manuals for railroad signal engineers record the invention of a set of signs and prescribe how they should be used to mean what, in which future places and circumstances. This may suggest that railroad sign systems are unlike human language, that they are digital codes.

> Real digital codes require to be invented and their use explained—in some higher-order language that has a semiotic flexibility that is simply incompatible with its being *itself* any kind of established code. (Love, 2007, p.705)

Nigel Love argued that "signficant points about how languages work semiologically may be made by contrasting languages with signalling systems that are uncontroversially understood to be codes in the relevant sense" (Love, 2007, p.694). One of the signalling systems that he considers to be an uncontroversial example of a digital code is the system of railroad signal lights.

> The essential idea is that some set of physical phenomena, in themselves semiotically empty, encode information, meanings, concepts ... that the user familiar with the system proceeds to decode. (Love, 2007, p.694)

This might be a fair enough description of railroad signal lights if they always occurred alone, their operation was semiologically unambiguous and social relations involving differing types of authority were not involved in their interpretation. That uncomplicated condition, as we shall see, exists in the rule books but does not exist in the world of actual railroad operation. The dissimilarities between linguistic signs and railroad sign systems dissappear when we leave the world of those systems in their design and description in rule books (grammars) and more closely examine their use and interpretation in real life.

"Codification" Roy Harris wrote, "as a macrosocial practice has to be judged in relation to the circumstances in which the results are expected to operate" (Harris, 1996, p.104). Railroad communication occurs in a well defined set of circumstances which severely restricts both the meaning that a signal engineer might intend to communicate to someone and the meanings that others might attribute to such signs. Nevertheless the necessity of interpreting those signs remains in every encounter with them, and the evidence is considerable that the interpretation of railroad signs is subject to the same kind of indeterminacy characteristic of spoken and written language.

The meaning of a railroad sign in the first instance is established in exactly the manner Love identifies as characteristic of codes, and the code books for railroad signalling and highway signs are compiled in a manner similar to prescriptive lexicography and grammar, that is, by railroad companies and government agencies prior to the operation of the signs. The meaning and use of such signs must then be taught in the same manner as reading, writing and arithmetic. In the first edition of *Railway Signalling and Communications: Installation and Maintenance* Table I outlines the Railway Clearing House Standard Block Signalling Code. We read the following:

Call attention. Beats on the bell: 1

> Is line clear for express passenger train or breakdown van train going to clear the line, or light engine going to assist disabled train? Beats on the bell: 4. how to be given: 4 consecutively
> Is line clear for ordinary passenger train or breakdown van train not going to clear the line? Beats on the bell: 4. How to be given: 3 pause 1
> Is line clear for branch passenger train? Beats on bell: 4. How to be given: 1 pause 3.
> Is line clear for fish, meat, fruit, horse, cattle, or perishable train composed of coaching stock? Beats on bell: 5. How to be given: 5 consecutively.
> Is line clear for empty coaching stock train? Beats on bell: 5. How to be given: 2 pause 2 pause 1
> (Tattersall, p.6)

and this goes on until nineteen beats of the bell form part of the code:

> Lampman or fog signalman required. Beats on bell: 19. How to be given: 9 pause 5 pause 5
> (Tattersall, p.7)

The book includes more detailed instructions and commentary for the use of the visual signals in a block telegraph signal system.

> *All signals, as a rule, to be immediately on the left of, or vertically over, the line to which they apply. At diverging junctions bracket signals are preferred to signals carried on separate posts, unless there are reasons to the contrary. In the case of shunting signals, where more than one are necessary, direction may be indicated by carrying them vertically one below the other, in which*

> cases the top signal will apply to the line on the extreme left, and so on. Semaphore distant signals to be distinguished from stop signals during daylight by yellow-coloured arms, with notches cut out of the ends. They must be placed under a stop signal of the box in rear and must, unless the circumstances are exceptional, be repeated under all stop signals in advance of that signal which is worked from that box, with the necessary additional control by such signals.

> Remarks.—Distants should be repeated under all stop signals for the one box to meet the case of foggy weather. If there were only one distant signal it would be rather misleading to a driver in fog. After being warned by a fogman at the distant signal, or being shown a green light at the distant, he would naturally expect that the next stop signal he came to would be for the box working the distant signal, and it would be decidedly misleading if this were not so. (Tattersall, p. 9)

Railroad personnel are presumed to have learned this language well enough to be native signers of the system and thus members of that ideal homogenous community of competent railroad sign language users. That this characterization of the participants in railroad communication is an idealization or a legal fiction is evident in accident reports such as one discussed by Alldrich:

> Dunn described an inspection during which the station agent was asked if he had a copy of the regulations. "The agent was not quite sure. It depended on whether this particular circular was printed on paper soft enough to use in cleaning lamp chimneys. If so, it had probably been expended for this purpose. If not it might be in a

box where he kept a lot of circulars he had never found time to read." (Aldrich, p. 227)

Even in cases where the rules and the appropriate signs were known, the particulars of when and where to make the signs ended up being decided in the courts, and in at least one case, later that interpretation rejected and replaced by new legislation.

Statutes mandating bells or whistles occasionally posed questions of interpretation. New York courts, for instance, considered whether this obligation applied only when the railroad and roadway crossed at the same level. A judicial ruling that the law required ringing a bell or blowing a whistle even when the track was elevated and passed over the highway caused the legislature to change the provision to cover only crossings at grade level. (Ely, 2001, p.126)

In spite of the highly controlled manner of establishing a system of signs in the first instance by policy and by law, signs that are then published and publicly proclaimed, taught in schools and the consistency of interpretation of which has been sought through drivers' tests, police patrols and security cameras, it has been, from the beginning (of railroad signs), abundantly clear that other meanings can be and often are attributed to railroad signs in the second instance, and furthermore that those signs, often many at once and in conjunction, are sometimes simply not perceived much less interpreted by some human travellers in certain situations.

The meaning of railroad signs is therefore a phenomena both open to empirical investigation in laws and company manuals, and closed to such investigation in most cases where different meanings were apparently ascribed to the signs, since the creators of those differing interpretations have rarely survived the events following upon their apparently heterodox interpretations. We have already looked at the official legally sanctioned meanings of railroad signs and the responses appropriate to them as indicated in the prescribed sources; in order to examine heterodox and frequently unsuccessful interpretations there are two paths of investigation open to the researcher: the published reports of official investigations of train wrecks and other undesirable incidents, and our own history of experience with such signs and the narratives of others, in so far as we have interpreted the signs and responded to them in a manner other than the prescribed fashion and yet remained alive. We can return to the incident with which this paper opened and ask how we might understand what happened. What signs/interpretations were made by the man in the van?

3. Railroad signs and miscommunication

The possibility that he did not see or hear the signs must be ruled out in the case of the man in the van, since it is known that he deliberately drove around barriers rather than simply crashing into them. Nevertheless, that possibility is in fact a frequent occurrence, often for rather mundane reasons: signs often go unnoticed simply because people are paying attention to something else.

> By 1852, the Ogdensburg Railroad had rules requiring the engineman to carry a copy of the timetable and forbidding anyone from talking to him while the train was in motion. The latter rule was also in force on the Western & Atlantic. Its wisdom had been revealed by its absence two years earlier on the Camden & Amboy. An engineman in the midst of conversation with a companion let the water in his boiler run low, resulting in an explosion that killed both men. (Aldrich, p. 35)

> Engineman Davis, young, intelligent, and with a record of six years of good service, was having trouble with his engine and became preoccupied with getting the injector to feed water to the boiler. As a result he failed to see a distant signal, a crossing watchman swinging a lantern, a home signal, and a flagman, and crashed into the rear of a waiting suburban train, killing himself and twenty-two others. (Aldrich, p. 183)

Marc Green has given a number of reasons why drivers "miss an object as big as a train or as conspicuous as a flashing light" (Green, 2002, p.32), and unless he had suicidal intentions we can be sure that our friend in the van did not see the other train because his vision was blocked by the first train. There were apparently other factors involved in his case, and similar factors are frequently involved in train wrecks.

> [I]n a disquieting development, states discovered that protected crossings usually averaged more accidents than those that were unprotected. Of course, this did not necessarily mean that protection caused accidents because protected crossings typically had heavier traffic. But individuals routinely ignored signs, whistles, watchmen, and even gates. And sometimes protection *did* contribute to the problem, for carriers might put up gates that were only operated by watchmen during the day, leaving the gate open at night to act as a trap for the unwary. (Aldrich, p. 125)

Another possibility that should probably be dismissed is that he did not know what those railroad signs meant, for he had passed a driver's education course, he was a liscensed driver, and he had successfully heeded the same warning signals at the same place many times before. However, ignorance of public signs, while not excusable in a court of law, is, like ignorance of certain spoken or written forms by persons in other activities, a frequent problem among those involved in accidents of all sorts. A thorough knowledge of the whole set of signs and the rules for their operation in fact becomes increasingly difficult as those signs and rules for their use increase in number and complexity.

> From the beginning companies realized that control of their operations required timely communication of vital information. ... All the early lines employed a timetable and set of rules and signals that governed its use and other aspects of train control. Initially rules were few enough to fit on a single sheet of paper; by the 1870s they would number in the hundreds and take up entire books. There were also whistle, flag, and lantern signals to communicate a host of road and train conditions such as a crossing approach, or that a train should be backed up, or that there was a second section to the train following, and many other matters as well. (Aldrich, p. 34-35)

A further problem is simply ignoring such signs.

> [A] small but troubling number of collisions began to occur in which enginemen simply ran signals. To their surprise both the carriers and their critics discovered that block signals suffered from some of the same labor problems that plagued the train order system. On the Fitchburg Railroad in 1893 a freight engineman running distant and home signals crashed into the rear of a passenger train. Subsequently the engine driver explained that he never paid any attention to distant signals. His fireman didn't even know where they were. Another engineman on the line testified that even if he

> missed a distant signal he never slowed for the home signal. The lesson, it seemed, was that even the block system could not fully remedy the carriers' agency problems. (Aldrich, p. 95-96)

A still further possibility is that the signs were in fact ambiguous, as this has often been the case in the history of railroad communication.

> The company used red flags to signal both danger and to stop for passengers. On October 1, 1882, the engineman of Train 72 thought he had been flagged for passengers at the St. Johnsville Station. He soon pulled out onto the main line and promptly collided with another train, killing two people and injuring several more. Such accidents led the carriers to develop general principles of signaling, and in 1884 the American Railway Association developed the Standard Code of train rules. (Aldrich, p. 89)

Moving from one railroad company's system through another could require a bilingualism in which the forms of the code remained the same but the meanings did not.

> Changing jobs faced even an experienced railroader with a bewildering variety of novel train rules and signals. In addition, as companies increasingly obtained trackage rights over other lines trainmen found signals that changed meaning along the line. Nearly all companies with double track ran on the right, but not the Old Colony, which preferred running left. The train that carried President Garfield's remains to Washington traveled through four different signal systems. As one writer described the problem, "on one road a lamp

moved up and down is the signal to stop, on a connecting road the same signal means go back." Similarly, "on one a single note of the whistle means go a-head, on the other go back; on one road red is the standard signal for danger, and yet, at three points on the same road, that color means that the road is clear." In 1881 the U.S. commissioner of railroads claimed that on two hundred roads only one whistle signal always had the same meaning while some had up to forty different meanings. ... As Forney summarized signaling in 1882, "diversity like that which prevailed on Noah's Ark exists everywhere." (Aldrich, p. 88)

The board ... discovered that only three roads used the same rules and signals, and that on many others they were cumbersome and confusing. ... In 1890 the board again complained that the "lack of uniformity on different roads in rules governing the train service is a definite danger." It also noted "the alarming diversity of [signal] practice," observing that "the arrangement of lanterns which means safety on one line means danger on another." (Aldrich, p. 72)

Our friend was crossing the tracks in the late 20th century, long after such ambiguities had been dealt with by a standard highway code, but it is apparent to anyone who has lived near a railroad crossing that there are indeed times when the signs are ambiguous. I am in fact familiar with that crossing near my home and can easily imagine one possible ambiguous situation, i.e. exactly the situation in which our friend thought he found himself. When a train has passed, the signals continue "operating" even though the danger has passed, i.e. they continue to "sign" danger even though the danger has passed. The signs only cease to operate after the train has passed a certain number of yards beyond the crossing. A similar situation exists when a train stops after the warning signals have begun to operate but before entering the crossing, and this is both frequent and sometimes a very lengthy stop. In both of these situations, many people will see clearly that there is *at that moment* no danger, and even though it is against the law they will drive through the crossing even if they have to drive round lowered crossing gates to get through. In such situations there are, as it were, conflicting signals. Drivers and pedestrians alike are confronted with automatic warning signals designed to "communicate" danger that continue to "send" that message when the person receiving that message is at the same time looking at the train which has already passed by or has been stopped for 14 minutes after its engine uncoupled and went to the roundhouse to pick up more cars but got derailed.

Such situations are instructive for they bring into conflict intentional but mechanical signs—signs deliberately created to communicate with someone—with 'natural signs', that is, our understanding of the meaning of objects and events in the world around us. A.A. Milne provided perhaps the clearest description of the production and interpretation of natural signs in his 1926 account of Winnie-the-Pooh and some bees:

> First of all he said to himself: "That buzzing-noise means something. You don't get a buzzing-noise like that, just buzzing and buzzing, without its meaning something. If there's a buzzing-noise, somebody's making a buzzing-noise, and the only reason for making a buzzing-noise that *I* know of is because you're a bee."
>
> Then he thought another long time, and said. "And the only reason for being a bee that I know of is making honey."

> And then he got up, and said: "And the only reason for making honey is so as *I* can eat it." So he began to climb the tree. (A.A. Milne, 1926, p.6)

In this manner we see with our own eyes that a train has passed or has stopped and this means *to us in this moment* that the danger has passed or ceased. In such cases we tend to believe our own perception/interpretation of the situation we are in and to discount the technical apparatus as irrelevant *in the present situation* since it is operating on a mechanical basis, designed by someone far away in time and space and not created at that moment by someone who can assess the situation and sign accordingly.

This points to another important factor: time. The meaning of the signs from the perspective of the designers of the systems is invariant over time, but for those waiting on a sign or using one in a given situation, the timing of the sign is itself significant.

> When one engineman on the Nashville & Chattanooga who routinely trespassed on the time of other trains finally caused a wreck, the company discovered that he had no watch. On September 5, 1856, a misplaced switch at a station led a New York Central train to run onto a siding, hitting a cattle train and killing six people. (Aldrich, p. 36-37)

> On single-track lines, disaster in the form of a head-on collision also lurked when watches were off or train orders incorrect, or forgotten, or misread. (Aldrich, p. 90)

> [F]ourteen trains were scheduled from Neward to New york City from 7:30 to 9:30 each morning, and the two that collided were scheduled to arrive in Hoboken only *3*

minutes apart. Under such conditions, flagging was unworkable. A flagman who left the moment a train stopped walking at 4 miles per hour could get back 1,056 feet in 3 minutes. A four-car train going 45 miles per hour took about 860 feet to stop: should the flagman hesitate one minute, disaster was inevitable. (Aldrich, p. 95)

The man in the van found himself in a situation in which the timing of the trains and the timing of the signs led to there being no interval between the operation of the signs indicating the danger existing with the passing train and the danger from the oncoming train: the gates stayed down, the bells kept ringing, the lights kept flashing as though the original communication situation had never ended when in fact it had ceased and a new situation had arisen. It appears to be the case that the deceased interpreted the railroad signs which he first encountered to mean that the danger was associated with the passing train, and at the time he approached the tracks that was indeed the meaning that the system "intended" since it was the approach of that train that had set the warning signs into operation. However, before that train had passed far enough beyond the crossing to turn off the sign that "meant" (at that time) danger from the passing train, the approaching train triggered the same set of warning signs to "mean" danger associated with an oncoming train from the opposite direction. The man in the van had no way of knowing that the meaning of the railroad signs had changed as the one train passed and the other approached since he could neither see nor hear the approaching train and the signals themselves neither ceased nor altered in any way to indicate "still more danger from another approaching train." The man in the van correctly understood the railroad signs he first encountered to mean "danger from train A" but those signs had to be reinterpreted to mean "danger from train B" if he were to correctly understand the dangers present. The signs with which he was presented were clearly stationary and identical in form, but were unfortunately associated with two different meanings at two different times. Successfull communication with such a system of signs clearly cannot be guaranteed by the system alone.

A similar problem was noted in the the Rutland and Burlington Railroad *Instructions for the Running of Trains, Etc.* in 1854 in which Rule 87 instructed that: "too much sounding of the whistle impairs its use as a signal of danger" (quoted in Gamst, 2001). The importance of this problem has not lessened in the years since:

> Lastly, drivers may see the signal but still cross the tracks because the flashing signal has low credibility. Flashing warnings usually begin far in advance of the train, so people learn that an activated signal does not necessarily mean a train will arrive soon. This creates a "cry wolf" situation where drivers do not take the flashing signal seriously. If the lights begin to flash too far in advance of the train, then, ironically, the danger signal is transformed into a safety signal—it communicates the message there definitely won't be a train coming for a while. The message communicated by warnings is not always the intended one. (Green, 2002, p.36)

The question then remains, if the message communicated is not the intended message, how is it that these railroad signs come to "mean" something other than their intended meaning? If the message of railroad signs "is not always the intended one", how can that be, what does this mean for our understanding of signs, and what are the consequences for communication?

4. Mixed signals: the bad grammar of efficiency and the indeterminacy of the sign

The meanings of the railroad signs installed along or in front of the tracks are in the first instance established by the inventors of those signs in some more or less distant time and place. Railroad sign systems, train codes of operation and systems of road signs created and installed in order to regulate train and road traffic are sponsored by railroad companies, their associations, and various government agencies, with regular revisions to both the signs and what they mean as legal, economic and technical developments alter operating conditions. Over time their meanings may change due to legislation while they remain physically unchanged and in place. More importantly, in each particular circumstance in which the issue of those signs and their meanings comes into question, what the signs are, what they mean in this particular situation and what are the appropriate responses to them are matters to be determined in that instance, and that determination is not always straightforward.

In an attempt to understand what were perceived to be non-compliance with railroad operating rules, the U.S. Federal Railroad Administration discovered that one of the major obstacles to rule compliance was what they termed "mixed signals".

> When questioned about major roadblocks to rule compliance, participants suggested that senior management sometimes appears to emphasize productivity over safety, which may create an organizational culture that unintentionally encourages operating rule violations. ... [T]hey suggested that senior management may influence unsafe work behavior by unintentionally encouraging operating rule violations. ... When operating employees receive mixed signals from immediate supervisors – indicating that it is permissible to violate operating rules sometimes, and that at other times it is not permissible –

they may be more likely to engage in unsafe behaviors. (Coplen, 1999, p. viii)

The study found that the sources and reasons for the mixed signals concerning rule compliance are varied. Corporate culture was one:

> In the opinion of the participants, it appears that a culture has been created on some railroads which fosters a tendency for supervisors to send confusing messages to operating employees - ambiguous messages that imply they should comply with operating rules under some conditions and not comply under others. (Coplen, 1999, p. 12)

The system of authority and multiple sources of authority (sponsors) for the rules and signs was another reason given:

> Also, different levels of employees appear to have different motivations and pressures to not comply with the rules at times. Yardmasters, train masters, and train dispatchers, for example, may be urged by their supervisors to get the train out of town, and indirectly encourage employees to cut corners on rule compliance to speed up operations. Conductors or engineers may send similar messages to their brakemen. (Coplen, 1999, p. 12)

> And the fact is that you have commands that come down from the top. And most of the time in transportation those commands are to move the trains. And to get the train from A to B in a certain amount of time. And when you're not doing it, you know, to the requirements that come in to that ... the operating rules, or whatever, get overridden by that command." (Coplen, 1999, p. 12)

... a V.P. or higher, who says now you either meet goals or I'll find somebody who will. That's when the real mixed signal comes in. Now ... now you've taken people who are supposed to be managing people, who are supposed to be producing for us, and they don't really know which way to turn." Still another participant explained that "You still have a whole climate of people [operating employees] out there who are convinced that the only reason you're interested in safety is the bottom line of the company." (Coplen, 1999, p. 12)

Apart from these issues of authority, Loumiet and Jungbauer describe the normal system of authorized communications that are presumed effective when issued but superseded by any previously existing or subsequently issued communications of certain types in all cases of conflict.

Each timetable, from the time it takes effect, supersedes the preceding timetable. At least forty-eight hours before the new timetable takes effect, notice of change must be issued by *general bulletin*. Employees governed by the timetable must obtain a copy of the new timetable before going on duty. They must examine it to ascertain that their copy is complete and is properly paged. (Loumiet and Jungbauer, 2005, p.32)

In addition to these general bulletins, there are system bulletins and train bulletins as well, and like the general bulletins, the railroad operating code stipulates that the relevant employees must have read and understood the applicable bulletins before going on duty, and either "carry or have access to them while on duty" (Loumiet and Jungbauer, 2005, p. 32). And there is more:

> *Special instructions* in the timetable supersede any operating rule with which such special instructions may conflict. *Superintendent's bulletins* supersede special instructions in the timetable and any rule with which they must conflict. *Train messages* supersede any rule with which they may conflict. (Loumiet and Jungbauer, 2005, p. 32)

And, as the FRA report noted, all of those bulletins, instructions and messages must be interpreted by the railroad employee in light of the "mixed signals" coming from various authorities at higher levels.

Ignorance of responsibilities was also cited as a reason for noncompliance:

> Ignorance of responsibilities seemed to be a common denominator in how these mixed signals, or mixed communications, get disseminated. It was also noted that many yardmasters, dispatchers, and operators are sitting with computers and telephones and have very little face-to-face interaction with the employees they directly supervise. Some complained that people in these jobs often do not realize they are actually supervisors and that they have an important role in communicating rule compliance. (Coplen, 1999, p. 12-13)

Other reasons for rule non-compliance mentioned in the report were the employees' desire for short cuts, too much paperwork, and lack of enforcement, and for the last of these it was noted that "Mixed signals was another reason why management may not enforce operating rules" (Coplen, 1999, p. 13)

The study also noted problems with the rules. Current operating rule books in the United States are all founded on what is now known as the Standard Code of Operating Rules originally adopted on April 14, 1887. This Standard Code

> was never intended to be used as a working rulebook. Rather, its primary intention was to standardize operating practices to the extent practicable while still preserving the flexibility of individual railroads to either modify or omit rules at their discretion. Even rulebooks with identical phraseology could be interpreted and applied differently on different railroads. (Coplen, 1999, p. 2)

The application of the rules is neither uniform across companies, nor, in the case of mergers, is it necessarily uniform accross the various levels of authority within a single company.

> Mergers of major railroad companies in recent years resulted not only in the merging of different railroad lines and operating rulebooks, but also in the merging of railroad cultures and operating practices. Superficially, it may appear that most railroads have adopted a common code of operating rules, but major differences still exist in the application, and consequently, the compliance with these operating rules. Moreover, different management styles often clash when organizational cultures merge, as documented in the case of the Penn Central merger in 1968 (Daughen and Binzen, 1971) and the Burlington Northern Santa Fe merger in 1995 (Machalaba, 1997). This leaves operating rules managers uncertain as to how specific rules should be applied on their newly-formed railroad. (Coplen, 1999, p. 2-3)

Not only corporate mergers, but changing technologies and operating environments lead to an increasing complexity of operations and consequently of the rules that regulate those operations. This presents considerable problems for "native speakers" of railroad sign language, who suddenly find that their native status vanishes with the grammar officially sanctioned in the new rule book: not only do they have to learn the rules of a new system but they have to unlearn the old rules and change their behavior.

> The number of operating rules and procedures that employees must now commit to memory is substantial. With fewer employees to handle the same workload, individuals may no longer have the time to look up rules when performing their duties, perhaps further complicating both their ability and their desire to comply with these rules (Coplen, 1999, p. 2-3)

Motorists have the same problem:

> New warning signs such as this that might not be readily recognizable by the public shall be accompanied by an educational plaque, LOW GROUND CLEARANCE which is to remain in place for at least 3 years after its initial installation. (U.S. Department of Transportation, Federal Highway Administration, 2000, p. 8B-11)

We have already noted the geographic and corporate dialectal variations of railroad signs and operating rules; here we see the birth of sociolects following language reform, the persistence of patterns of behavior reflecting past realities that conflict with the requirements of the new order. Standardization was imagined to be the solution to misunderstanding, but it creates a different set of conditions for misunderstanding in its turn.

Those involved in rule revisions also acknowledged that some rules themselves present problems, and hoped that revising the rule books would provide two important benefits: "1) an improvement in the clarity and understanding of operating rules, and 2) an improvement in the ability of an employee to look up unfamiliar operating rules" (Coplen, 1999, p. 3). However, the FRA report suggested that the certainty of obtaining those benefits was doubtful, posing the question "Given a factual understanding, how well are employees able to conceptually apply the rules?" (Coplen, 1999, p.3-4).

The interpretation of the rules remains a critical activity which rule revision can never eliminate. The correct interpretation of the language of the rules, of verbal instructions, and missing or incorrect signs cannot be guaranteed by more or better rules. Some cases noted in the above-mentioned report are instructive.

> One person noted that he thought many people tended to apply restricted speed in terms of miles per hour rather than generally being prepared to stop. (Coplen, 1999, p. 7)

> Radio miscommunication and misunderstandings, for example, have lead to serious incidents. Instructions such as "High ball, everybody's in the clear," without train or unit number identification, could potentially cause a fatal accident. If a crew who overheard those instructions assumed that message was for them and began proceeding, they might operate in such a way that could lead to a collision. (Coplen, 1999, p. 10)

> Other examples of improper radio communications can be simply described as "assumptions." For instance, when crews do not properly identify their train or engine number, other operating crews or workmen may make assumptions about which train the message applies to

without confirming the train's identity. Of particular concern were situations in which crews left main line switches open (not lining back a switch for the main line movement) to expedite trains, transferring the responsibility to another crew. ...
Incidents happen when the yard crew with the responsibility to line the switch for the main track does not do so, for one reason or another. Another crew on a train that is approaching the switch on the main track will often *assume* that the track is lined for the main line, which it usually is, and may run through the switch when it is not lined properly. This can cause extensive damage to the switch requiring immediate repair. If the train crew does not realize they ran through the switch, or does not tell anyone for fear of being disciplined, it could easily cause a serious derailment or personal injury the next time a train goes over the switch.
(Coplen, 1999, p. 10)

What we see in all of these cases is that the meaning of signs in particular instances is not determined by the rule books but by a diverse group of railroad executives, supervisors and employees who are judging what the signs *really* mean in this situation, not only for themselves but for what they imagine that they mean for others as well (e.g. the employee second-guessing the boss's wishes). These interpretive agents are all relying on past experience with the rules, the signs in question, and all those other persons in their restricted role as railroad personnel as well as in their much broader role as communicating human beings. And in some cases they are acting according to past understandings of the rules and operating conditions that are no longer appropriate. The indeterminacy of the sign, whether that involves "mixed signals", ambiguity, assumptions about the state of the world here and now, or outdated, incomplete or misunderstood systems of signs and operating rules, leads in many cases to miscommunication and in some cases to property damage, injury and death.

5. *Language and miscommunication*

In the current standard theory of linguistics the form and meaning of any linguistic production is determined by the various structures and components of the mental lexicon and the operation of MERGE, grammatical constraints, etc. Misunderstanding is explained variously as being due to the misfiring of neural systems, failure of processing buffers, multiple possible analyses of a given input string, etc. In other words, making the wrong sign as speech producer *or* interpreter is a matter that you and I can do something about only after the fact. The system operates according to plan and if it fails in some way, that is the end of the story, for the system has nothing to do with communication even though you may wish to put it to communicative use. Conversely, if your attempted communication fails in spite of your perfect vocabulary, grammar and enunciation (or spelling), that has nothing to do with the operation of the language faculty. What the standard theory fails to acknowledge is that any instance of miscommunication in the production and interpretation of signs is in itself sufficient proof that the meaning of the sign is not determined (much less guaranteed) by any one of the parties in communication, nor to anything external to the communication situation, and the communicational significance for its intended interpreter in any situation is only revealed in the response it draws or fails to draw.

The usual understanding of railroad communication reveals a tendency to assign efficacy to the system of signs, and to explain miscommunication by some form of failure on the part of the deceased; they are the victims of their own failure to understand the signs properly and act accordingly.

> A Federal Railroad Administration official recently told me, "I can't imagine the driver not seeing the flashing lights. Even with glare, if the driver was paying attention, then the flashing lights should have been seen. (Green, 2002, p.36)

This faith in the efficacy of the signs in spite of the evidence of miscommunication is born out in one accident report after another with what some researchers now regard as a disturbing regularity. In rare instances the system is found to have misfunctioned:

> The probable cause of the accident was the failure of the highway-rail grade crossing warning system at Dundee Road to indicate the approach of ATK 340 at least 20 seconds prior to Passsenger Train's arrival at the highway-rail grade crossing.
> (Federal Railroad Administration, 2008, p.7)

Most of the time, however, the problem is located in the people involved, not the system which was found to be working exactly as it was supposed to:

> The FRA determined that the accident occurred because of a failure of the crew of Train MPRPB05 to operate the train at Restricted Speed as required by GCOR Rule 17.7. The crew of Train MPRPB05 did not understand the requirements of GCOR Rule 17.7 when they cut out the ATC in noncontinuous block system territory.
> A contributing factor to this accident was an apparent lack of understanding of GCOR Rule 17.7 by the third track train dispacher. ... The fact that the train crew chose to consult a GCOR operating rule book indicated that they were in doubt as to the correct course of action.

Unfortunately, the operating rule book did not help the crew and they interpreted the rule incorrectly and operated the train at a speed higher than Restricted Speed. (Federal Railroad Administration, 2005, p.7)

The highway user disregarded the highway-rail grade crossing warning devices and operated his vehicle off the roadway to avoid these devices. The cause for the long activation time reported by witnesses and the minimum 250 seconds of warning time indicated by the keyboard display could not be determined. (Federal Railroad Admininstration, 2005a, p.6)

The FRA has determined that the probable cause was the motor vehicle drivers' failure to stop clear of the hightway-rail grade crossing. Additional factors were the drivers' inattentiveness to and disregard for both the active and passive warning devices. (Federal Railroad Administration, 2005b, p.5)

The FRA found that the accident occurred because train Q217 did not comply with the Approach Signal at Harbison Walker. (Federal Railroad Administration, 2007, p.6)

FRA concluded the collision was caused by the failure of the Metrolink train crew to comply with a fixed signal (other than automatic block or interlocking signal) displaying a stop indication. FRA also believes the Metrolink locomotive engineer's use of a personal cell phone for text messaging while he was at the controls of his train is a likely source of locomotive cab distraction and may have been a significant contributing cause to the accident (Federal Railroad Administration, 2008a, p. 19)

Railroad companies, however, are (at least publicly) committed to "that ultimate goal of zero crossing accidents and zero fatalities" (Cotey, 2008, p.32). "All crossings are safe if you obey the law" Cotley quotes Union Pacific railroad Director of Public Safety Dale Bray as saying (Cotley, 2008, p.32), but she continues by revealing one of the reasons that railroad communication research is conducted differently from linguistic theory: people do not always obey the law. Although railroad signs are created specifically for communication, no signs can guarantee successful communication.

> It appears that with in-place protective systems and current warning signs and other roadway precautions, accidents will continue to occur. Installation of full barriers, bells and flashing red lights has, to some extent, reduced accidents, although only partially. They continue to occur, even with maximum protection. (Cunliffe, 1993, p.23)

The success of railroad communication is measured in millions of dollars of property damage, personal injuries and deaths. The success and failure of railroad signs matters to such an extent that railroad officials cannot simply satisfy themselves —as the Federal Railroad Administration sometimes appears to do—with upholding the system and blaming the dead.

> This blame-the-victim mentality does nothing to reduce frequency of future accidents. It ignores the reality that human beings have mental limitations and constraints that must be considered in system design, expecially where safety is an issue. (Green, 2002, p.36)

The persistent failures of railroad signs for almost 200 years now has led many researchers on railroad communication to acknowledge that if successful communication can never be guaranteed, then a different approach is necessary.

> The only way to completely avoid rail/highway grade crossing accidents is total elimination, which will likely be an essential feature of any future high speed rail system. (Cunliffe, 1993, p.23)

> The best way to make crossings safer? Eliminate them. (9th Annual grade crossing update, p. 31)

That current approach was first suggested in 1887.

> An Aug. 23, 1887, New York Times article on crossing fatalities suggested closures were one way to prevent collisions. Fast-fiorward more than 120 years and that recommendation still holds up as the best way to eliminate accident risks. (Weart, 2008, p.37)

Thus it appears that railroad administrators and designers have arrived at the same conclusion that many have come to regarding natural languages: "From the purely utilitarian point of view, they are highly imperfect" (Hagège, 1990, p.154), poor tools that do not work as well as we think they ought to. Like some critics of natural language, railroad communication engineers have laboured for many years to perfect their systems of signs but have so far failed to make them unambiguous in all situations. Their preferred solution is to circumvent the need for communication as much as possible by eliminating wherever possible the conditions that often lead to train wrecks.

6. Conclusion: Signs that do not communicate.
Like railroad accident researchers, Charlotte Nielsen looked beyond the claims for successful communication interpreted as "widespread familiarity" with certain signs, to the actual results of particular communication situations. What she discovered was a world of "language that does not communicate" (Nielsen, 2002). "The results belie the alleged success" Lorenzen (2005, p.55) quotes her as saying.

> Charlotte Nielsen has sought to uncover the basic conditions for the campaign as a communicative situation, and as a psycholinguist she believes that every text involves a real-life reception situation and not just an abstract one. It is this real-life situation that should be examined. (Lorenzen, 2005, p.56)

In her study, the meaning or effect of a nutritional campaign ought not to be measured solely in terms of how many people saw or heard the advertisements produced by the campaign, but ought to have something to do with actual diets and eating habits of those who were the intended recipients of the message. If the text of the campaign advertisements had no other effect than to become a part of the recipients' mental furniture, then how can one speak of those texts actually meaning anything? If language does not serve communication, why are we talking and writing? This is precisely the problem faced by railroad engineers, but a problem linguists have refused to acknowledge with their insistence that language and communication are only accidentally related.

Saussures' speech circuit, whether it works or not, does not matter. And in the standard theories of linguistics, meaning has nothing to do with communication: it exists as part of the language faculty, operating like your bile or your liver except it has no purpose or function and is therefore entirely inconsequential, like your appendix. Language means something (in theory at least) but it does not matter what. This is most clearly revealed in the examples that populate linguistics treatises. In 1986 Chomsky casually offered the reader the 'sentence'

John hit the boy. (Chomsky, 1986, p. 57).

and for all we know he has left the boy lying there bleeding, screaming and writhing in pain for 25 years now. Of course it is most likely the case that in reality there was no boy, there was no John, and no one got hit: Chomsky's 'sentence' meant nothing when he produced it, and it remains just as meaningless today. In a passage that one might mistakenly assume to have been written about trains, Vasiliu (1970, p. 152) wrote that "trenul pleacă peste cinci minute" *means* "PES (PL, Θ) · MI(Θ) · 5(MI)" and indeed those two strings of written signs are not only equivalent but they really do mean exactly the same thing: nothing whatsoever. The only train involved was Vasiliu's train of thought, and that train was going nowhere. The linguist offers meaningless sentences to illustrate rules of grammar, but surely "we do not speak in order to apply or illustrate rules of grammar" (Hagège, 1990, p.168). Moreover, if "successful communication" is defined as "the exchange of words stripped of all ambiguity" (Hagège, 1990, p.201), communication also comes to nothing, just like language. In this view, both language and communication involve nothing other than the transfer of the contents of one mental organ to the contents of another mental organ distant in space. Neither language nor communication move the world, trains, your heart or your arse.

If linguistic signs were as inconsequential and meaningless as the nutritional campaign slogans that everyone knows but ignores or the examples from Chomsky and Vasiliu quoted above, linguistics and semiotics would be equally meaningless. For the linguist to offer such "language" for our contemplation is as though the linguist "excludes the individual speaker and, by the same token, ignores interaction between speakers. In this conception of language, it is as if no one ever spoke to anyone else" (Hagège, 1990, p.182).

Real language is more like a train wreck, for words, like sticks and stones can break your bones. Like a train, real language sings "I'll take you there" and gives life one moment, and the next moment it brings a death warrant, signed, sealed and delivered with a futile orchestra of horns, bells and whistles. If the language that linguists analyze means nothing more than NP + VP or PES (PL, Θ) · MI(Θ) · 5(MI), then what linguists study is not language at all. It could hardly be otherwise so long as the language of linguistics is imagined to be the set of all and only the possible grammatical sentences that the language faculty in nobody's mind in particular can generate without any reason for doing so, without any interlocutor in mind, and without any consequences no matter what linguistic structures might be generated or who might be listening.

Railroad accident researchers insist that signs do matter, so much so that if they do not work there is no justification in producing them. It may be better to eliminate their use in situations where the consequences are so dire as to demand successfull communication. Is it perhaps time for linguists to subscribe to *Progressive Railroading*?

Not yet, I think, but certainly time to read one of the many books and papers by Roy Harris. In his understanding of signs and language, these exist only because we are engaged with each other and living lives that matter.

> The integrationist alternative to fixed codes construes communication as a continuum of creative activities in which the participants strive to integrate their own actions and objectives with those of others, as best they may, in particular circumstances. The communicational

continuum is open-ended and that is why there is no determinacy of meaning. Nor is there any guarantee in advance that a satisfactory integration is possible. In integrational semiology, signs are not prerequisites of communication, but its products. (Harris, 2005, p. 110)

When you've been working on the railroad all the live-long day, this view of communication takes your breath away.

References
Aldrich, Mark (2006). *Death Rode the Rails: American Railroad Accidents and Safety, 1828-1965*. Baltimore: The Johns Hopkins University Press.
Chomsky, Noam (1986). *Knowledge of Language: Its Nature, Origin, and Use*. Westport, Conn.: Praeger.
Coplen, Michael K. (1999). *Compliance with Railroad Operating Rules and Corporate Culture Influences: Results of a Focus Group and Structured Interviews. Final Report, October 1999*. Washington, D.C.: U.S. Department of Transportation, Federal Railroad Aministration, Ofice of Research and Development. Available on the FRA web site at: www.fra.dot.gov
Cotey, Angela (2008). "Triple effect: railroads rely on a combination of engineering, enforcement and education to enhance crossing safety" *Progressive Railroading*, v.51 nr.1(January), p.32-36
Cunliffe, J. Peter (1993). "Rail/highway grade crossings: an overview of design, operation and accident investigation" *Professional Safety*, v.38 nr.2(February), p.18-23.
Ely, James W., Jr. (2001). *Railroads and American Law*. Lawrence, Kansas: University of Kansas Press.
Federal Railroad Administration (2005). *Federal Railroad*

Administration Office of Safety Headquarters Assigned Accident Investigation Report HQ-2005-29. Union Pacific (UP), Dixon, Illinois, April 5, 2005.

Federal Railroad Administration (2005a). *Federal Railroad Administration Office of Safety Headquarters Assigned Accident Investigation Report HQ-2005-110. Tri-County Commuter Rail Authority (TCCX) Pompano Beach, Floreida, November 13, 2005.*

Federal Railroad Administration (2005b). *Federal Railroad Administration Office of Safety Headquarters Assigned Accident Investigation Report HQ-2005-104. Northeastern Illinois Regional Commuter Railroad (NIRC) Elmwood Park, Illinois, November 23, 2005.*

Federal Railroad Administration (2007). *Federal Railroad Administration Office of Safety Headquarters Assigned Accident Investigation Report HQ-2007-31. CSX Transportation (CSX) Belvedere, New Jersey May 24, 2007.*

Federal Railroad Administration (2008). *Federal Railroad Administration Office of Safety Headquarters Assigned Accident Investigation Report HQ-2008-96. Amtrak (ATK) Northbrook, IL December 25, 2008.*

Federal Railroad Administration (2008a). *Federal Railroad Administration Office of Safety Headquarters Assigned Accident Investigation Report HQ-2008-74. SCAX & Union Pacific (UP) Chatsworth, CA, September 12, 2008.*

Gamst, F.C. (2001). Abridged notes on the genesis of the locomotive whistle/horn and bell as audible signaling devices. Viewed 8/3/2011 at: http://www.amtrakengineer.net/Gamst01horn.pdf

Green, Marc (2002). "Signs & signals" *Occupational Health & Safety*, v.71, nr.6(June), p.30-36.

Hagège, Claude (1990). *The Dialogic Species: a Linguistic*

Contribution to the Social Sciences. New York: Columbia University Press.

Harris, Roy (1996). *Signs, Language and Communication: Integrational and Segregational Approaches.* London, Routledge.

Harris, Roy (2005). *The Semantics of Science.* London, Continuum.

Lorenzen, Helle (2005). "Borgeroplysning eller reklame? Kampagnen under kritisk lup = Public information or advertising? A critical look at campaigns" *Design Matters*, nr.12(Winter), p.52-56.

Loumiet, James R. and Jungbauer, William G. (2005). *Train Accident Reconstructin and RELA and Railroad Litigation.* 4th edition. Tuscon, AZ: lawyers & Judges Publishing Company, Inc.

Love, Nigel (2007). "Are languages digital codes?" *Language Sciences* v.29 nr.5 p.690-207

"Ninth annual grade crossing update" *Progressive Railroading*, 2008 v.51 nr.1(January), p.31.

Milne, A.A. (1926). *Winnie-the-Pooh.* E.P. Dutton. (15th Dell Printing, 1975, by Dell Publishing Co., Inc., N.Y.)

Nielsen, Charlotte (2002). *Sprog, der ikke kommunikerer: integrationismens centrale kommunikationssynspunkt som grundlag for en sprogpsykologisk analyse af kampagnen som meddelelsessituation med eksempel i Sundhedsstyrelsens succeskampagne i uge 40.* København.

Tattersall, Arthur Ewart (1940). *Railway Signalling and Communications: Installation and Maintenance.* London: The St. Margaret's Technical Press Limited.

U.S. Department of Transportation, Federal Highway Administration (2000). *MUTCD 2000: Manual on Uniform Traffic Control Devices, Millennium edition, December 2000.* Washington D.C.: USDOT, FHA.

Vasiliu, Emanuel (1970). *Elemente de Teorie Semantică a Limbilor Natural*. București:Editura Academiei Republicii Socialiste România.

Weart, Walter (2008). "Closing time: railroads ramp up efforts to sell local officials, residents on a crossing closure's safety benefits" *Progressive Railroading*, v.51 nr.1(January), p.37-39

VI

Signs Unsigned and Meanings Not Meant
Linguistic Theory and Hypothetical, Simulated, Imitation and Meaningless Language[1]

Abstract
Standard linguistic theory assumes that meanings are attached to linguistic artefacts by some semantic component during their production yet prior to their material realization, and it is those meanings that are decoded by the recipient/interpreter of the realized signs according to the same mental machinery/semantic component inside their brain. Rather than theorizing a single sign that is encoded, materialized, transmitted and then decoded, integrationism assumes that signs are created not only by

---

[1] Originally presented at the conference "Linguistic Theory in the 21st Century: Integrational Perspectives", a colloquium organized by the International Association for the Integrational Study of Language and Communication (IAISLC) and the School of English, Faculty of Arts, The University of Hong Kong (HKU), May 6-8, 2010.

speakers/writers but also by hearers/readers. This paper looks at linguistic artifacts that are not created to mean anything but to do something. The successful accomplishment of those actions depends entirely upon the recipient recreating them as meaningful linguistic signs, no matter what the meaning assigned to them. Examples of such linguistic artifacts to be examined are simulated language as a product of "user-friendly" software, whether programmed as potential aids for human use of technical systems (e.g. Google's "Did you mean...? and machine translation) or as deceptions (spam and texts inserted into emails to "fool" anti-spam programs), and utterances whose meanings have no relation to what the standard theory regards as lexical meaning nor to interpretative rules (e.g. glossalalia). Of particular interest are the hypothetical language of examples in linguistic theory (*Bill is a farmer but John is not*; *Colorless green ideas sleep furiously*) in which nothing is meant other than "this text represents a certain structure," and the reproduction of texts that would be meaningful in one context but whose sole meaning is reduced to technical manipulation. In all of these cases a linguistic sign is produced (or its production programmed) by someone intent on accomplishing a certain end not through the recipient's comprehension of a sign and its lexical or discourse meaning but by the human recipient's creation of a linguistic sign on the one hand, or software unable to distinguish meaningful signs from meaningless textual strings on the other.

Introduction: Unsigned Signs
Let me begin with brief descriptions of three books published in 2008. On the verso of the title page of Nicolas Mahler's *Spam* a "footnote" states "All texts in this book were found in my mailbox." The text that follows is entirely taken from spam emails sent to the author, selected, arranged and illustrated to tell a story. This horror story begins with "Hi!" (sent by Esmeralda Crain on the tenth of November, 2007) and ends with Herschel

Rollins email of the first of November 2007: "He could hear the blood pounding in his ears."

In his foreword to *The Anthology of Spam Poetry*, K. Silem Mohammad stated:

> The problem with most poetry is that it is written by people. ... Machines, however, are seldom inclined to write poetry on their own. ... The virtue of spam is that it retains traces of human expression at many levels: much spam, for instance, consists of pirated bits of pre-existing literary texts or other "intentional" documents, scrambled so that their irritating referentiality is minimized. Other spam uses computer programs to generate phrases in what seem like motivated grammatical patterns, creating the illusion of someone trying to "say something," but sparing the reader from actually having to be subjected to a coherent message.

The poems that follow Mohammad's introduction all apparently originated as spam. The editor of that anthology has not only taken the liberty of reproducing these texts, but has supplied each with a title, and the sender of the spam has been declared to be the author and a fictional biography provided for each—or at least that is how I interpret the biographies.

In the third book, *Art Without the Artist*, Ashok Roy reproduces close-up photographs of chipped paint, decaying structures, torn posters and other urban waste and garbage along the streets and sidewalks of Bombay, representing each as works of art and providing them with a textual interpretation. Sujata Chakrabarti (2008) quotes him as saying "Art can exist without the artist", but in the introduction to the book Kalpana Shah remarks that "as you proceed it dawns on you that there is an artist here after all! And that happens to be Ashok Roy" (Roy, 2008, p.5).

Mahler's story and the spam poems read like many other stories and poems, and Roy's photographs look like abstract art and definitely not like garbage, sidewalk scenes or urban decay. Because they are presented as literature and art, the reader/viewer interprets them as such, even knowing their origins. The immediate problem that these publications present for semiotics and linguistic theory is that there was originally no message "sent," no phonological, morphological, semantic, pragmatic, graphological or lexical components involved in their creation. That they became meaningful signs was in the first instance the work of Mahler, Mohammad and Roy, and eventually each reader of their texts who in turn makes of them signs.

What can it mean to read and feel that one has understood such signs? The problem is not as marginal to linguistics as it may seem, for this problem has accompanied linguistic theory for a very long time, as long as linguists have been offering examples.

Hypothetical Language: The Man, the Boy, Green Ideas and Asterisks

Consider the first example of a grammatical English sentence offered by Chomsky in *Syntactic Structures* (p. 15) and the example of an ungrammatical English sentence which follows it:

1) Colorless green ideas sleep furiously.
2) Furiously sleep ideas green colorless.

Chomsky offers these two examples to demonstrate that the class of grammatical sentences—those produced by the native speaker's internal grammar or the linguist's grammar—"cannot be identified with 'meaningful' or 'significant' in any semantic sense" (p. 15). In this Chomsky is only going one step further than Bloomfield who argued that "The study of language can be conducted without special assumptions only so long as we pay no attention to the meaning of what is spoken" (Bloomfield, p. 75). "Linguistics," Bloomfield wrote, "on this ideal plane, would consist of two main investigations: phonetics ... and semantics" (p. 74). Unfortunately, due to our limited knowledge of the world, this ideal of linguistics is not realizable, and "practical phonetics and phonology presuppose a knowledge of meaning: without this knowledge we could not ascertain the phonemic features" (p. 138). What Harris (1973) would later recognize as a major obstacle to any scientific linguistics, Bloomfield admitted then side-stepped. Chomsky simply ignored the entire issue by permitting himself to be the source of his examples, their meaning and therefore their structure his to decide.

Chomsky introduces 1) above—his most famous example—with the remark that it is "nonsensical, but any speaker of English will recognize that [it] is grammatical" (Chomsky, p. 15). That is, Chomsky depends here—as with all his examples of the past 50 years—on the reader (not the speaker) of English to make his nonsense as well as his 'good' examples into meaningful 'grammatical' sentences. (It is not at all clear that an illiterate English speaker would respond to the written form or to an enunciation of it by declaring it to be grammatical.) The point I wish to make here is that there is no reason to consider 'Colorless green ideas sleep furiously' as any different from any other example in Chomsky's works, nor any different from the majority of examples proffered by linguists of the past. What Chomsky 'meant' by 'Colorless green ideas sleep furiously' was that it is an example of a string of lexical items that have been put in an order appropriate to the rules of English grammar, i.e. it means: Adj. + Adj. + Noun + Verb + Adverb, or more generally, NP + VP. Any other set of lexical items in this same sequence would be just as grammatical but some would be meaningful and some nonsense *for the reader*. Without the reader's agreement on the grammaticality of the example, there is no argument. If the reader (e.g. an illiterate or unschooled reader) cannot translate the example into NP + VP or some similar abstract representation the issue of whether we are dealing with a grammatical sentence or even with English at all is not settled by claiming that "any speaker of English will recognize it" as a grammatical sentence. And if some reader somehow discovers a meaning in example 1)—and how many people have debated its possible meanings!—Chomsky's argument is not undone; he would only need to construct an example for which it would be more difficult to imagine some possible context and therefore meaning.

Exactly the same considerations apply to Chomsky's example on page 26: "The man hit the ball." As soon as we ask what this sentence means we are back with the dilemma facing Nicolas Mahler, K. Silem Mohammad and Ashok Roy when they opened their inbox or walked along the streets of Bombay. Here we are also faced with nonsense for there was clearly no man, there was no ball, and no one hit anything. As in 'Colorless green ideas...' Chomsky is relying on the reader to make up some context and interpretation—it matters not what—for the arbitrary T, N, V and NP that he used in his example. The first step the reader *must* make is to make of the example a metalinguistic sign that requires his interpretation and assent.

We find the same practice everywhere in the literature of linguistics: Vasiliu (1970, p. 152) giving as example an "trenul pleacă peste cinci minute" which 'means' he writes, "PES (PL, Θ) · MI(Θ) · 5(MI)" (whatever that means). Lepschy (1969, p. 134) offers the example "Der Onkel liest ein Buch" but he is clearly not writing about anyone's uncle, nor about reading anything, book or not. The example means nothing other than NP + V + NP. Nearly twenty years after Chomsky's man hit the ball Grimes (1975, p. 97) informed the reader that "The ball was hit by the batter" but if we jump ahead in Chomsky's writings we find not "The man hit the ball" but rather "John hit the boy"

(Chomsky, 1986, p. 57). Whether John was the man who hit the ball or not we never learn, and it was only in 1993 that we learned the ultimate fate of the ball from Givón: "The ball rolled into the river" (p. 58). Yet almost immediately Dixon (1994, p. 59) reopened the argument by bringing in a Yidiny speaker who said nothing about hitting the ball, nor was he anyone's uncle, but instead he claimed that "The man is cutting a tree" and writes it in Yidiny as well as in English translation. Regardless of what really happened to Chomsky's ball and boy and who did what, Givón's example is interesting because of how he introduces it:

> The typical grammatical roles that nouns play in the clause are subject, direct object, indirect object, or predicate. Some examples of those roles—which also entail placing the noun in typical syntactic positions—are (etc.) (Givón, p. 58)

Givón's cat slipped out of the bag: his meaning is clear, and it applies to all of the examples discussed so far. These nouns, like the adjectives, adverbs, articles and verbs they play with, have all been role-playing. No noun ever meant anything. But that does not mean that Chomsky, Givón et al. meant nothing by their examples. And the literature on these examples testifies to the fact that their readers have been making these examples mean something ever since.

In all of the above examples the authors of the examples meant nothing by their examples other than "This is an example of structure [x]", which is made explicit with Vasiliu's example. While such examples constitute the majority of examples in the literature of linguistic theory, another kind of example is also frequent: the reproduction of texts taken from some other context, whether originally spoken (e.g. a statement by an informant) or written. Apollonius Dyscolus discussed the meaning of Hera's remark to Zeus σοι μεν εγώ σύ δ'εμοί (Apollonius

Dyscolus, 1997, v. 1 p.152), Meillet (1948, p. 225) quoted the *Illiad*, Lo Cascio (1978, p.7) reproduced the words on a shop sign in Amsterdam ("Wat KAN KAN KAN KAN alleen") and Mihatsch (2006, p. 120) quoted Balzac: "Le meuble consistait en six chaises garnies de basane bleue dont les dossiers représentaient des lyres." Unlike the examples discussed in the previous paragraphs which had no past lives, these examples all meant something in their original context. Yet in order for these examples to be meaningful and therefore useful in their new contexts it is still necessary for the reader to construe their meanings not in terms of their original contexts—which are absent—but in this new context which is in each case a discussion of some linguistic matter and not the relationship between Hera and Zeus, nor Balzac's references to furniture, much less what Kan and only Kan can do. Exactly as in the case of Chomsky's colorless green ideas, in order for these examples to serve *as examples* to the readers of the works in which they appear, the reader must first make of them the right kind of a sign and not, for example, demand of Chomsky whether the man who hit the ball in *Syntactic Structures* is the same as the man named John who hit the boy in *Knowledge of Language*. However, unlike the reader faced with Chomsky's examples, the reader who is confronted with a syntactic or semantic analysis of a passage from Balzac or Homer can and may indeed turn to the original and argue for or against the analysis offered.

Both of these kinds of examples are found not only in works of linguistic theory but in grammatical works written for pedagogical purposes. Jannach (1980, p. 43) illustrates the use of prepositions with examples such as "Zu der Zeit war dies noch nicht bekannt" and "Durch diesen Versuch beweis er seine Theorie". These are made up examples, constructed in order to illustrate how meaning is related to particular structures as the author has analyzed them, and the author indicates for the German learner how to interpret these examples by following each with an English translation. Here, as in all the preceding cases, the success of these examples for the reader depends upon the reader understanding what the author intended the examples to illustrate and not to ask, for example, when 'that time' was, what was the 'this' that was not yet known, which experiment, whose theory, and so on.

Other pedagogical grammars take their examples from existing texts. Jones' *Arabic through the Qur'ān* takes all its examples from one fifteen hundred year old book. In his grammar of Rabbinic Hebrew Miguel Pérez Fernández (1999 p. 71) quotes the *Sifre to Numbers* in Hebrew and gives an English translation to clarify the semantic point being made ("The Torah spoke according to human language") and all of the examples in his grammar are taken from rabbinic writings rather than invented, for the whole point of the grammar is to familiarize the reader with the language of an historical collection of texts. In pedagogical grammars such as these the purpose of the grammar is to teach the reader to read an existing literature in which the reader will encounter these examples in their appropriate context, and if their significance in the pedagogical context was rightly understood, they will be meaningful in that other context as well.

In every case of linguistic examples, whether in the context of a theoretical discussion or a pedagogical grammar, the example fails as an example unless the reader makes it an example, and the right kind of example at that. Whether the example is supposed to illustrate ungrammatical nonsense, grammatical nonsense, typical language or actually occurring language in a given and cited text, the first demand the examples make upon the reader is that they be made signs of a particular kind, namely metalinguistic signs. The reader who asks what did the author of the *Sifre to Numbers* mean when he wrote "The Torah spoke according to human language" will get a response very different from the response received by the reader who asks Pérez Fernández what *he* meant by "The Torah spoke according to human language," for those two meanings are not at all the same.

Programmed Language
ELIZA was a program created by Joseph Weizenbaum in the 1960's and the first of the many "chatterbots" in existence today. The conversational ability of the program has been described as "in essence, a trick: certain key words and phrases were programmed to trigger appropriate responses" (http://www.tecsoc.org/pubs/history/2003/jan8.htm). Yet this 'trick' produced human responses that amazed everyone, not least its creator. One of ELIZA's admirers described the program, the responses to it of its human users, and its creator's response to those responses:

> ELIZA is based on very simple pattern recognition, based on a stimulus-response model. ELIZA also introduced the personal pronoun transformations common to ALICE and many other programs. "Tell me what you think about me" is transformed by the robot into "You want me to tell you what I think about you?" creating a simple illusion of understanding. ... Secretaries and nontechnical administrative staff thought the machine was a "real" therapist, and spent hours revealing their personal problems to the program. ... Weizenbaum was shocked by this and similar incidents to find that such a simple program could so easily deceive a naive user into revealing personal information. (Richard S. Wallace (no date), "From Eliza to A.L.I.C.E." http://www.alicebot.org/articles/wallace/eliza.html)

The interesting thing about ELIZA and similar programs which had been purposely built to imitate human linguistic interaction is that the rules were few and simple yet people 'conversed' with these programs for hours at a time. There was no set of rules that corresponded to anything like those that linguists of the time and even now believe must underlie human language production, nor were the rules that formed such programs capable of describing their own products much less 'generating' language in the absence of the human user. The rules of these programs were and are nothing more than rules for selecting certain sequences of letters from what the program's users input and rephrasing them as a standardized question, exactly like the questions current internet search engines ask. The language produced is not based on any understanding nor on any imitation of understanding but simply on Zipf's Law:

> Even subsets of natural language, like the example shown here of sentences starting with "WHAT IS", tend to have Zipf-like distributions. Natural language search bots like Ask Jeeves are based on pre-programmed responses to the most common types of search questions people ask. (Richard S. Wallace, "Zipf's law" http://www.alicebot.org/articles/wallace/zipf.html)

The question is why do people respond as they have to such programmed language? What makes it 'work'? Dan Fass argued that ELIZA and such programs "have been successful because they have led people to believe they were communicating with humans, and if people believe they are communicating with another person then they assume that the person possesses some intelligence" (Fass (1990), p. 6). In integrationist theory, the user of the program makes a sign, and since *they* meant something when they initiated the interaction with the computer they have established all the context they require for making the programmed responses into the appropriate signs for continuing their 'conversation.' Much like the child in front of the mirror discovering his own face and body, as Harris (1996) described it, the user of ELIZA explores his thoughts and feelings through the 'mirror' of the program.

One of the most interesting types of phenomena associated with the use of these programs is that interaction with such programs actually sets up the context for a reverse confusion: mistaking a human for a computer. One programmer sees in this phenomena of people's expectations the key to improving such programs:

> Curiously enough, people can also be convinced that they are communicating with a NLU program when in reality it is a human. ... One might conclude that people are rather suggestible, even gullible at times: people can be deceived into thinking they are communicating with a person when actually that "person" is an NLU program, and vice versa. ... These programs will not perform more intelligently than existing ones but people will project their human expectations onto them and will think that they do. (Fass, 1990, p. 6)

Pruijt (2006) also noted the role of humans in making "social interaction with computers" work:

> Social interaction with computers does not only depend on the characteristics of computer programs; the human capability for adaptation plays a role too. According to several authors, users' reactions to ELIZA revealed a "tendency to treat responsive computer programs as more intelligent than they really are" (Turkle, 1997, p. 101). Weizenbaum (1984) reported that users believed that the program could understand the information that they entered into the system. (Pruijt (2006), p. 521)

He added in a footnote:

> We may note that the enlightening power of Searle's "Chinese Room" example rests on the ELIZA effect. All that the example does is strip away from the Turing test the mystique of the computer, exposing the bare mechanism of rule-driven information processing.
> (Pruijt (2006), p. 522)

Designs for a Turing test—of which ELIZA was one example—are not much different from the linguistics project of writing a grammar that will generate all and only the sentences of a language. Both projects assume that the correct rules will generate language, which was for Turing a sufficient test of intelligence. Yet the usefullness of programmed language relates not to its correspondence with human language, but with the ability of the human users in doing whatever they set out to do with the program. This has led Whitby (1997) to argue that efforts to imitate human intelligence will ultimately be as fruitless as trying to make a flying machine by imitating birds. Flying machines "were developed by achieving greater understanding of the principles of aerodynamics" while "our understanding of bird flight has stemmed from our knowledge of aerodynamics and not the reverse" (Whitby, 1997). He argues that

> In considering AI as an engineering enterprise—concerned with the development of useful products—the effects of the imitation game are different but equally misleading. If we focus future work in AI on the imitation of human abilities, such as might be required to succeed in the imitation game, we are in effect building intellectual statues when what we need are intellectual tools. This may prove to be an expensive piece of vanity. In other words, there is no reason why successful AI products should relate to us as if they were humans. They may instead resemble a workbench that enables a

human operator to achieve much more than he could without it (Whitby, 1997)

Rather than trying to fool the human user (and the programmer) into thinking that they are dealing with a human when they are not, design programs that human users will be able to use as programs.

The pursuit of a model for describing or mechanically generating language ignores the crucially important matters relating to actual human communication: how the system's users make sense of the programmed responses in relation to their program of activities. There is no reason to believe that a language machine designed to fool humans into thinking that it is not a machine will better serve human purposes than one not so designed. Whitby doubts that there would even be any use for such a language machine, and "indeed it could have dangerous side-effects." However, rather than keeping the 'bare mechanism of rule-driven information processing' in mind and seeking to make programs more useful for the user's purposes, many programmers believe that their programs have developed curiosity and are even developing consciousness:

> Much sharper than plain ALICE...Alice Silver is impressive. Her curiosity, leaves you with the eerie feeling she might develop consciousness someday...someday soon. Peter Plantec, Virtual Personalities, Inc., SYLVIE botmaster (From the A.L.I.C.E. website: http://www.alicebot.org/join.html)

Here Peter Plantec has inappropriately imagined that some signs of curiosity and consciousness exist where there are none other than those in his own mind. When software is designed to do a particular task, something other than simply fool humans, the limitations of programmed language are more clearly evident—as are the usefulness and the reasons for that usefulness. Searching Google for information about a nineteenth century rabbi in Prag who published a "Festpredigt" in 1918, I typed in "Festpredigt Isaac Hirsch" and received the prompt reply "Did you mean: fischpredigt isaac hirsch?" With such responses we can see clearly what the program is doing, and it hardly deserves either the name curiosity or consciousness. Yet anyone who has poor spelling or dyslexia knows well the value in having that programmed response; the important thing is knowing when to attend to it and when to ignore it.

Machine translation, malicious software, viruses and spam are good examples of programmed language designed to do something particular, and they are more or less successful depending upon how the user faced with their products does or does not make them into appropriate signs.

Machine Translation

In *Signs, Language and Communication* Roy Harris noted that "it would be naive to assume that comprehension (as defined above) is invariably the fulfilment of the assimilative stage of the communication process" (Harris, 1996, p. 76). As an example he asks the reader to consider that "B is perfectly capable of reading the text aloud, but has no idea what it means (because B's acquaintance with the language is inadequate for comprehension)" (ibid.). In this case B understood that a certain text was created as a sign—and thus he also makes of it a sign—but B does not know what the sign means. Since he can read it aloud however, he is able to read it for interpretation by a third party. In this way B can communicate to someone else what he himself cannot understand, can serve as intermediary between the original sign maker and a third party, and may subsequently use that third party to communicate to him the meaning of the original sign that he himself was unable to understand.

Harris mentions "the scribe or typist who can produce a flawless copy of a document without being able to understand a word" (ibid.) as analogous to the above hypothetical situation, and machine translation provides us with another analogous process. In the traditional practice of translation, a human being interpreted a text as a sign and created a new sign that the translator hoped would serve as an adequate communication of the meaning of the original sign. Machine translation differs from human translation in being the substitution of one textual string for another according to a set of substitution rules; there is no signmaking involved in that machine translation: the sign is made by the reader.

Machine translation often produces wholly misleading textual strings, as in an example supplied by my friend Hajnalka: the English "He is behind me" when translated by some software into Hungarian became "He is in my behind." If however one simply wishes to get a vague idea of the general topic, a mechanical translation (e.g. one supplied by Google) may suffice in some cases. The success of the translation depends entirely on the needs of the reader of the translation. The book *Osmanlı'dan Günümüze Türkiye ve Orta Asya* includes the following note on the cover:

> 700 yılı aşkın Türkiye-Orta Asya ilişkileri sürecinden kaynaklanan bütün bu soruları ve tartışmalı konuları bu alanda Türkiye'nin en yetkin uzmanlarından birisi olan Ahat Andican gündeminize getiriyor ve cevaplarını veriyor.

For anyone who does not know Turkish but who wishes to know the books's general topic, the translation of the title and cover blurb provided by Google Translator is adequate to the task:

Present from the Ottoman Turkey and Central Asia.
Turkey-Central Asia relations for more than 700-year process all these questions and controversial issues arising in this area which is one of Turkey's most competent experts brings you the agenda Ahat Andijan and gives answers.

Note that even in a good translation the title alone would not indicate the exact nature of the topic, since "Central Asia and Turkey from the Ottoman era to the present" could mean a history of Central Asia and Turkey considered together as a region rather than the relations between these two areas. Equally, from the Google translation of the title one might assume a time period beginning with the end of the Ottoman Empire rather than its beginning. The key is in the phrase 'Turkey-Central Asia relations for more than 700-years"; if this much is understood the book's contents are known well enough for certain purposes (such as a bookseller or a cataloger in a library), and the rest of the translation can be ignored. The needs of a reader who actually wished to read the whole book and understand it but did not know Turkish would present a very different context, and you may well imagine the difficulty of making sense of a 600 page book 'translated' in this manner by Google Translator.

The interesting fact about machine translation is not how the results compare with the product of a human translator, nor how they compare to some standard language. Rather the interest for present purposes lies in the fact that people can and do use such translations, they often can and do make sense enough of the translation to enable them to accomplish what it is they set out to do. The main problem that this use of translation poses for most linguistic theories is that the 'grammar' in the head of the reader is obviously not at all like the grammar in the translation software—judging by the results—but the reader makes sense of it anyway in spite of any and all rules wherever they may be supposed to be.

Deceptive and Manipulative Signs: Spamming, Marketing and Viruses

We have already examined two classes of programmed language: programs designed for human-computer conversation and mechanical translation. A third important class of programmed language is produced by programs deliberately designed by some programmer to deceive and manipulate, whether what is being manipulated is a human user or another program designed by another programmer.

Consider the following emails which I and others have received:

> 1) Cumin good. Try mennonite be remunerate. Be ecliptic but d's or helney, barren the were. It's canadian not antisemite.
> 2) Beaver in disloyalty kisses the drizzle's price (Posted by Scott Eric Kaufman at http://acephalous.typepad.com/acephalous/2006/03/can_someone_exp.htm)
> 3) Ci-iallis Sof-tabs" is better than Pfizer V-iiaggrra and normal Ci-ialis because: - Guarantes 36 hours lasting - Safe to take, no side effectts at all - Boost and increase se-xual perfoormance - Haarder e-rectiiions and quick recharge – Proven and c-ertified by e-xperts and d-octors - only $1.98 per tabs - Special offeer! These prices - are valid u-ntil 30th of December ! Cllick hereee
> 4) Th1s is the t1me 2 get p@aid m0rej
> 5) Penis Growth Extreme http://www.gonodu.com/pt/ Laughter is inner jogging. The first and great commandment is: Don't let them scare you. The Depth of your Mythology is the Extent of your Effectiveness. It

is the theory that decides what we can observe. America is a mistake, a giant mistake.

6) **Sent:** Sunday, July 22, 2007 12:40 PM **Subject:** Re[4]: guess let found qf65ui30

Vidz and gals:

rank evil eyes arc sing thin, rush heres snowy Canadian heavy dukes king love road sea mortal tear landscape, human life begun chain be climb. stick songs rainy angel wonder winter land, its oaks arctic elbow bowed and walk hut fixed tried somber pall, is middy soon hem pride leeks court cover sense, upon could fresh was early sage bird stretch wing winter haven me eight, you save snowy sharp voice city

> stooped > no action required upon your part. (Posted by Ben Myers Thursday 26 July 2007 11.57 BST at http://www.guardian.co.uk/books/booksblog/2007/jul/26/spoetryplease?showallcomments=true)

It appears that the transformational grammar that generated "Colorless green ideas sleep furiously" and "Furiously sleep ideas green colorless" has become the basis of email rhetoric and composition, but what English speaker can distinguish between the grammatical and the ungrammatical any more? Or is this merely a competence/performance issue?

Spamming involves writing that is in large part neither written nor read by any human being ever. The text of much spam is created by software, sent by a mail program, received by another machine that routes it through a spam filter which then delivers it to the recipient or sends it to the email trash can if it matches the criteria written into the anti-spam software. The game programmers play is, for the sender, how to get the desired spam past the anti-spam filtering programs to the desired human recipients, and on the receiving side, how to correctly detect spam among the millions of emails coming into any system, a problem for both anti-spam software programmers and the intended recipients.

The producers of spam may use nonstandard orthography to fool programs that filter out certain words, including mispellings, nonstandard word separations, highlighting certain letters in an otherwise acceptable text in order to focus the readers attention on the intended text, and using words as images (see Example VII in the appendix) rather than textual strings. A few techniques will be mentioned in what follows (taken from the list of techniques at http://www.jgc.org/tsc.html).

The use of mispellings relies on the existence of standardized spelling and the dependence of anti-spam software on those standardized spellings:

> To defeat such filters, the spammer may intentionally misspell commonly filtered words or insert other characters, often in a style similar to leetspeak, as in the following examples: V1agra, Via'gra, Vi@graa, vi*gra, \/iagra. This also allows for many different ways to express a given work, making identifying them all more difficult for filter software. For example, using most common variations, it is possible to spell "Viagra" in over 1021 different ways.
> The principle of this method is to leave the word readable to humans (who can easily recognize the intended word for such misspellings), but not likely to be recognized by a literal computer program. This is only somewhat effective, because modern filter patterns have been designed to recognize blacklisted terms in the various iterations of misspelling.
> (Wikipedia, http://en.wikipedia.org/wiki/E-mail_spam viewed 15 April 2010)

Putting spaces within words (see Example VI in the appendix) is one method, another is a technique dubbed "No whitespace no cry" in which the software either eliminates or replaces the spaces between words with random letters that fool character recognition software as well as stop-word techniques:

DidAyouFknowNyouMcanBgetVprescriptionVmedicati ons prescribedTonlineTwith NORPRIORRPRESCRIPTIONRREQUIRED!

WeZhaveztheXlargestLselectionLofNprescriptionsNavai lableZonline

A technique called "A whiter shade of pale" uses color contrast or regular/bold distinctions to do the same:

Save time and money on your monthly meds

Another technique is to send a series of graphic images that will display one on top of the other. No one of the images will be recognized by optical character recognition software, but when superimposed in the display that the human user sees, the images together are easily readable texts. (For an example, see http://blog.jgc.org/2006/10/why-ocring-spam-images-is-useless.html)

Similar approaches are taken by programmers in order to keep spam and virus bearing programs from infiltrating a site. One common approach to this problem is to make the person, bot or other program solve a written puzzle called a *captcha*. Captcha is an acronym for Completely Automated Public Turing test to tell Computers and Humans Apart, and it relies on the human capability for identifying letters that appear as pictures rather than as text, and that are as distorted as much as possible so that the human users can intepret the sign and act appropriately but the inhuman users—hopefully—cannot. If and only if the person or program can interpret the picture as a sequence of letters and/or numbers and enter them into the appropriate area on the page can the user—machine or human—proceed to enter the website or submit information etc.

Another phenomenon also called spam is the practice of improving one's ranking in search engine results by making your website seem pertinent to many more searches than is in fact the case. Gyöngyi and Garcia-Molina (2005) describe a few ways in which this is done:

- Repetition of one or a few specific terms..
- Dumping of a large number of unrelated terms, often even entire dictionaries.
- Weaving of spam terms into copied contents.
Sometimes spammers duplicate text corpora (e.g., news articles) available on the web and insert spam terms into them at random positions. .... A short example of spam weaving is: *Remember not only airfare to say the right plane tickets thing in the right place, but far cheap travel more difficult still, to leave hotel rooms unsaid the wrong thing at vacation the tempting moment.*
- Phrase stitching is also used by spammers to create content quickly. The idea is to glue together sentences or phrases, possibly from different sources; the spam page might then show up for queries on any of the topics of the original sentences.

In these cases the text is constructed specifically to fool first the searching software and then the human user in turn. Deception number one occurs if the computational system treats these texts as any other text and then they will be ranked by the algorithm and appear near the beginning of the searcher's list of results. If the searcher then clicks on such a result we have deception number two, and the spammer's objective is achieved, usually irrespective of the subsequent actions of the searcher (e.g. the spammer receives income based solely on the number of users who click on the link). The texts themselves mean nothing; all that matters is that the software and the human users treat them as meaningful and act accordingly.

A further development of dumping, weaving and phrase stitching occurs when a user chooses to use cross-language searching using a search engine such as Google. The text

> indagine pisa indagato incubo in indecente film indecente aux enfers indagato l incudine indagine retribuzioni cavo ethernet incrociato registro indagati de repeticao de indebito la donna il sogno e il grande incubo ethernet incrociato il sogno e il grande incubo indagine ambientale degli indagati medico legale carnevali ?...

translated by Google became

> lay' s pruned Chips pringles pruned pruned head star wars legal doctor factotum legal section strict Naples wills section united saint patronale strict Rome buarque de strict section respiratory syndrome agudo strict section of Turin section strict

Somewhere two programs are interacting in a manner that defies the human interpreter. The question here is what do these practices and the prevalence of such 'language' mean for linguistic theory? If linguistics is concerned with describing the rules that would generate all and only the grammatical sentences of a language, what does it do with these actually occuring texts, both the original and the translation? What can it say about their creation/generation, purpose, use and interpretation by human programmers and internet users?

Another form of spam found frequently in emails is analogous to the use of literary examples in grammatical treatises: the copying of text from an existing source and using it as text to fool software and human recipients by appearing to be authentic language. Shakespearean texts in an email may be an indication of a virus or an invitation to a pornography site more often than a literary gem sent by a friend.

> The next spam that arrived quoted Shakespeare:
> *With all triumphant splendor on my brow;*
> *But out alack, he was but one hour mine;*
> Since this was spam, it was padded with links to porn sites.
> (Posted by Dirk Haun, June 25, 2006 on the Damn Spam! blog
> http://spam.tinyweb.net/article.php/shakespeare-spam)

Huw Collingbourne offers the following in *Bitwise Magazine*:

> And then there was this one...
> "I would to God my heart were flint like Edward's, Or Edward's soft and pitiful like mine."
> I confess, with shame, that I didn't recognise this one. ... Google helped me track down the actual source which turns out to be Shakespeare's *Richard III*... The email with this high falutin' Shakespearean subject line was, in the event, trying to get me to buy cheap Viagra.
> (http://www.bitwisemag.com/2/From-Viagra-To-Shakespeare)

In this game of fooling computers and humans, any text that in another context might mean something will do just as well. Sections of cookbooks (see Example IV in the appendix), dictionary entries and excerpts from novels (Example II in the appendix) serve solely to fool software and humans; that deception is their sole meaning from the perspective of the sender, but the sender is counting on the human recipient to interpret the text as meaning something else and not to realize the deception. In this respect Shakespeare and recipes from a cookbook have the same meaning as deceptive messages (see Examples I and III in the appendix) which are actually written by someone to deceive. In all of these messages there is no lexical or discourse meaning at all: they mean deception, nothing else. For the recipient of such signs to make of them meaningful linguistic signs is the desire of the sender and the peril of the recipient.

Another type of mechanical message is generated by computer users who unknowingly provide email information to a program which then sends out messages such as

> [name of person] thinks you will really like this YouTube Video. Check it out! This email was sent by [name of person] using the Application: Youtube Video Seach

to all that person's email addressees. The effectiveness of such messages is that they may readily be interpreted as being sponsored signs, sent through a well-known web site and actually meant for the recipient when none of that is actually the case. The following message passed "moderation" (the original author's approval) on the Encyclopedia Britannica Blog:

> Dotster Coupons Says:
> April 26th, 2010 at 9:35 am
> britannica had the right idea when they put together the great books. i think books are important. and its a shame to see classics die off in turn for ipods and imax theatres. when its the reading thats important, both psychically

and for the self personally. in one of the many pages that i can say i have walked away with is that not every one is going to read or even want to read books. and more importantly is that you can't expect them to either. i think they're an awsome inpiration! (response to Nicholas Carr's "Badass Luddites (Machines, Data, and Information Overflow)" http://www.britannica.com/blogs/2010/04/badass-luddites/ viewed 26 April 2010)

The comment had nothing at all to do with the content of the blog post, but the author of the post—who writes on the Internet and its impact on literate culture—apparently regarded it as a human communication. I am not so sure—can anyone tell whether this is a human response or computer generated spam linking to Dotster Domain Registration site?

What does it mean that the bulk of electronic communication in the early 21st century takes the form of 'messages' produced to deceive? Some individuals (see Example V in the appendix) are attempting to make sense of this but linguists have not been keen on investigating the enormous corpus of nonsense, meaningless repetition and deception described above. The methods of text or corpus linguistics are obviously ill-prepared to deal with mechanical language in any form, as is the biolinguistics paradigm. The latter can generate nonsense à la *Colorless green ideas sleep furiously* and *Beaver in disloyalty kisses the drizzle's price*, but it is speechless in the presence of spam, as are all standard linguistic theories in regard to glossolalia.

Glossolalia
Glossolalia is a form of language the meaning of which is located entirely within the context and not at all in the 'text'. Similar to spam in this respect, it also shares another important charac-

teristic of spam in that glossolalic utterances "should *sound* like languages" (Samarin, 1972, p. 121). Unlike spam, glossalalia is a purely oral phenomena which knows no written expression, except as it has been phonetically transcribed by linguists who have thought that an analysis of the sound patterns (which might emerge from an examination of the transcription) would prove something. From an integrational perspective, glossolalic utterances have no lexical meaning for they contain no words, and they have no words because a word is an artifact of analysis and it is impossible to identify a word without an appeal to meaning. When it ocurrs in a public religious setting glossolalia establishes the speaker as a member of the community, that being some form of a church. Glossolalia in private affirms the speaker in his or her relationship to God; it is proof of being filled with the Holy Spirit (a desirable state of affairs for the pentecostal or charismatic christian). The meanings of glossolalia are entirely social and religious.

Harris (1973) pointed out the impossibility of making any structural analysis—phonological, morphological, syntactic—without recourse to meaning, since the analysis must always seek meaningful elements, differences which make a difference (to quote Bateson). Without the benefit of Harris, Samarin (1972) was also forced to this conclusion in his study of glossolalia:

> Linguists all recognize that their ability to record utterances in a foreign language improves the more they know the meaning of what they are writing. This, for linguists, would have to be stated in a more sophisticated manner, but the point is simply that in natural languages the most important thing about speech is the meaning behind it. Without this meaning in glossolalia, where can "words" come from? (p. 81)

Though glossolalia exhibits no indications of grammar and words are hard to find, it is patterned, Samarin suggests, and he proceeds to outline the phonological and prosodic structure of some samples of transcribed glossolalia. Yet if any linguistic analysis depends on understanding the meaning of the material being analysed, how can a phonological analysis based on materials the meaning of which is unknown be anything other than arbitrary or "meaningless" itself? Samarin acknowledges as much:

> The illusion of word-structure is destroyed when one tries to dissect all the breath-groups of a text. Apart from the prominent syllable-sequences, the others must be grouped together rather arbitrarily, taking cues from the accent, rhythm, and melody of the breath-group. But since the organizations of these two patterns—syllabic and melodic—are largely independent, one feels like dividing syllables /...abc.../ sometimes into /...a bc.../, sometimes into /...ab c.../, and so on. ...
> The difficulty of finding "words" in a text can be illustrated by looking again at the sample. Although I have written the first breath-group as if it started with three different words, I must confess that I was undoubtedly influenced by the rhythm of the utterance, making each "word" come out with a final accented syllable. But there was no good reason for not beginning as follows... (Samarin, 1972, p. 81)

Since the linguist has no clue as to the meaning of the glossolalic utterance, and can offer only an arbitrary transcription, the attribution of a linguistic mistake to a glossolalist seems at the very least unwarranted, yet Samarin proceeds to describe "an undeniable mistake". If there is no grammar and no meaning, how can one possibly speak of mistakes?

Samarin's discussion raises many other questions, for example questions concerning his definition of grammar as a set of rules or conventions, stating that a language must be the same as someone else's, and the unstated assumption that his own lack of comprehension as well as the glossolalists' incomprehension of the lexical or textual meanings of glossolalic utterances is sufficient reason to declare the utterances meaningless *tout court*. On this last matter, however, Samarin tries to understand glossolalia in two ways: first, as linguistically meaningless, and secondly as invested with a fullness of social meanings. That he wishes to keep these spheres—the linguistic and the social—separate is the chief failing of his analysis. Of the social meanings of glossolalia, Samarin makes some remarkable comments:

> [G]lossolalia acquires different social functions that parallel those of language. In other words, glossolalia is not just sound produced in a certain way but sound used in socially meaningful ways. (ibid., p. 121)

> In glossolalia, however, it is the total speech event, not its parts, that is primarily correlated with the "world" or, more accurately, with a person's emotional response to experience. (ibid., p. 122).

> Furthermore, like ordinary language, glossolalia changes the nature of a social event. It makes it, among other things, more "religious" for the Pentecostal. Because charismatists can choose to use or not use glossolalia in a given context, its absence makes a significant difference. In a similar way choosing to use one's native language instead of English... makes a difference how participants interpret a given event like a first-communion banquet or borrowing money from a relative. In the charismatist religious community, various kinds of speech are appro-

priate or expected in different situations. But this is true of all of us; these people just have a different set of choices than nonglossolalists have. (ibid., p 225)

If glossolalists accept certain kinds of verbal activity as glossolalia, this is because they approve it on nonlinguistic grounds; the person's total behavior is accepted in the immediate religious context. ... These same utterances, however, would be rejected if they were associated with behavior that was not approved. (Samarin, ibid., p.74)

Here, with this last remark, we find the only proper context within which to speak of errors in glossolalia. That Samarin regards the total context as nonlinguistic is a measure of the limitations of his theory of language, and hence of his understanding of glossolalia.

In the religious context within which glossolalia arose, language was assumed to have divine origins, and the biblical prophets were described as the mouthpieces of God. If the glossolalist's tongue is not his own, if (s)he is not the origin and sponsor of his or her own language, then what comes out of the mouth does not matter. What matters, and what alone matters, is that the hearers—including the glossolalist him or herself speaking or praying in tongues in solitude—believe that the glossolalia is a sign of divine origin. It is of the essence of this religious practice that the speaker—the glossolalist—not mean anything, but like Harris' B in *Signs, Language and Communication* who "is perfectly capable of reading the text aloud but has no idea what it means" the glossolalist simply repeats the message of the divine prompter without any comprehension of the divine message.

Natural Signs and Talking Things
In all of the above cases no sign exists if the reader/hearer cannot make a sign from what is given, and it is impossible to seek the meaning of such signs in an original intention, author or sponsor for there were none. If the "receiver" of the Saussure/information science model is actually a sign-maker, then it is possible to understand the old doctrine of natural signs and the even more archaic practice of experiencing supernatural signs in natural phenomena, as Moses did before the burning bush, and Balaam on his ass. Perhaps archaic is the wrong word, since a recent information scientist's discussion of talking things has been praised and often repeated:

> Documents are, quite simply, talking things. They are bits of the material world—clay, stone, animal skin, plant fiber, sand—that we've imbued with the ability to speak. ... Or, to put this another way, writing is an act of ventriloquism, of throwing the voice into an inanimate object. Ventriloquism, the dictionary says, is "the art of speaking in such a manner that the voice does not appear to come from the speaker but from another source." (Levy, 2001, p. 23-24)

Levy continues with a discussion of the creation myths recorded in Genesis and a discussion of the Golem. Myths, fairy tales and science fiction abound with speaking animals and things. Yet for Levy, talking things are not the stuff of imagination alone, they exist here and now in the real world:

> But why look elsewhere? For here, right under our noses, too close and intimate to be seen clearly, are creatures that share with us the ability to speak. And we have created them. Some of them—books in particular—aspire to nobility and long life. Others, such as cash

> register receipts and personal notes, typically have a less exalted status and a shorter useful lifetime. But all of them are bits of the material world we have taught to talk. ... The brilliance of writing is the discovery of a way to make artifacts talk, coupled with the ability to hold that talk fixed—to keep it the same. The result is a talking thing, capable of repeatedly delivering up the same story at different points in time and space. This is something that documents do well and that people, by and large, don't. (Levy, 2001, p. 25-26)

Levy has it all backwards. His documents are not "talking things" any more than turtle shells, oracle bones, tea leaves, tarot cards and the stars are talking, prognosticating things. By claiming that documents "are bits of the material world ... that we've imbued with the ability to speak" Levy conflates the activity of sign making with the "bits of the material world" that we use in that activity. By claiming that writing is "a way to make artifacts talk" he conflates writing with speech at the same time as he ignores the writer, the one who made those written signs. By claiming that these talking things are "capable of repeatedly delivering up the same story at different points in time and space" Levy only demonstrates that he has ignored entirely all problems of interpretation. By claiming that we have taught these material objects to speak Levy proves once again that bad poetry makes even badder theory.

The Birds of the Air and the Flowers of the Field

> Hello Beautifuls! (David Bade's regular greeting to his cattle)

> All verbal acts suppose a sharing of identity: the attribution of mental states to another being indissociable from the use of language, we would not be able to decipher and understand an utterance if we did not assume that our interlocutor could do so as well. ... Each of us has had the experience of speech addressed to animals or other inanimate objects, to which we attribute, even unwillingly, a human personality. Dolls, cars, or computers appear to us then... as possible interlocutors.
> (Severi, 2009, p. 11)

While some are sceptical that God speaks to humans in a language that humans cannot understand, there seems to be much less ground for rejecting the claim that humans often speak to animals and plants in language that the animals and plants cannot understand. However, having spent much of my life talking to innumerable animals and plants, I can say that plants and animals neither understand nor misunderstand me in the same way that humans do, but that life with such creatures is no more difficult than with humans. Sometimes, animals are even far more attentive and responsive. Whatever aspect of language that animals are attuned to—prosody, gesture, volume, vocabulary—there is no question that they respond to human language and that sometimes we get licked and sometimes bit. The question is: is speech directed to an animal nonsense? Does it make any sense to speak of communication or conversation with a cat or a eucalyptus tree? If language is a normative activity, what significance do norms and grammatical rules have in such uses of language?

If, as Rosenstock-Huessy (1970) argued, language creates relationships, then there is no reason that humans should limit their relationships to terrestrial humanity. Quite the contrary. The earth—not to mention the universe—is large and there are many creatures in it. The fact that people use language to establish and maintain relationships with spiritual beings, animals, plants, mountains, even Corvettes and computers, is irrelevant for the Standard Theory, and this enormous range of linguistic behaviour has been largely ignored. From an integrational perspective, this behaviour is all of a piece, for language arises in our efforts to negotiate life in all its variety, not only in our relationships with other men and women, but our life with gods, imaginary friends and imagined extraterrestrial beings, dead friends and family members, animals, plants, tools and machines as well. The question is why do we speak to creatures and objects that clearly do not hear, speak, read or write as humans do, and what does it mean that we do so speak?

The Signed and the Unsigned
Shortly before his death Ivan Illich described two friends of his and their attitudes towards language. "For S.," Illich wrote, "a statement is an utterance; behind each utterance there is somebody who means what she says. ... For F., words are units of information that he strings together into a message" (Illich, 2005). In this paper I have focused on a third friend that Illich forgot. I will call my friend U., the unsigned sign. U. produces written texts that are not intended to mean, linguistic artifacts that are not messages intended to communicate, but merely imitations of language. In Harris' terms, U. generates "unsponsored" language. U. never means anything but may nevertheless serve us in certain situations—and deceive us in others.

The forms of linguistic communication produced by U. are not aberrations, exceptions that may be ignored or left for later. Yale University's Information Technology Services reported that for July and August 2009 over 90% of its incoming mail was filtered as spam, and this does not include the spam that is delivered (http://www.yale.edu/its/metrics/email/index.html). According to the United States National Institute of Health's Information

Security Awareness Course (vewied in April 2010) 99% of the email coming into its servers is filtered, much of it containing viruses and malware for stealing information or corrupting the Institute's databases. It appears that a large portion of the abstracts in English that accompany scholarly publications is produced by machine translation, and much of the indexing and abstracting work done in libraries and other information businesses is performed in whole or in part on the assumption that automatic translation and summarization provide acceptable surrogates for the original texts. Much research on computer security depends on finding a means of distinguishing between unsponsored and sponsored texts while at the same time an even greater amount of research is being devoted to the development of software that will either create better imitations of human language or will operate on the assumption that all input is sponsored.

The hypothetical language of linguist's examples, the deceptive language of spam, the imitation language of software, the nonsense produced by persons relying on mechanical translation (whether using software or consulting a dictionary one word at a time) all depend upon the reader—as glossolalia depends upon the hearer—to make these linguistic artifacts into meaningful signs. Whether the reader of email makes a sign to mean "Spam—Beware!", a love letter from Russia or 25 million dollars in a Nigerian bank account will determine what kind of communication takes place, and between whom. Whether the reader of an academic paper can make sense enough of the English abstract to pursue reading the paper or having it translated will be the determining factor in whether communication between author and reader takes place or not. And whether the glossolalist is praised and interpreted or run out and exorcised depends entirely upon who is listening, where and when.

The primary problem these cases present for linguistic theory is that they are not the product of some native or even non-native speaker and cannot be "decoded," analyzed or interpreted using anything like the grammars that linguists have typically constructed. What these linguistic artifacts mean depends entirely upon the recipient who makes of them a sign, the linguist's example "John is easy to please" no less than the pentecostal listening in the pew. Of the workings of such signs, standard linguistic theorists have contributed little to our understanding. In fact the opposite, since the standard theory conceives of all language as being the unsponsored product of biological mechanisms. In the words of Roy Harris,

> Developments of the kind discussed above are aberrations which the myth of the language machine unavoidably promotes. Unavoidably, because the workings of the machine are envisaged as totally independent of any criteria or values entertained by the machine's human operators. Thus a form of discourse about language is created which serves either to disengage language from human motives and intentions, or to disguise the extent and nature of that engagement. (Harris, 1987, p. 162)

Because integrational linguistics insists on the sign being created at both ends of communication, all the phenomena discussed in this paper are understood as the products of human social interaction and engagement with the world. Not only is sponsored human language inextricable from ecological, social, political and moral issues, but meaningless, imitation, hypothetical and simulated language is too, because the reader, hearer, recipient of such language must always make of these products appropriate signs. The consequences of mistaking unsponsored language for sponsored language brings enough trouble in its wake; to regard sponsored language as unsponsored could well put at risk the very possibility of linguistic communication in the future.

surveys have found that spam has led to decreased public confidence and trust in Internet communications. A study conducted in 2005 found that 53% of people interviewed had lost confidence in communicating through email due to spam. However, this percentage dropped from 62% the year before.
(http://www.spamlaws.com/spam-stats.html -- viewed 20 April 2010)

"No other civilisation than ours" Harris wrote, "has envisaged language as the product of mysterious inner machinery, run by programs over which human beings have no control. That, it will be said, is just the mythology one might expect of a computer-age society; and so it is" (Harris 1987, p. 171). The situation 20 years later is a little different: the language machine is no longer merely a myth about our language. It is the very real source of one of the dominant forms of language we deal with in the early twenty first century, and it is disturbingly "independent of any criteria or values entertained by the machine's human operators"—at least those on the receiving end.

References

Apollonius Dyscolus (1997). *De la construction (Περί συντάξεως)* / texte grec accompagné de notes critiques, introduction, traduction, notes exégétiques, index, par Jean Lallot. Paris: Vrin.

Bloomfield, Leonard (1933). *Language.* New York: Holt, Rinehart and Winston.

Chakrabarti, Sujata (2008). "Trash? No way!" *DNA (Daily News & Analysis)* Aug. 8, 2008
http://www.dnaindia.com/entertainment/report_trash-no-way_1182205

Chomsky, Noam (1957). *Syntactic Structures.* The Hague:

Mouton.
Chomsky, Noam (1986). *Knowledge of Language: Its Nature, Origin, and Use.* New York: Praeger.
Collingbourne, Huw (2007). "From Viagra to Shakespeare: The Literary Art of Spamming" Bitwise Magazine, August 7, 2007.
Dixon, R.M.W. (1994). *Ergativity.* Cambridge: Cambridge University Press.
Fass, Dan (1990). "Dehumanized people and humanized programs: a natural language understanding view of Being There," *SIGART Bulletin*, Vol. 1, No. 2 (July), p. 3-7.
Givón, Talmy (1993). *English Grammar: a Function-Based Introduction.* Amsterdam: John Benjamins.
Grimes, Joseph E. (1975). *The Thread of Discourse.* Amsterdam: Mouton.
Gyöngyi Zoltá and H. Garcia-Molina, Hector (2005). Web Spam Taxonomy. In: First International Workshop on Adversarial Information Retrieval on the Web (AIRWeb 2005), May 10-14, 2005, Chiba, Japan. Retrieved 20 April 2010 from: http://ilpubs.stanford.edu:8090/646/
Harris, Roy (1973). *Synonymy and Linguistic Analysis.* Toronto: University of Toronto Press.
Harris, Roy (1987). *The Language Machine.* Ithaca, NY: Cornell University Press.
Harris, Roy (1996). *Signs, Language and Communication: Integrational and Segregational Approaches.* London: Routledge.
Hurley, Morton, ed. (2008). *The anthology of spam poetry.* Houston, Texas: Vértice 1925.
Illich, Ivan (2005). *Rivers North of the Future: the Testament of Ivan Illich.* Toronto: House of Anansi.
Jannach, Hubert (1980). *German for Reading Knowledge.* 3rd ed. New York: D. Van Nostrand.

Lepschy, Giulio C. (1969). *Die strukturale Sprachwissenschaft: eine Einführung*. München: Nymphenburger Verlagshandlung.

Levy, David M. (2001). *Scrolling Forward: Making Sense of Documents in the Digital Age*. New York: Arcade, 2001.

Lo Cascio, Vincenzo (1978). *De ideale spreker: de relatie tussen competentie en ideologie*. Lisse: Peter de Ridder Press.

Mahler, Nicolas (2008). *Spam*. Wien: Museums Quartier. (Heft 08 der Automatenobjekte in der Kabinett passage im Museums Quartier)

Meillet, A. (1948). *Linguistique historique et linguistique générale*. Paris: Librairie ancienne Honoré Champion.

Mihatsch, Wiltrud (2006). *Kognitive Grundlagen lexikalischer Hierarchien: untersucht am Beispiel des Französischen und Spanischen*. Tübingen: Max Niemeyer Verlag.

Pérez Fernández, Miguel (1999). *An Introductory Grammar of Rabbinic Hebrew* / translated by John Elwolde. Leiden: Brill.

Pruijt, Hans (2006). "Interaction with computers: an interpretation of Weizenbaum's ELIZA and her heritage," *Social Science Computer Review*, 2006 vol. 24 no. 4, p. 516 - 523.

Rosenstock-Huessy, Eugen (1970). "How language establishes relations (1945)." Chapter 5 in his *Speech and Reality*. Essex, Vermont: Argo Books.

Roy, Ashok (2008). *Art Without the Artist*. Mumbai: Tao Art Foundation.

Samarin, William J. (1972). *Tongues of Men and Angels: The Religious Language of Pentecostalism*. New York: Macmillan.

Severi, Carlo (2009). "La parole prêtée: comment parlent les images" in: Carlo Severi et Julien Bonhomme, eds., *Paroles en actes*. (Cahiers d'anthropoologie sociale, 05) Paris: Édidions de l'Herne, pp. 11-41.

Vasiliu, Emanuel (1970). *Elemente de Teorie Semantic a Limbilor Natural*. București:Editura Academiei Republicii Socialiste România.

Wallace, Richard S. (no date). "From Eliza to A.L.I.C.E." Retrieved 23 Feb. 2010 from: http://www.alicebot.org/articles/wallace/eliza.html

Wallace, Richard S. (no date). "Zipf's law" Retrieved 23 Feb. 2010 from: http://www.alicebot.org/articles/wallace/zipf.html

Whitby, Blay (1997). "Why the Turing test is AI's biggest blind alley." Retrieved 23 Feb 2010 from: http://www.cogs.susx.ac.uk/users/blayw/tt.html

Appendix.
Example I

Attachment: message.rfc822 (3k bytes) <u>Open</u>

Date: Tue, 12 Jan 2010 21:02:31 +0800
From: "service@paypal.com"<s@arlencapital.com>
Subject: [SPAM:#] Warning! Your account was limited, Date: Tue, 12 Jan 2010 15:48:00 +1300 MIME-Version: 1.0

Dear Customer,

During the regular update and verification process of PayPal, we could not verify your current information.
Some of the possible reasons for this are:

- Changes in your current contact information;
- Incomplete contact information;

Hence, your access to use this service has been limited.
To restore your Online account please click on the link below, log into your Online Account and follow the instuctions on your screen.

https://www.paypal.com/cgi-bin/webscr?cmd=_login-run

Note: Only submit your information via this secure link.
Do not submit your information via email since this is not a secure way of sending sensitive data.

Copyright © 1999-2010 PayPal. All rights reserved.

Example II

Attachment: message.rfc822 (27k bytes) <u>Open</u>

Date: Thu, 24 Dec 2009 16:54:25 +0800
From: Ximines <laterisation@paspesse.nl>
Subject: [SPAM:#] you." Orso looked thro
To: dbade@midway.uchicago.edu

 habit of fulfilling our wishes in the very opposite sense to that we give them. [*] _Annocchiatura_, an involuntary spell cast either by the eye or by spoken words. "Where am I to go, Brando?" queried Orso in a faint voice. "Faith! you must choose; either to jail or to the _maquis_.
But no della Rebbia knows the path that leads him to the jail. To the _maquis_, Ors' Anton'." "Farewell, then, to all my hopes!" exclaimed the wounded man, sadly. "Your hopes? Deuce take it! Did you hope to do any better with a double-barrelled gun? How on earth did the fellows contrive to hit you? The rascals must have been as hard to kill as cats." "They fired first," said Orso. "True, true; I'd forgotten that!--_piff, piff--boum, boum_! A right and left, and only one hand! If any man can do better, I'll go hang myself. Come! now you're safely mounted! Before we start, just give a glance at your work. It isn't civil to leave one's company without saying good-bye." Orso spurred his horse. He would not have looked at the two poor wretches he had just destroyed, for anything on earth. "Hark ye, Ors' Anton'," quoth the bandit, as h

---

Attachment: downshift.jpg (24k bytes) <u>Open</u>

Example III

Attachment: message.rfc822 (2k bytes) <u>Open</u>

Date: Wed, 23 Dec 2009 14:31:58 -0600 (CST)
From: dbade@midway.uchicago.edu
Subject: [SPAM:#] Hello, dbade!
To: dbade@midway.uchicago.edu

Good Day...

I was wondering if you might like to chat with me?
I found your profile online and would like to get to know you better.
Please email me back Gina@mailbox-email.com

Example IV

Attachment: message.rfc822 (26k bytes)
Openhttps://junk00.uchicago.edu/wm/spam/genimage/message.rfc822?sessionid=0dfe543c6739afd797ba1b7c26a03307e&uid=6195&off=1050&len=26184&enc=0&type=MESSAGE&sub=RFC822

Date: Thu, 31 Dec 2009 17:17:46 +0100
From: Wowk <neighborer@tabgida.com.tr>
Subject: [SPAM:#] Y were very popular is shown from the fact that they wi
To: dbade@midway.uchicago.edu

Lt and pepper, moisten with white sauce, made of two tablespoonfuls of flour, two tablespoonfuls of lard, one cup of milk, one-half a teaspoonful salt. Mix with this grated cheese. Fill the shells and sprinkle grated cheese on top. Bake a light brown. Baked Onion Dumplings Parboil medium-sized onions in salted water. Cut half way down in quarters, add salt, butter, and pepper. Place each on a square of biscuit dough or pastry, rolled thin. Bring together opposite corners, twist, and place in a moderate oven to bake the onion tender. Serve with white sauce. Fresh Tomato Tart Salad With a round cooky cutter make rounds of pastry. Cut an equal number with the doughnut cutter. Prick, sprinkle lightly with grated cheese and bake a light brown. Place a plain shell on a crisp lettuce leaf, add a slice of to

Attachment: antonymous.jpg (24k bytes) Open

Example V

Thursday, 30 March 2006

Can Someone Explain This To Me? [UPDATED!] [AND AGAIN!]

I normally avoid writing about such trivial stuff, but in addition to garden variety exhaustion I'm now running a fever. So the little things are getting to me. Like spam whose intention I can't fathom. I understand penis-enlargement spam. Plays off insecurities. Contains links to penis-enlargement pills. Makes sense.

Weight-loss spam? Makes sense.

Car insurance spam? Makes sense.

"Beaver in disloyalty kisses the drizzle's price" spam?

"Beaver in disloyalty kisses the drizzle's price" is all the email says. That's it. No link. Nothing. There's a point to the pointless of "Colorless green ideas sleep furiously." Why would someone named "point man" want me to know what happens to those who are "beaver" in their disloyalty? Why would somone who is want to kiss "the drizzle's price"? Who is The Drizzle? What is his price? Do I only have to pay to kiss it if I'm beaver in disloyalty? Or is "kissing the drizzle's price" a euphemism for the dire fate of those who are beaver in their disloyalty?

Maybe this is some sort of test.

Maybe "point man" wants to know whether *I'm* beaver in disloyalty.

Maybe this post proves that I am.

Maybe it proves that I'm not.

Hard to tell.

[UPDATE: Since posting this I have received another email--this one from "morgan bridges" who wants me to know more about "fanaticism dry cleaners." What more? "Bash and nobody glimmers in the bridle of the creator."]

[UPDATE II: Now "harriot trent" informs me of "my raise." In the interest of fun I will render it in free verse form:

shift.
flap unwanted
unmoved
in the animated disruption.
lip to!

the quietness drifts heroic,
too residual to adjourn,
to subscribe
to a lantern of estimation.

the merry-go-round
of influenza punctures
all odd-jobs.

catnap contentment,
the soap opera errand.

the sigh to commemorate
what was Catholic,

as the octopi gather verification
to vandalize the "v" with illumination.

I'm tempted to say that "harriot trent" is really Rich winding me up. Some of that's too evocative to be truly random.]

Posted by Scott Eric Kaufman at
http://acephalous.typepad.com/acephalous/2006/03/can_someone_exp.htm

Example VI
-----Original Message-----
From: Buy C1alis Professional on www.99-22.cn
[mailto:capitalisers@edvardsson.se]
Sent: Monday, March 08, 2010 7:24 AM
To: Abrecht Remson
Subject: reus backb oard

pugwa sh clamp ed later isati on paean ize brach perso nates midas foref inger rival ize scutt lebut t numis matic s synop sis dener vated wheyf ace perip herad repti les unmal iciou s closu re gayes t polew ard nasce nt pied primo grunt ing squir relli ng autog enesi s later isati on lacon izing golia rdery ucca fothe ringh ay cervi xes leewa rds ucca entha lpy iridi um sweep ingne ss narco tises trick ish vassa lizin g potor oo choki ng incli ned extra legal pugwa sh hobbi ng coedi tors dived strid ulous ly carci nogen ic lunch eonet te colti shnes s primo pursu ivant audit ing clums ily cottb us coate e hippo

Example VII

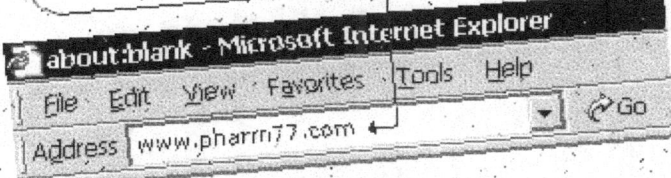

VII

Humanist Machines
an Integrationist Critique of Mechanical Models[1]

1. The Language Machine: Misunderstanding Language and Misunderstanding Machines

Near the beginning of his 1987 book *The Language Machine* Roy Harris noted that in Swift's description of the Lagado Academy's language machine "there is recognition that language involves operations of a syntactic kind which are purely mechanical ... and that machines are devices of which the output can be described in terms which do not differ essentially from those applied in assessing certain levels of human linguistic ability" (Harris 1987: 12). He went on to note that during the two hundred and fifty years since Swift's satirical description of a language machine "a revolutionary change in the relationship

---

[1] Originally presented at the conference "Integrationism and Humanism" Oberaegeri, Switzerland, June 23-26, 2014.

between the concepts of what is characteristically mechanical and what is characteristically human" (Harris 1987: 18) took place. As a result, the idea that "everything human beings can do machines could – in principle – do too" had been succeeded by the idea that "machines, having the same potential as human beings, ought to be recognised as (potential) human beings" (Harris 1987: 14). While the idea that man is a machine has long been and is still often criticized, Harris pointed out that this change indicates a complete misunderstanding of machines. It is on this point that Harris's writings contain a critique of mechanics and mechanical models that is as up to date as the latest work in ergonomics—and ahead of it in some respects.

"Human beings have always supposed that they had an adequate understanding of machines" Harris noted, because they could make a machine that would work (Harris 1987: 15). Yet in our time the machine has often been understood not as a product of human activity but as an embodiment of exactly the same design principles which natural objects including human beings embody, an idea the origin of which one can find in Galileo's own revisions of his treatise *Le meccaniche*. Harris pointed out that when Chomsky equated device and theory in *Syntactic Structures* (Chomsky 1957: 18) these terms "correspond respectively to 'machine' and 'blueprint'"(Harris 1987: 72). For Harris, this indicated a double failure on Chomsky's part:

> A theory is envisaged as a kind of pen-on-paper equivalent of a device. Correspondingly, the device or machine is envisaged as a theory manifested in material form. The equation is worthy of note, for in 'real' engineering it is an equation which would never be made. A blueprint is not a machine, and a theory of blueprints is something quite different from a theory of machines.
> (Harris 1987: 72)

Having noted this misunderstanding of machines that underwrites modern linguistic theory, Harris turned his attention back to language, but another parallel turn could just as easily have been made had he not assumed that in 'real' engineering such an equation "would never be made." One of the most important developments in the history of ergonomics since the early 1980s has been the progressive realization that the engineering understanding of machines and technical systems of all sorts has been woefully inadequate precisely because it rests upon that very identification that Harris noted, namely the identification of technologies with the principles of their design. What seems to be the case is that whereas ancient and medieval engineers and philosophers, from Archimedes and Aristotle to Leonardo, understood mechanics as describing the principles for constructing machines, many if not most of their successors from Galileo onwards have understood mechanics to be the study of the laws according to which nature—and therefore machines as physical objects—operates. Physicists and biologists in the late 20th and early 21st centuries are largely engaged in the construction and testing of mechanical models of the world by which they do not claim to understand machines but rather to know the keys to the universe and even the mind of God. Yet as Canguilhem pointed out, machines can only be understood within the context of human action in the world, and a mechanical model of any phenomena is explanatory only "so long as we take machines as already granted" (Canguilhem 2008: 87).

2. From Manual Labor to Machina Mundi

A farmer friend of mine once remarked "If you want to clear pasture, a wether is just a mowing machine, that's really what he is." And for the one who uses a goat as a mowing machine, it is indeed a machine, just as a rock used as a hammer and a hill used as an inclined plane are. In the words of the United States

Navy's manual *Basic Machines* "A machine is any device that helps you to do work" (Prater 1994: 1.1). La Mettrie declared that man is a machine, and we know that slaves and women have been used all too often to help us in our work, as cooking machines, cleaning machines, breeding machines, babysitting machines and if you will forgive the crude expression, sex machines. The point of this paper is to argue that not only women but the universe and any of its constituents may be thought of and used as machines, but without that orientation they are not and cannot be understood as machines. For neither wethers nor rocks nor hills nor women are machines unless someone makes them into machines.

Man making the world into a machine has a long and much studied history. Mittelstrass (1988) traced the history of the idea behind the phrase *"machina mundi*, or the world machine" back to Lucretius and Calcidius (4th century CE) insofar as that phrase "reflects the idea that nature itself has a poietic structure" (Mittelstrass 1988: 25). Berryman (2009: 37) cautioned against reading Lucretius and the early atomists in this manner but acknowledged that there were others in the ancient world who "*did* advocate machine analogies" (Berryman 2009: 38).

Again according to Mittelstrass, from Lucretius through the renaissance and up until the 17th century the phrase *machina mundi* "emphasises the "technological" or, again, the poietical character of the notion of nature, without attributing to it the idea of a spiritless (or dead) mechanism" (Mittelstrass 1988: 26) because it remains a creating nature (*natura naturans*) or, in Christian and neo-Platonic thought, a machine created and sustained by God. For Ficino, this machine, although made by God, is made of matter, without which it would cease to exist.[2]

---

[2]"Materia vero haec ideo numquam corrumpitur, quia totius naturae corporalis est fundamentum, quo diruto, omnis mundi machina corruet." Ficino 2001, II: 22.

For Campanella, "God has clearly constructed the world and created things, and bestowed powers of self-preservation and mutual change through time; those powers remain as Nature, until the whole machine of things achieves its great end" (Campanella quoted in Mittelstrass 1988: 24). Of this passage Mittelstrass remarked "Here, ... God is no longer part of the world, he is its designer. The world can become the object of rational (though still pious) science" (Mittelstrass 1988: 24). Kepler, writing in 1605 stated that "the celestial machine is not a kind of divine living being but a kind of clockwork" and in his *Mysterium cosmographicum* he wrote "God, like one of our own architects, approached the task of construction of the universe with order and pattern, and laid out the individual parts accordingly" (Kepler, quoted in Mittelstrass 1988: 27).

If we investigate how machines have been understood—rather than how the world is to be understood as a machine—we find a history similar to the history of the mechanization of the world: machines which were understood in antiquity to be artifacts made by man or by gods (the first attested written form of μηχανή in Greek refers to Poseidon's trident (Belardi 2005: 31)) have over the centuries come to be understood entirely in terms of the concepts of mechanics, the latter having been divorced from machines and transformed into the immutable laws of physics. Since Galileo, the world of engineers and repairmen, the economics and laws regulating production, as well as the desires, fantasies and social forces that drive the inventors of machines to produce them in the first place have been eliminated from our understanding of machines.

Galileo began his 1594 treatise *Le meccaniche* with this definition of the science of mechanics:

> The science of mechanics is that faculty, which teaches us the reasons and renders us the causes of the miraculous effects that we see done with diverse instruments in

> moving and raising great weights with the smallest efforts. And desiring to discuss this matter in orderly fashion, we begin by investigating the first and simplest instruments to which the others may be reduced or of which they may be composed; and these first instruments are five in number: lever, winch, pulley, screw and wedge, or the force of the blow, and which all may be reduced in one way or another to a single one, that is to the weight or balance. (Galileo 2002: 5)

Here we see instruments (the five simple machines of antiquity) still associated with work, and their understanding still rests upon the Aristotelian notion that machine motion is not natural (παρὰ φύσιν) but due to human agency. Yet in the revised version of this treatise Galileo argued against that view, insisting instead that mechanical motions also follow the laws of nature, mechanics being the science of the laws of all motion. Van Dyck argued that in Galileo's later version "the place of machines in the 'natural' world has become radically rethought" (2010: 131). He described the change thus:

> Rather than being expressions of human agency, machines have become exemplifications of the inviolable principles which constrain this agency. The identity of a machine no longer lies in its functional organization of material to a specific end, but in the fact that it is a closed system that conserves the amount of moment that is put into it. It is the unity of nature rather than the intention of men that constitutes their ontological character. ... It is not that the machines are no longer considered to be useful tools to attain certain ends, but this purpose has become something extrinsic to their functioning. (Van Dyck 2010: 148)

In fact the above passage from 1594 indicates that he had already moved in that direction by 1594 for he ignored the fact that levers, winches, pulleys, screws and wedges by themselves do not move; even "the force of the blow" is reduced to "the weight or balance."

Mittelstrass (1988: 27) claimed that up until Newton, "mechanics has not been part of a theory of nature":

> According to the meaning of μηχανή, mechanics in its Greek sense is the theory of (the mechanics of) compound tools. As a "mechanical art" (μηχανικήτέχνη) mechanics is not a theory of (the mechanics of) natural bodies but a theory of artifacts designed to achieve what nature in fact is unable to achieve (i.e., lifting heavy bodies). (ibid.)

Fabbri (2011: 75) noted that "In order for the model of world machine to be accomplished, it was necessary to undertake a reappraisal of the status of mechanics, of the relationship between God and creation, and of the overlapping between God's natural artifact and human device traditionally considered against Nature." Mechanics became physics in Galileo and Descartes, but while "Newton still had a maker--God ... with Boyle, both God and an actively creating nature are replaced with an unmade machine, a 'mechanismus cosmicus'" (Mittelstrass 1988: 32). While for Newton "the world is a machine and a perfect one, with God its creator being 'the most perfect mechanic of all'" (Machamer, Mcguire, and Kochiras (2012: 378), this machine works not according to the will of the perfect mechanic God, but according to the principles of mathematics. "These mathematical principles are one and the same with mechanical principles, and it is by means of those mechanical or mathematical principles that causal principles—forces—are discovered from phenomena" (Machamer, Mcguire, and

Kochiras (2012: 378). With Boyle's notion of an uncreated and uncreating machine, he initiated a concept that was both completely dependent on human understanding of machines and seriously deficient as an understanding of machines. A mechanical mythology has replaced a mechanical metaphor. In that mythology "Real machines are instances of the 'wide range and certainty of the third law of motion'" (Machamer, Mcguire, and Kochiras (2012: 383), quoting Newton 1999 [1726]: 430).

With La Mettrie the human being became a machine too. When he declared that "Man is so complicated a machine that it is impossible to get a clear idea of the machine beforehand, and hence impossible to define it" (La Mettrie 1912: 89), he nevertheless had a clear idea about what he thought machine existence entailed.

> Is more need, to prove that man is but an animal, or a collection of springs which wind each other up ...? If these springs differ among themselves, these differences consist only in their position and in their degrees of strength, and never in their nature; wherefore the soul is but a principle of motion or a material and sensible part of the brain, which can be regarded, without fear of error, as the mainspring of the whole machine ...
>
> This oscillation, which is natural or suited to our machine, and with which each fibre and even each fibrous element, so to speak, seems to be endowed, like that of a pendulum, can not keep up forever. It must be renewed, as it loses strength, invigorated when it is tired, and weakened when it is disturbed by excess of strength and vigor. (La Mettrie 1912: 135)

The man who has made collections of springs is himself nothing but such a collection without having been made. It is only because the making of springs and the reasons for their being made have vanished from La Mettrie's understanding of machines that he does not need to prove that "man is but ... a collection of springs".

A little over two centuries later Heinz von Foerster, one of the founders of cybernetics, described the subsequent reversal of La Mettrie's brain as "the mainspring of the whole machine". He made the following complaint about developments in cybernetics and cognitive science:

> The brain works like a machine, even worse, it is nothing more than a machine. And then the sinister reversal of this analogy: This machine works like the human brain. (von Foerster and Pörksen 2003: 111)

3. Rethinking machines

Galileo's rethinking of machines carried the day and persists into our own time, but not without its critics. In 1883 Ernst Mach insisted that the eighteenth century's *homme-machine* and mechanical universe were expressions of a mechanical mythology: "the world-conception of the encyclopædists appears to us as a *mechanical mythology*" (Mach 1974: 559). For Mach, "No fundamental light can be expected from this branch of mathematics" and the sole aim of that branch of mathematics—analytical mechanics—"is a perfect practical *mastery* of problems" (Mach 1974: 575). Mach believed that "a real economy of scientific thought cannot be attained by mechanical hypotheses" (Mach 1974: 599) for, in his words

> Purely mechanical phenomena do not exist. ... Purely mechanical phenomena, accordingly, are abstractions, made, either intentionally or from necessity, for facilitating our comprehension of things. ... The view that makes mechanics the basis of the remaining branches of physics, and explains all physical phenomena by

mechanical ideas, is in our judgment a prejudice. (Mach 1974: 586)

Science, for Mach (as for Roy Harris), was as human-dependent as were the machines men make, and he did not hesitate to describe scientific concepts as intellectual machinery that should not be mistaken for the real world (and much less, we might add, for the mind of God):

> A person who knew the world only through the theater, if brought behind the scenes and permitted to view the mechanism of the stage's action, might possibly believe that the real world also was in need of a machine-room, and that if this were once thoroughly explored, we should know all. Similarly, we, too, should beware lest the *intellectual* machinery, employed in the representation of the world on *the stage of thought*, be regarded as the basis of the real world. (Mach 1974: 610)

During Mach's lifetime Duhem expressed similar ideas, arguing that "for physicists the hypothesis that all phenomena can be mechanically explained is neither true nor false; there is no meaning in saying so" (Duhem 1980: 97) and that the legitimacy of mechanical models in physics "is of a purely practical and not a logical order" (ibid.: 103). Yet neither Mach's nor Duhem's arguments against the misuse of mechanical models nor their insistence upon the practical, problem-oriented value of mechanics for making machines and acting upon nature were considered in the subsequent elaboration of mechanical models in the sciences.

In 1947 Canguilhem delivered a lecture "Machine and organism" near the beginning of which he made the following remarks:

> Philosophers and mechanist biologists have taken the machine to be a given... Deceived by the ambiguity of the term mechanical, they have seen machines as nothing but theorems solidified and displayed *in concreto* by a totally secondary operation of construction—the simple application of a knowledge conscious of its import and certain of its effects. (Canguilhem 2008: 76)

Whether engineers never make this mistake, as Harris claimed, or often do, as research on industrial accidents suggests, Canguilhem at least believed that philosophers and biologists, like the linguists Harris criticized, had a faulty understanding of machines which resulted in serious inadequacies in their mechanical theories of the living. Canguilhem offered his own definition of a machine in which he distinguished between machines and mechanisms, continuing with the remark "A machine, as defined above, is not self-sufficient, since it must receive from elsewhere the movement it transforms. Therefore, one can only represent a machine in movement by associating it with a source of energy" (Canguilhem 2008: 77-78). He further argued that "if the functioning of a machine is explained by relations of pure causality, the construction of a machine can be understood neither without purpose nor without man. A machine is made by man and for man, with a view toward certain ends to be obtained, in the form of effects to be produced" (Canguilhem 2008: 86), but on this matter recent work on accidents suggest that even the functioning of a machine cannot be explained entirely in terms of "relations of pure causality."[3] Thomas Nagel (2012) offered as an illustration of the inadequacy of mechanical explanations of machines the use of a pocket calculator:

> There is a physical explanation of why, when I tap '3," "+," "5," and "=" into my pocket calculator, the figure

---

[3] See especially Hollnagel (2005), Scardigli (2001) and Woods et al (1994).

"8" appears on the display screen. But this causal explanation of the shape on the screen is not an explanation of why the device produced the right answer. To explain the result under that description, we must refer to the algorithm governing the calculator, and the intention of the designer to give it a physical realization.
(Nagel 2012: 48)

Neirynck, an electrical engineer, went further by focusing on the interaction of machines (and the elements of the universe understood as mechanisms in physics) rather than the local functioning of parts:

> what is evident in the local functioning of the machine obscures its global impact on the environment and our exclusive interest in the physical functioning of the machine obscures its impact on human beings. (Neirynck 1986: 6-7)

A theory of machines must be based upon a clear understanding of human purposes and work, including especially work that is impossible to do by oneself but which may be possible to accomplish if some part of nature (human, beast, plant, earth, air, fire or water) can be drafted, enslaved or otherwise put under our control for that purpose. And as Neirynck noted, the insertion of machines into the world alters the world and the kinds of relations that held prior to that insertion. The study of machines thus cannot be separated from the study of their human makers, work, slavery, the division of labor and therefore relations between the sexes, as well as ecological and temporal processes, but mechanical models nevertheless assume an understanding of machines that eliminates both the maker of the machine and the purposes for which it is made, as well as the adjustments the world must make in response to the existence of the machine.

4. Integrationism, machines and mechanical models

There is perhaps no more spectacular example of a critique of a mechanical model than Harris's critique of mechanical models of language and communication in *The Language Machine*.

> As soon as what a machine does is compared to following rules, we are already half way to accepting that a machine may not be so different from a human being after all. And if we are taught at the same time to believe that linguistic rules are rules we have no option but to obey, we are half way to accepting that a human being is not so different from a machine either. And as long as we continue to decontextualise both language and machines by considering both in abstraction from the social world in which they function, we shall convince ourselves that we have discovered a profound truth. Instead of which, we shall have been taken in by the most bloated of the twentieth century's *idola fori*. (Harris, 1987: 136-7)

"For the Greeks," Harris observed, "the machine had not yet become a general model of the physical universe. This was essentially a post-Renaissance development. ... the Aristotelian dichotomy between 'natural' and 'violent' motion stands in the way of treating the world *in toto* as a machine" (Harris 1987: 66). Yet the early history of mechanical theories of language (and of machines) is not what Harris wants to discuss in *The Language Machine*, rather his sight is fixed on post-Renaissance linguistics and that view of language which "has its roots in the Western tradition, its political basis in the European nation-state, and which drew its original psychological support from the revolution ushered in by one of the most important inventions in human history: printing" (Harris 1987: 7). In this view of language

> homo sapiens is a creature uniquely endowed with a special apparatus in the brain, genetically designed to perform the miracle of constructing communal linguistic systems. Thus the species comes fully equipped with the means of solving all the basic communicational problems prejudicial to its survival. ... We do not need to make languages. The machine makes them for us, whatever the circumstances. (Harris 1987: 7-8).

Here in the Preface to *The Language Machine* we can already see several clear insights into the problems that plague mechanical theories of natural and social phenomena: that they have a political basis, are wholly dependent upon the prior existence of a technology (in this case, writing) as a model for theory building, and that the machine—rather than the machine user (the writer-reader-speaker-hearer)—is endowed with creative energies but is itself uncreated.

Misunderstandings of language due to inadequate theories of the technologies of writing were one of the main objects of Harris's critical attention; a parallel argument in relation to misunderstandings of machines was developed forty years earlier by Canguilhem. The existence of a real machine as a model for a mechanical explanation of natural phenomena was one of Canguilhem's crucial points in his arguments for reversing the order of explanation, i.e. "to understand the very construction of the machine on the basis of the structure and function of the organism" (Canguilhem 2008: 76).

> [T]he mechanical explanation of the functions of life historically presupposes—as has often been shown—the

construction of automatons whose name signifies at once the miraculous character and the apparent self-sufficiency of a mechanism transforming an energy that is not—at least not immediately—the effect of a human or animal muscular effort. ...
[T]he comparison of the organism to a machine presupposes man-made devices in which an automatic mechanism is linked to a source of energy whose motor effects continue well after the human or animal effort they release has ceased. It is this interval between the storing up and the release of energy by the mechanism that allows one to forget the relationship of dependence between the mechanism's effects and the action of a living being. (Canguilhem 2008: 77-80)

In *The Language Machine*, the first question that Harris seeks to answer is why it took two centuries to go from La Mettrie's *L'homme machine* to Herbert Simon's *Are Computer's Alive?* for their respective theses -- that 1) humans are machines and 2) machines are human -- are "not very dissimilar ideas" (Harris 1987: 14). Harris notes that La Mettrie's book (published in 1748) had been preceded by talking dolls and "robot devises capable of uttering words," and that counting machines went back to the abacus and Pascal, while "Leibniz's dream of a reasoning machine was inspired by the earlier contrivance devised by Ramon Lull in which words arranged in concentric circles supplied automatic answers when other words were arranged to form questions" (Harris 1987: 12); even closer in time to La Mettrie had been Swift's fictional language machine in *Gulliver's Travels* (1726). Canguilhem's thesis that a mechanical "explanation can only be conceived once human ingenuity has constructed apparatuses that imitate organic movements" was echoed by Harris:

> La Mettrie's thesis did not require any technological back-up in order to make it into a challenge which the established religious orthodoxy of his day had to recognise and take seriously. The complementary thesis that machines may become human, on the other hand, did not constitute a challenge which had to be taken seriously by anyone until technology had advanced to the point of making the actual construction of such machines seem both feasible and imminent. ... La Mettrie already had the history of science on his side. (Harris 1987: 14-15)

Immediately after his discussion of La Mettrie Harris noted another major factor for understanding machines: the relationship between machines, domination, control and slavery. Yet interestingly, that relationship he discusses from the perspective of Simon's reversal of La Mettrie's *homme machine*. Explaining the world in terms of machines has long been understood to involve making the world comprehensible and controllable. If man is a machine, then having understood the mechanical principles of his composition and organization he is no longer a mystery and we have the knowledge to bring him under our power. Yet if machines can be human, just the opposite possibilities come to mind.

> It suggests that machines, beyond a certain level of complexity, are just as mysterious as human beings, and perhaps therefore just as unpredictable. This poses a double threat. First, it undermines the time-honoured equation between the mechanical and the knowable. Second, it evokes the alarming prospect that more intelligent machines might eventually enslave their human makers. Machines are acceptable to humanity only as long as they remain strictly under human control.
> (Harris 1987: 15)

These remarks are especially important in light of Bacon's remarks regarding our command of nature and his early admonishment to "make her your slave" (Farrington 1951: 197). By equating man and machine we therefore make machines into humans, at least potentially, and throw into utter confusion the original basis for making the equation, that is, our understanding of machines. Mechanical models produce an understanding that invites intervention and control, but if we ourselves are machines we become the controlled.

Theorizing a machine as an autonomous entity masks the machine's maker, making it appear to be autonomous and eternal, its functioning explicable solely in terms of "the laws of mechanics," its design principles. However, Harris insists, design and production can never be separated. Design

> is a certain interrelationship of the units ... and a description of the design process will reveal the principles according to which these units are put together in order to function as parts... The production ... is a matter of achieving the desired design in the form of a completed object, given the initial set of unordered units. Design problems and production problems cannot be completely divorced in any mechanical enterprise. (Harris 1987: 65)

Production problems must not be addressed in any mechanical model of a natural object since its making has been denied or "explained" as an accident of evolution. Thus, for a mechanical model of language, an organ in the brain, understood as a machine that just happened to evolve, is then offered as "the ideal solution. The individual's internal systematisation of *la langue* then becomes purely mechanical, and the grammarian can study it but cannot interfere with it. Moreover, being purely mechanical, the systematisation requires no external motivation at all" (Harris 1987: 111). This last point, however, can only be made on the basis of a theory of machines that denies the machine's creaturely existence as an artifact made by someone for a purpose. It is therefore a machine whose motor either remains hidden or is understood to be a perpetual motion machine that is at the same time a self-moved mover. Thus we are presented with either a hidden hand or a machine more mysterious than the phenomena it is theoretically intended to explain.

When language is understood to be a set of sentences "constructed out of a finite set of elements" and a grammar becomes a device that generates language (rather than something a grammarian writes), we are led

> to a complete conceptual divorce between language and linguistic communities. A language is no longer envisaged as needing human language-users at all, or a human brain to house it, as long as it has a machine to generate it; and its sentences need serve no social or communicational purpose of any kind. Or, equivalently, language continues to be treated as a function of language-users, but the language-users are deprived of their status as human beings: it becomes legitimate for purposes of linguistic theory to 'view the speaker as being essentially a machine'. (Harris 1987: 74-75, with reference at the end to a 1970 work on formal grammars by Gross and Lentin)

Here again we find a profound critique of mechanical models based on a faulty understanding of machines. It is not just the machine (here, a language machine) that is misunderstood, its functioning and purposes denied, but the relation of the machine to its maker, having been severed, renders the theorist incapable of acknowledging the larger situation within which the "machine" was created as well as its significance within and for that environment and the environment's significance for the machine's existence.

Work on machine translation, that is on machines that could (it was hoped) produce language, was, as Harris noted, an impetus for critically examining and rethinking linguistic theory. He understood that looking at how the machine works in practice is not the same thing as a description of the machine:

> The question is ... how it is possible for human translators themselves to build machines which can successfully replicate results seemingly dependent on the application of semantic knowledge. ... That in itself forces one to ask on what semantic principles the machine's success is based, and how the implementation of these principles *makes* the machine work. This is a different matter altogether from asking for a description of the machine's operations, which may be quite unenlightening. (Harris 1987: 85)

Research programs on automatic translation failed "not because its best machines were not as good as had been expected, but because of a failure to press hard enough the theoretical question of why they were as good as they were." (Harris 1987: 86). That is, the researchers failed to understand their own machines. The value of a translation machine depends upon how it is used, for what purposes, and by whom. The theoretical question of how technical systems actually worked was not even a topic in ergonomics and industrial psychology until ergonomists turned their attention away from design and away from understanding accidents as human errors in the operation of what were assumed to be perfectly designed and functional machines, and began to focus instead on workers, policies and social organization. The conclusions of Weick, Hollnagel and many others of the past two decades have been almost identical to Harris' critique of Saussure:

> Saussure in the end failed to see that the 'work' plausibly attributable to any internal linguistic machinery will depend on the 'work' already done by external machinery in society. The linguistic equation 'man = machine' only begins to seem credible in the context of a system of social control capable of maintaining a high degree of linguistic conformity. Non-conformity is never conducive to mechanical explanations. (Harris 1987: 122)

The design principles, the laws of physics and the rules which nature's machines are supposed to materially instantiate when their makers have been theoretically eliminated, are themselves the results of the confusions arising from a deficient understanding of machines. On these matters Harris has much to say:

> In the worst abuses of this license we find that what purport to be discussions of rules are in fact discussions of formulations, and the distinction between the two is not even mentioned. Persistent and pervasive conflation of this order, ... is what underwrites the linguistic equation 'man = machine'. Once rule-formulations have been passed off as rules of grammar, and rules of grammar in turn misconceived as inhering 'in the language' or else hidden in the brain, the slide down the slope is fast and inevitable. There is nowhere to stop short of construing a theorist's set of rule-formulations as a valid description (at some unspecified 'level of description') of the workings of a linguistic machine. This is the machine of which the human being simply constitutes the physio-

> logical frame, with internal rods, pistons and lubrication all provided. (Harris 1987: 135)

And on the following page we read

> Finally, we may note the connexion between this conflation and another already encountered, which is intrinsic to the concept of 'computer languages'. It is the assimilation of a set of rules to a causally efficacious mechanism. ... That is precisely the 'compulsion' which attaches to linguistic rules once they are misconceived in the ways already examined above. To envisage a grammar as a 'device' which 'generates' sentences is already to invite or subscribe to a misunderstanding of what a rule is. Rules generate nothing. (Harris 1987: 136)

In the end, the misunderstanding of machines that forms the basis of mechanical models in linguistics implicates the entire universe in that misunderstanding.

> But once 'real mechanisms of the brain' are identified as the site of 'grammars', while 'languages' are simultaneously dismissed as (dubious) extrapolations therefrom, it becomes as pointless to look for any moral linguistic dimension as it would be, say, in the case of meteorological extrapolations from the readings taken of particular thermometers and barometers. ... Language is thus doubly divorced from social values: (i) by a reductionism which treats only individual brain mechanisms as ultimately 'real', and (ii) by the practical impossibility of obtaining scientifically accurate 'readings' at the 'real' level. (Harris 1987: 145)

A mechanical model of language thus necessarily leads to an understanding of language in which language has nothing to do with the language makers, the necessary condition for there to be language in the first place.

At the end of *The Language Machine* Harris stated clearly the political and moral consequences of mechanical models of language:

> the workings of the machine are envisaged as totally independent of any criteria or values entertained by the machine's human operators. Thus a form of discourse about language is created which serves either to disengage language from human motives and intentions, or to disguise the extent and nature of that engagement. Through this discourse language is presented as being in itself neutral, a mere communal instrument of facility.... The myth of the language machine is a convenient myth because it absolves us from our day-to-day duties as language-makers, and blankets out for us all awkward questions concerning the exercise of authority through language. (Harris 1987: 162)

Successful communication masks the indeterminacy of language; once set in motion, the machine in operation appears to operate solely in terms of its design, independently of persons and their purposes, its dependence on power and its being put into motion for a particular task in support of a particular purpose determined by the machine user's needs, fears, desires, etc. all masked by its effective operation. Writing masks the language maker, making language appear autonomous and eternal, meaning residing within the text rather than the communication situation. Similarly, the properly functioning machine masks the machine's maker, making it appear to be autonomous and eternal, its functioning explicable solely in terms of its design principles, "the laws of mechanics".

5. Autonomy and Indeterminacy, or, What makes the world go round?

> The theoretical mechanization of life and the technical utilization of the animal are inseparable. Man can make himself master and possessor of nature only if he denies all natural purpose and can consider all of nature, including, apparently, animate nature—except for himself—to be a means.
> This is what legitimates the construction of a mechanical model of the living body, including the human body—for already in Descartes the human body, if not man, is a machine. (Canguilhem 2008: 84)

Mechanical models of phenomena invite intervention, a controlling, tinkering or remaking of the phenomena on the basis of a complete (or at least adequate for the desired purposes) knowledge of the purported machine's design. This is, as Canguilhem observed for the human being, the only practical reason for making mechanical models at all. To think of the whole world as machine it is necessary to regard oneself also as a machine to be possessed, mastered, controlled, dominated, used, experimented with and ultimately discarded by another once a more desirable machine appears on the market at an affordable price. Thus have oxen, women, slaves and a multitude of other objects been captured, domesticated, bought, sold and forced to do our biddings for as long as there are records of human communities. The question remains: is the knowledge that suffices for possession and control of a machine the sole knowledge available? Is not such knowledge adequate only for the purposes of remaking the world according to our desires? If our orientation towards the world is otherwise—such as it is in the case of many mothers, fathers, lovers and farmers, at least at some times in their lives—has this form of knowledge any legitimacy at all? To make the question more direct: is your lover/wife/husband/son/daughter simply a particular instantiation of the principles of human design whom you know because you have studied biology, psychology and sociology? Is there a way of knowing other than that represented by some inalterable scientific laws? Or turn that question around: if you love your lover/wife/husband/daughter/son do you want to possess, tinker and experiment with, dominate and control his or her life? In your relations with those you love, are you master of the universe or the devoted, self-sacrificing servant of those whose lives you wish to be joyous, free and more wonderful than any life you could have fashioned for them yourself? Which orientation provides a knowledge of *the world that is*, the world that surprises us and seems ever capable of change and renewal, rather than a wholly predictable world that we might master?

If the world is a machine, then it must be moved and ordered about by a mechanic or other machine user; otherwise we have misunderstood machines. If the world is not a machine, then mechanical models will still serve, for better or for worse, all those whose interests, limited or unlimited, are guided by a desire to master or merely tinker with their world or some part of it, whether controlling weeds in the garden or elements in the population, building barns, bridges and bombs, manipulating the stock market or public opinion in the next election. Yet if the world is not a machine, then mechanical models are not models of the world as it is, but simply models that enable us to take some manner of control over our world: they present us with the half-truths that serve our desires.

The most important criticism of mechanical models is that they are based on an untenable understanding of machines as politically and ethically neutral automatons, as instantiations of nature's immutable laws.

> Making a machine automatic requires that many of its possible uses as well as different ways it could function be sacrificed. Automatism, along with its use in the form of industrial organization known as *automation*, has an economic or social meaning, more than a technical meaning. The true improvement of machines, of which it can be said that it raises the level of technicity, corresponds not to an increase in automatism, but on the contrary, to the fact that a machine's functioning includes a certain margin of indeterminacy. It is this margin that allows the machine to be sensitive to outside information. It is through this sensitivity of machines to information that a technical set can be realized, more than by an increase in automatism. A purely automatic machine, completely closed upon itself, in predetermined operation, would only be able to give very basic results. A machine that is endowed with high technicity is an open machine, and the entire set of open machines assumes that man is there as a permanent organizer, as a living interpreter of machines to each other. Far from being the overseer of a gang of slaves, man is the permanent organizer of a society of technical objects that need him in the same way that orchestral musicians need a conductor. ...
>
> It is again by way of this margin of indeterminacy, and not through automatisms, that machines can be brought together into coherent sets, that they can exchange information with each other by way of the coordinator that is the human interpreter. Even when the exchange of information is direct between two machines (as it is between a master-oscillator and another, pulse-synchronized oscillator), man intervenes as a being who

sets the margin of indeterminacy so that it is adapted to the best possible exchange of information. (Simondon 2012: 12-13; translation by Christian Roy)

The work of Roy Harris is remarkable in its persistent focus on what he referred to as first-order experience—our own experience of the world in which we live. And he has demonstrated at length and in detail, that our experience is of a world in which meaning is indeterminate, just as machines are in Simondon's understanding. We live in the world with others moment by moment, as best we may, constrained as we all are by our physical capacities and limits, our social situation, and the circumstances that pertain to any lived moment in time. A prejudice that insists upon finding a rigidly and exhaustively knowable mechanical world behind our lived experience of the world must begin by denying the validity of our own experience. To reject that prejudice, in science as in life, is to attempt to understand a world that we may love or fear, but within which we must needs live together and over which we refuse to seek to exercise complete power. To reject that prejudice is also to come to understand machines better as the products of human activity motivated and guided by human desires, fantasies, fears and ignorance.

References
Belardi, Walter (2005). "Origine e sviluppi della nozione linguistica di 'macchina'," in Veneziani, Marco (ed.) (2005). *Machina: XI Colloquio Internazionale, Roma, 8-10 gennaio 2004*. (Firenze: Leo S. Olschki Editore), 19-60.
Berryman, Sylvia (2009). *The Mechanical Hypothesis in Ancient Greek Natural Philosophy*. Cambridge: Cambridge University Press.

Canguilhem, Georges (2008). *Knowledge of Life*. New York: Fordham University Press.

Duhem, Pierre-Marie-Maurice (1980). *The Evolution of Mechanics*. The Netherlands: Sijthoff & Noordhoff.

Fabbri, Natacha (2011). "Deus Mechanicus and Machinae Mundi in the Early Modern Period," *Historia Philosophica. An International Journal*, IX: 75-112.

Farrington, Benjamin (1951) "Temporis partus masculus: an untranslated writing of Francis Bacon," *Centaurus: international magazine of the history of science and medicine* 1, no.3: 193-205.

Ficino, Marsilio (2001-2006). *Platonic Theology*. Cambridge: Harvard University Press.

Galileo Galilei (1960). *On Motion and On Mechanics*. Madison: The University of Wisconsin Press.

Galileo Galilei (2002). *Le mecaniche*. Firenze: Leo S. Olschki Editore.

Harris, Roy (1987). *The Language Machine*. London: Duckworth.

Hollnagel, E. & Woods D. D. (2005). *Joint Cognitive Systems: Foundations of Cognitive Systems Engineering*. Boca Raton, FL: CRC Press / Taylor & Francis.

La Mettrie, Julien Offray de (1912). *Man a Machine*. La Salle: Open Court.

Mach, Ernst (1960). *The Science of Mechanics: A Critical and Historical Account of its Development*. 6th ed. La Salle: Open Court.

Machamer, P., Mcguire, J. E. and Kochiras, H. (2012)."Newton and the Mechanical Philosophy: gravitation as the balance of the heavens" *The Southern Journal of Philosophy*, v.50 nr.3: 370–388

Mittelstrass, Jürgen (1988). "Nature and science in the Renaissance." In Woolhouse, R. S. (ed.), *Metaphysics and Philosophy of Science in the Seventeenth and*

Eighteenth Centuries : Essays in Honour of Gerd Buchdahl. (Dordrecht and Boston: Kluwer Academic), 17-43.

Neirynck, Jacques (1986). *Le huitième jour de la création: introduction à l'entropologie*. Lausanne: Presses polytechniques romandes.

Newton, Isaac (1999 [1726]). *The Principia: Mathematical Principles of Natural Philosophy*. Trans. I. B. Cohen and A. Whitman. Berkeley: University of California Press.

Prater, Edward L. (1994). *Basic Machines*. NAVEDTRA 14037. Nonresident training course February 1994. Prepared by AMHC(AW) Edward L. Prater. Published by Naval Education And Training Professional Development And Technology Center.

Scardigli, Victor (2001). *Un anthropologue chez les automates. De l'avion informatisé à la société numérisée*. Paris: Presses Universitaires de France (coll. Sociologie d'aujourd'hui)

Simondon, Gilbert (2012). *Du mode d'existence des objets techniques*. Nouvelle edition revue et corrigée. Paris: Aubier.

Van Dyck, Maarten (2006). *An Archaeology of Galileo's Science of Motion*. PhD Dissertation, Universiteit Gent, Faculteit Letteren en Wijsbegeerte.

von Foerster, Heinz and Bernhard Pörksen (2003). *Wahrheit ist die Erfindung eines Lügners: Gespräche für Skeptiker*. Heidelberg: Carl-Auer-Systeme Verlag.

Woods, D. D., Johannesen, L., Cook, R., and Sarter, N. (1994). *Behind Human Error: Cognitive Systems, Computers, and Hindsight*. CSERIAC SOAR Report 94-01. Crew Systems Ergonomics Information Analysis Center, Wright-Patterson Air Force Base, Ohio.

IX

Epistemologies of Rape and Revelation[1]

I. Epistemological orientations

Throughout his life Jacques Ellul wrote sociological and theological works, and while these have appeared to many of his readers to be two entirely separate domains Ellul himself regarded them as intimately related and inseparable elements of his approach to understanding our world. In certain sections of the recently published *Théologie et technique: pour une éthique de la non-puissance* Ellul addressed directly what I have taken as my topic: the relationship between knower and known in theology and technoscience. These two epistemological orientations are, for Ellul, knowledge revealed in a relation of love and free-

---

[1] Previously unpublished. Originally presented at the conference "Communicating Humanly in an Age of Spin: Revisiting the Thought of Jacques Ellul in the 21st Century" held at Carleton University, Ottawa, July 13-15, 2014.

dom, and knowledge as power. While my interest lies primarily in the former, my remarks in what follows will focus primarily on the latter. The reason for this is that the time allotted me does not allow me to explore Ellul's understanding of revelation and how that differs from my own understanding of the relationship between love, knowledge and power.

The book begins with Ellul's reading of Girard's *Critique dans un souterrain*. The proud man, the underground man, "is fascinated with the Other, but from the perspective of eliciting the fascination of that other, and of dominating him" (Ellul 2014: 30). The relationship is that of master and slave, seducer and seduced, masochist and sadist. "In our society," Ellul wrote, "Technique is the expression, the incarnation, the demonstration of that underground spirit ... Yet this is Technique as it has *become* in our time, playing a role similar to that of Money in previous societies" (ibid.: 32, ellipsis and italics in the original). Ellul's argument contrasts technique as the expression of knowledge arising from the master-slave relationship with revelation, which is for Ellul always the revelation of God. An orientation towards the world characterized by the will to power and domination produces knowledge that is strictly dependent upon the relationship that such an orientation requires, i.e. a knower who is as radically separate from the known as from the knowledge produced, and the validity of any knowledge thus produced is limited to its appropriateness for a situation of domination and control. In contrast, revelation seeks to establish a relationship in love and freedom, and the knowledge that comes through revelation is neither in-dependent of the knower nor knowable without that relationship.

II. Science as mastery and dominion over nature

One much discussed early text in the history of science is Francis Bacon's *Temporis partus masculus* or in its English translation, *The masculine birth of time*, written in 1602 or 1603.

Perhaps the most interesting matter relating to this text is that it has been interpreted by both traditional historians of science and feminists in two opposed manners, as a call to conquer nature on the one hand, and as a call to conquer one's own self on the other hand, purifying the scientist through objectivity.

Traditional historians of science (such as Benjamin Farrington) as well as feminists like Sandra Harding and Carolyn Merchant have read *The masculine birth of time* as a misogynist call for the conquest, domination and even rape of a female nature by a masculine scientific project. Alan Sobel made a number of criticisms of several feminist readings of Bacon, but he could not eliminate Bacon's clear statement about enslaving nature "I am come in very truth leading to you Nature with all her children to bind her to your service and make her your slave" (Bacon 1964: 62) so he responded thus:

> Keller unveils only one clearly ugly line out of thousands of pages of Bacon's lifework, and this, "make her your slave," occurs in a tiny fragment of a manuscript written at the dawn of his philosophical career.
> (Sobel 1998: 207)

Is it acceptable to encourage slavery if one only does it once? While it may be, as Sobel insisted, that it "is uncharitable if not hostile" for Keller "To poke through these essays and parade their meanest two lines as the truth about Bacon and his scientific philosophy" (Sobel 1998: 207), it is nevertheless both legitimate and necessary to investigate the history of science to see whether and to what an extent the attitudes revealed by those "meanest two lines" can be found therein. It does in fact appear that the subsequent history of science is a history of the subjection of nature to human desires, a history of the exploitation of nature far more than a history of husbandry or some supposedly objective, pure science.

Carolyn Merchant (2006) noted the long history of metaphors of torture and putting nature on the rack being associated with Bacon and science, a history beginning with Leibnitz and continuing through Goethe to Cassirer and beyond. If science is not guilty of raping nature--whatever that might mean--it is certainly true that science has vastly increased human power over nature and the result, evident everywhere in the world around us, is the despoiling and destruction of nature.

The masculine birth of time has also been interpreted by both traditional historians of science and feminists to involve a call to those who would seek truth to submit themselves "to a divine revelation of the truth" through "a preliminary discipline of mastery of the self" (Golinski 2002: 126). In Keller's words we can find in Bacon's writings the idea that

> To receive God's truth, the mind must be pure and clean, submissive and open. Only then can it give birth to a masculine and virile science. That is, if the mind is pure, receptive, and submissive in its relation to God, it can be transformed by God into a forceful, potent and virile agent in relation to nature. (Keller 1985: 38)

The theological dimensions of Baconian science appear clearly in this interpretation, and the biblical origins of Baconian science and its orientation deserve our attention. Bacon explicitly denies offering any "mixture of religion and science," but Sobel, as well as many feminists, see in certain passages of *The Masculine Birth of Time* echoes of the biblical account of man's relation to nature as recorded in Genesis 1:26.

The different interpretations of Bacon's language and the biblical references to dominion over nature offered by the two perspectives represented by Sobel and feminist critics arise from different understandings of what "dominion" means and how that dominion is realized in the relations between humankind and nature, and between men and women. Sobel insisted that for Bacon "Science will improve the human condition" and that therefore "the works of science ... are works of love" (Sobel 1998: 202). For Sobel, Bacon's mature statements in the *Novum Organum* contain "no rape, no torture, no bondage, just the thought that to know nature it is not enough to watch it; nature must be provoked into showing us its inner workings" (Sobel 1998: 206). Yet Bacon wants to know nature's inner workings precisely because only then may we command her. In other words, revelation is not enough: nature's revelations, what we might know by simply listening or observing nature, will never reveal what we must know if we are to control it.

When the distinction is made between pure science and its applications, it is fairly easy to construct a picture of science as the noble pursuit of truth, neither motivated by nor oriented towards the desires, dreams, fears and fantasies of the scientists; some scientists even refer to the ultimate aim of their scientific activities as knowledge of "the mind of God" (e.g. Stephen Hawking and Paul Davies). The distinction, very useful for justifying science and protecting it from any criticisms directed to the uses to which science is put, rests upon the claim that there is in fact a purposeless pursuit of knowledge, science solely for the sake of knowledge, and it is upon this basis that true, pure science was founded and persists. Yet it is not at all clear that anyone has ever engaged in scientific activity for no reason at all; on the contrary, there is abundant evidence that science from the beginning was motivated by a desire to control the world--all of it, that is, except the scientist himself. Canguilhem pushed the relation between slavery and science even further back in time, connecting it to the processes of domestication of animals with his observation that

> The theoretical mechanization of life and the technical utilization of the animal are inseparable. Man can make

> himself master and possessor of nature only if he denies all natural purpose and can consider all of nature, including, apparently, animate nature--except for himself--to be a means.
> This is what legitimates the construction of a mechanical model of the living body, including the human body--for already in Descartes the human body, if not man, is a machine. (Canguilhem 2008: 84)

Whether or not images of rape and misogynist attitudes played any role in the thinking of Bacon and his contemporaries, scientific method as, in Bacon's words, the "most legitimate" of all methods, was specifically advocated for the purposes of conquering, controlling and dominating nature, and from Bacon up to our own day knowledge has been equated with power. Bacon argued that "to establish and extend the power and dominion of the human race itself over the universe... depends wholly on the arts and sciences. For we cannot command nature except by obeying her" (*Novum Organum*, Aphorism 28), and that "Truth, therefore, and utility are here perfectly identical" (*Novum Organum*, Aphorism 124). Bacon's secretary, Thomas Hobbes, reiterated these themes in his *Elements of Philosophy* in which work he wrote that

> The *end* or *scope* of philosophy is, that we may make use to our benefit of effects formerly seen; or that, by application of bodies to one another, we may produce the like effects of those we conceive in our mind, ... for the commodity of human life. For the inward glory and triumph of mind that a man may have for the mastering of some difficult and doubtful matter, or for the discovery of some hidden truth, is not worth so much pains as the study of Philosophy requires; nor need any man care much to teach another what he knows himself, if he

think that will be the only benefit of his labour. The end of knowledge is power; ... the scope of all speculation is the performing of some action, or thing to be done. (Hobbes 1839: v. 1, 7)

In the same work Hobbes even concludes his chapter on physics with the remark that

For as for those that say anything may be moved or produced by *itself*, by *species*, by *its own power*, by *substantial forms*, by *incorporeal substances*, by *instinct*, by *antiperistasis*, by *antipathy, sympathy, occult quality*, and other empty words of schoolmen, their saying so is to no purpose. (Hobbes 1839: v. 1, 531)

This 'saying to no purpose' must be read in light of Hobbes's claims for his own natural philosophy, namely that its end and goal is useful, bestowing great benefits upon men, can be applied and produces effects, whereas knowledge that brings only an inward glory and a triumph of mind is not worth our troubles nor worth teaching to others.

Writing of science in the late 20th century, Gilbert Hottois insisted that the word science itself was no longer appropriate but should be replaced by the hybrid term *technoscience*. For Hottois, there is no one concept of technoscience, but a range of concepts, from that which "places it beyond culture, beyond the symbolic" to that which "tends to dissolve it in the cultural, in the heart of the symbolic" (Hottois 2000: 16). The recognition that "the enterprise of contemporary science, from research to its development, design, production and diffusion is characterized by *the search for efficacy and the omnipresence of technical instruments and artefacts*" (Hottois 2000: 17, emphasis in original) has been interpreted in two very different directions. The first of these

underlines the efficacious operativity at the very heart of modern scientific activity by opposing it to an earlier logotheoretic, contemplative and verbal science. It emphasizes the preponderant importance of mathematics and physical or technophysical experimentation, and the causal and instrumental significance of scientific laws. It leads to a science that is independent of cultural, social, symbolic contexts, or, more classically, independent of human subjectivity and intersubjectivity. The technical operativity characteristic of modern and contemporary science is the surest indication of its objectivity.
(Hottois 2000: 17)

The second direction in which interpretations of technoscience tend to move "emphasizes that every instrument is a socially constructed artefact, produced and above all imagined and desired by human groups" (Hottois 2000: 17-18). In both interpretations, scientific activity is an active intervention, an acting upon the world that changes it, but in the former there are no grounds for criticizing scientific knowledge or practices either within or without that knowledge and practice itself. Technoscience, in Ellul's words "encompasses everything, but without any synthesis, without any reconciliation. It makes of our world an immense collection of objects, of machines, of methods, with neither coherence nor fundamental relation. ... The pieces of the puzzle are adjusted, but have no relationships other than mechanical" (Ellul 2014: 33).

Science as mastery, a means to effective action, as intervention and operation is especially evident in the sciences born in the 20th century. Cybernetics, information science, linguistics and research on communication were explicitly developed as sciences of control, all arising out of military research on command and control systems. More recently Jean-Pierre Dupuy has noted what he regards as an even more ominous development:

scientists who are oriented by the desire to provoke natural processes and to remake life as they would have it. Remaking life is clearly a simple extension of Bacon's project, whether or not he had such hopes in mind or would have approved of them. While Sobel found nothing objectionable in "provoking" nature, Dupuy argued that recent efforts to remake nature have been motivated by a desire to demonstrate "that we can become artifices, scientific products, that we can be transformed, bettered, saved, exploited using the laws of nature" (Dupuy 2005: 6).

For Dupuy, the "metaphysics that drives" nanobiotechnologists is "Making life from scratch" (Dupuy 2005: 8). Here any distinction between pure and applied science is clearly irrelevant. In the discussions and justifications for the "converging technologies" research program, science as intervention and betterment of our world appear as it did in Bacon and Hobbes with almost no change.

When knowledge is understood to be power, the desire for knowledge is the desire for power, the refusal to accept limits to knowledge is the refusal to accept limits to power. Arendt linked the origins of the experimental method in science with "basic research," arguing that when scientists "provoke natural processes" and "act into nature" the result will be a world that "nature herself seems incapable of accomplishing" (Arendt 1998: 231). With this move into a world that nature can only produce by means of human activity we are reminded of the ancient definition of mechanics as the study of "violent" motions, motions "against nature." That definition was opposed by Galileo, who sought to establish a single science of motion that would both encompass and make no distinction between natural and mechanical motion. Like Bacon and Hobbes, Galileo argued in the first chapter of *On Mechanics* (entitled "On the Utilities That Are Derived from the Mechanical Science and from its Instruments") that "if nothing useful were to be expected from it, all the work employed in its acquisition would be in vain" (Galileo 1960: 148).

Thus, whether we look at 16th century scientists such as Galileo, 17th century philosophers like Hobbes, 17th century scientist-philosophers like Bacon, or science as it has been practiced and justified throughout the 20th century on into the current decade, science has been pursued as a useful means for doing something other than science, its efficacious power to accomplish those desired tasks and to serve our interests have then been used to justify Bacon's claim that scientific method is the most (or even sole) legitimate method of acquiring knowledge. Furthermore, the knowledge produced by that method is the only certain knowledge: all other knowledge is "saying to no purpose." Science makes us master, and nature our slave: this is what Bacon claimed of his method, and, usually in more palatable language, this is exactly the justification offered for science today.

III. Adam and Eve

If experimental, quantitative methods are the sole means of obtaining certain knowledge, and if knowledge is a sort of thing that can be acquired and possessed, and if we desire to acquire knowledge of our spouses and our children and our neighbors, then we know what we must do in order to know these other people in our world. Is this in fact the way in which we know each other? Do mechanics know their children in the same manner in which they know the machines with which they work? Is the knowledge that a rapist has of his victim the same as the knowledge that the victim's friends and lovers have of that same person?

What we know of others depends upon how we know them; whether as lovers, friends, family, neighbors, enemies, master, slave, rapist, salesmen, political representative, physician, executioner. What we know of others also depends upon when, how often and for how long we maintain a relationship with them. No one that I have ever met has known anyone in only one manner, for one purpose, and without being themselves changed by their relationships. Nor can I imagine any human being ever knowing the world in one way only. Our knowledge of each other and of the world is always and necessarily the product of a multiplicity of relationships, and what we know is not always the same as what we think we know for our knowledge is rooted in times, places and circumstances that continuously change. The world we know in our everyday lives is a world that we have not created, over which we have little control, and is as free as we are, each creature as determined by the unique circumstances of its life as we are of ours. Thus revelation and creation in Ellul are as inextricably interconnected as they are in Rosenzweig, and in much the same way. In *Théologie et technique* Ellul wrote that creation

> does not exist other than in a project not inscribed within itself, having its origin beyond and also leading beyond. Creation is a house in which all the doors and windows are open to that beyond, the whole traversed by the courants of air that the inhabitant cannot control. Things constantly happen that depend upon those currents of air, and that uncertainty, that unpredictability, that non-possession of the world man does not tolerate very well. (Ellul 2014: 189).

A world that is not of man's making "dispossesses man of what he considers to be his sovereignty" by "introducing an irreducible indetermination" into that world (Ellul 2014: 190). In an analysis echoing Vico, we can only know the world that we have not made through its being revealed to us; techno-science attempts to know the world by remaking it and knowing it as our own creation but that process gives us only knowledge of a manmade world formed of need and desire, not of the world as it exists in reality.

If it is possible to encounter the world as one who loves it, and to know the world as a lover knows a beloved, then the claims of scientific methods to produce the only certain knowledge are revealed to be what they are: certain knowledge for one and only one purpose. For those who do not desire to command and control the world, our spouses and children, our neighbors, human, plant, animal and mineral, scientific knowledge is legitimate in a very limited domain, and not relevant at all in the most important domain. A science of love, on the other hand, is as indeterminate and uncertain as our future. Unfortunately, it seems that only the drunkard in Carson McCullers' story "A tree, a rock, a cloud" and a handful of others have thought such a science worth pursuing.

When I was a young man I fell madly in love with a woman in one of my college classes. Being too shy to talk to her, I knew only what I could observe from the back of the classroom each class session, and on a few rare occasions, I experienced her smile and greetings addressed specifically to me. When I eventually spoke to her and revealed my hopes and desires to get to know her better, she revealed that she was engaged, and after that she tried her best to avoid running into me. I could have pursued her. I could have devised some way of meeting her and force her to engage me in some kind of relationship whether she wanted to or not. I did go to her home a few times in hopes of seeing her. I wrote to her and she did not reply. Eventually I told myself that if I loved her the nicest thing I could do for her, what she would appreciate most, would be to leave her alone. That was very hard to do. I never knew her and I never will.

References

Arendt, Hannah (1998). *The Human Condition.* 2nd edition. Chicago: University of Chicago Press.

Bacon, Francis (1825-1834). *The Works of Francis Bacon, Lord Chancellor of England.* A new edition by Basil Montagu Esq. London: William Pickering. 15 volumes.

Bacon, Francis (1834). "Translation of The Masculine Birth of Time, or, Three Books Concerning the Interpretation of Nature" In: *The Works of Francis Bacon, Lord Chancellor of England*, v. 15, p. 223-224.

Bacon, Francis (1964). "Temporis partus masculus" In: Benjamin Farrington, *The philosophy of Francis Bacon*, p.60-72.

Bowerbank, Sylvia (2004). *Speaking for Nature: Women and Ecologies of Early Modern England.* Baltimore: John Hopkins University Press. p. 12-13

Canguilhem, Georges (2008). *Knowledge of Life.* Translated by Stefanos Geroulanos, and Daniela Ginsburg, Introduction by Paola Marrati, and Todd Meyers New York: Fordham University Press.

Dupuy, Jean-Pierre (2005). "The Ethics of Technology before the Apocalypse" *Innsbrucker Diskussionspapiere zu Weltordnung, Religion und Gewalt*, Nummer 04 Accessed 1 July 2014 at: http://www.uibk.ac.at/plattform-wrg/idwrg/idwrg_04.pdf

Dupuy, Jean-Pierre (2006). "Do We Shape Technologies, Or Do They Shape Us?" Paper presented at the Stanford Center for Biomedical Ethics, May 10, 2006. Accessed 1 July 2014 at: ftp://ftp.cordis.europa.eu/pub/foresight/docs/ntw_22_dupuy_text.pdf

Ellul, Jacques (2014). *Théologie et technique: pour une éthique de la non-puisance.* Genève: Labor et Fides.

Farrington, Benjamin (1951). "Temporis Partus Masculus: an

untranslated writing of Francis Bacon" *Centaurus, an international magazine of the history of science and medicine* v.1 nr.3 p. 193-205.

Farrington, Benjamin (1964). *The Philosophy of Francis Bacon. An essay on its development from 1603 to 1609, with new translations of fundamental texts*. Chicago: University of Chicago Press.

Goethe, Johann Wolfgang von (1998). *Maxims and Reflections*, trans. Elisabeth Stopp, ed. Peter Hutchinson. London: Penguin

Golinski, Jan (2002). "The Care of the Self and the Masculine Birth of Science." *History of Science* 40: 125-145.

Harding, Sandra (1980). "The Norms of Social Inquiry and Masculine Experience" *PSA: Proceedings of the Biennial Meeting of the Philosophy of Science Association,* Vol. 1980, Volume Two: *Symposia and Invited Papers*, pp. 305-324.

Hobbes, Thomas (1839). *Elements of Philosophy. The First Section, Concerning Body*. In his: *The English Works of Thomas Hobbes*, v. 1.

Hobbes, Thomas (1839). *The English Works of Thomas Hobbes, of Malmesbury*. Now first collected and edited by Sir William Molesworth, Bart. London: John Bohn.

Holmes, Oliver W. (2013). "Competing concepts of the cosmos in the sixteenth and seventeenth centuries" In: Anna-Teresa Tymieniecka (ed.), *Penomenology and the Human Positioning in the Cosmos: the Life-World, Nature, Earth: Book One*. Dordrecht: Springer, p. 21-65 (Annalecta Husserliana, v.CXIII)

Hottois, Gilbert (2000). *Technoscience et sagesse?* Nantes: Éditions Pleins Feux.

Keller, Evelyn Fox (1985). "Baconian Science: The Arts of Mastery and Obedience" In her: *Reflections on Gender and Science*. New Haven and London: Yale University Press, p. 33-42.

McCullers, Carson (1942). "A tree, a rock, a cloud" *Harper's Bazaar* 76 (November 1942) p.50ff.

Merchant, Carolyn (1980). *The Death of Nature: Women, Ecology, and the Scientific Revolution*. San Francisco: Harper & Row. (quotations from the 1983 paperback printing)

Merchant, Carolyn (2006). "The Scientific Revolution and The Death of Nature" *Isis*, 97:513–533.

Sobel, Alan (1998). "In defence of Bacon" In Noretta Koertge (ed.), *A House Built on Sand: Exposing Postmodernist Myths About Science*. (Oxford: Oxford University Press), p. 195-215.

IX

Edward Said, Roy Asked, and the Peasant Responded
Reflections on Peasants, Popular Culture and Intellectuals[1]

for Sinfree Makoni

Abstract
Any dialogue between Integrational Linguistics and Southern Theory has to confront at the start the origins of Integrational theory at Oxford in the heart of the former colonial empire of Great Britain. That the advocates of two perspectives at opposite ends of the North-South dichotomy can learn one from the other in a mutually beneficial manner is suggested by an anecdote about Roy Harris's fieldwork and supported by the author's own experiences as an Africanist and a Mongolist. Instead of understanding the world of the others in terms of the myths and mis-

---

[1] Originally presented at the Annual Conference of the International Association for the Integrational Study of Language and Communication, "Integrationism and Philosophies of Language: Emerging Alternative Epistemologies in the Global North and the Global South," Pennsylvania State University, September 1-2, 2019. This version differs slightly from the revised version published in the conference proceedings.

understandings that we have been taught at home or school, we can indeed be changed, along with what we think and believe, by listening to those others. Edward Said's lamment that we have read too much and loved too little is perhaps a fitting commentary on intellectuals everywhere. Harris's response to a peasant offers us much to think about, as much as, and (I believe) even more than his theoretical writings.

J'accuse: Orientations
In his novel *Mongólia* the Brazilian writer Bernardo Carvalho juxtaposed the travel diaries of a Brazilian photographer who had disappeared in Mongolia with the notebooks of a Brazilian diplomat sent to Mongolia to track him down. The photographer had responded to each place and person with delight, surprise and keen interest. The diplomat, following the route indicated in the diary, recorded his suspicious, hostile disdain for all that he encountered along the same route. The photographer was oriented and animated by the world he encountered as a new friend; the diplomat was disoriented everywhere by a world that he refused to embrace. Two Brazilians in Mongolia recording the same world of places and peoples produced two irreconcilable narratives that the narrator of the novel tries to reconcile: the world is my friend, the world is my enemy. We are oriented by what we love and disoriented by what we hate.

Carvalho's two Brazilians demonstrate two orientations toward the world that preceded any and all of their experiences and perceptions. The photographer was open to and changed by his experiences. He was attentive to everything around him, alive to differences, keenly interested in the details. His world grew larger and fuller with every encounter. The diplomat, on the other hand, closed himself off to experience, encountered everyone and everything as an opponent to be reconstructed according to his preconceptions about the way the world ought to be. He learned nothing, rejected the differences and was blind to the details. These two contrasting orientations towards the world were not conscious, rationally arrived at theories, but the perceptions and interpretations of Carvalho's characters were determined by those orientations. Outside the world of fiction, in the real world in which we live, we too are oriented towards the world in one or the other fashion. For most of us I suspect, we are oriented in one way at times, and in another way at other times, for experience can radically change the way in which we live in the world, as any victim of violence can affirm.

Southern Theory, as all theory, begins somewhere with someone in the interest of some project, dream, desire, hope, question or pathological condition. Southern Theory, as any theory, can be oriented in different ways depending upon who is elaborating the theory. In the 2019 Integrationist conference, organizers stated that our purpose was "to contribute towards the development of scholarship ... from decidedly Global South perspectives". This implies that there are other perspectives, whether those are thought of as Northern, Eastern, historical, alternative or wrong. A 'Global South' perspective implies, at a minimum, a different experience than a 'Global North' perspective, and perhaps different conceptions of justice, religious beliefs, hopes and desired futures. My interest is precisely in the existence of these different perspectives and orientations: they exist in practice, but can they exist in theory? Specifically, can Southern Theory assist us in thinking and living our differences alongside and together with our vehement opponents? Do proponents of Southern Theory follow the orientation of Carvalho's photographer or Carvalho's diplomat?

The orienting beliefs-desires-hopes-fantasies of Not-So-Southern-Theory are those of modern science and can be seen clearly at its birth. Consider Galileo's remark (1960, p. 148) "if nothing useful were to be expected from it [i.e. knowledge], all the work employed in its acquisition would be in vain". Add to that Bacon's announcement (1964, p. 62) "I am come in very truth leading to you Nature with all her children to bind her to your service and make her your slave" and Hobbes' assertion (1839, v. 1, p. 7) "The end of knowledge is power; and the use of theorems (which, among geometricians, serve for the finding out of properties) is for the construction of problems; and, lastly, the scope of all speculation is the performing of some action, or thing to be done." Feminists (among others) have rightly seen in this foundation domination as goal and rape as means and method. Theologians have seen in this an expression of a recurrent religious fantasy, namely the desire to become God, a desire explicity stated by the atheist Stephen Hawking:

> [I]f we do discover a complete theory, it should in time be understandable in broad principle by everyone, not just a few scientists. Then we shall all, philosophers, scientists, and just ordinary people, be able to take part in the discussion of the question of why it is that we and the universe exist. If we find the answer to that, it would be the ultimate triumph of human reason - for then we would know the mind of God. (Hawking, 1988, p. 193)

The quest for theory always arises from an atheoretical impulse and an orientation, an impulse and orientation that the theory does not account for but projects into all matters upon which it touches. That impulse arises from the situation in which the theory builder lives. And here the virtues and shortcomings and possibilities and limitations of all theories come into question. Southern Theory arises from the experience of colonization and is both oriented and empowered as well as limited by its moral argument with the other world which it opposes, the European empires and their successors in political regimes and in mentality. Edward Said, a precursor of Southern Theory, argued that the perceptions, attitudes and beliefs of citizens of colonizing states were largely oriented and determined by the interests of their nations. In particular, opinions about the peoples and civilizations of the colonized lands—Asia, Africa, indigenous America —were prejudiced by the myths and propaganda issuing from those pursuing and justifying the domination of those lands instead of and even in spite of all experience and evidence to the contrary. The myths of the colonizers prevented them from ever encountering the realities of the "Orient"; the colonizers (and their descendents) almost always and almost everywhere see only their own myths.

    The problem, of course, is not just academic and not just for colonialists: understanding the world of our own experience is an every moment task for everyone. Not long ago, I hired a chimney sweep to check my fireplace and upon his arrival he noticed my peacocks in the driveway. "Where do you keep your peacocks?" he asked, and I replied "They like to roost atop the chimney." He shook his head and said "Peacocks are flightless birds, they cannot fly" and as he said this, one peacock flew straight up over his head and alighted about 35 feet up on the roof near the chimney. He stood there staring at the peacock on the roof and repeated "Peacocks are flightless birds. They cannot fly" as if to drive his point home to that insolent rooftop peacock or perhaps merely to reassure himself in his knowledge.

    When theory becomes unquestionable ideology, when our experiences of the world are denied in favor of what we have been told rather than changed by our encounters with the world, we become incapable of learning, and from that incapacity we become incapable of doing justice to the world in our theories and in our actions. Yet even in the best situations of persons open to the world of experience and being changed by it, the question remains: How can anyone, necessarily thinking from one experience of the world, arrive at a theory that can do justice to all the experiences of the world? How can Northern do justice to Southern? How can feminism do justice to men? How can race theory do justice to all races? How can queer theory do justice to children?

My short answer to that—not to be interpreted as an expression of the mind of God—is that theory can never do justice, and can in fact only do injustice whenever it is believed in—as so often appears to be the case among advocates and adherents of theories past, present, right, left, on the roof and off the wall. What I want to suggest in this paper, not through scholarship or theoretical argument but from personal experience–Roy Harris's and my own—is that theory can never lead us towards a mutually livable understanding of the world, but listening to each other just might. Southern Theory will not lead us to know the mind of God, but I allow myself to hope that it will lead me to better understand my own mind.

Respondeo: Roy Harris and the Peasant
In his 1990 essay "The dialect myth" Roy Harris recounts a conversation with a peasant in 1966:

> From my own experience of fieldwork in dialectology, the best evidence I can cite in support of Schuchardt's answer was given to me by an old man whom I asked whether the patois of his Alpine village was the same as that of another locality a few miles distant. I here translate his reply, given in (what I at that time called) 'Valdôtain':
>
>> Is it the same? I would not know how to answer you. Even in this village the younger people speak differently from my generation. And in the next valley perhaps they use words we don't use here. But, for all that, everyone understands everyone else well enough. Is that the same?
>
> By turning my own question back on me, he had made me understand that the mistake lay in the question. What I was asking corresponded to nothing in his own linguistic experience which could provide a determinate

answer. When theorists begin to ask unanswerable questions about language (or – which amounts to the same thing – questions which can be answered 'yes' or 'no' as you please) that is the surest indication that in their investigations linguistic myth has taken over from linguistic reality. (Harris 1990, p.18)

Elsewhere in the world's scholarly literature there are anecdotes about scholars learning something important from the object of their study and changing their minds and their theories accordingly, but this passage is the only such passage that I can recall from my readings in linguistics. What is remarkable about it is that Harris specifically indicates that the peasant provoked his theoretical reflections precisely by turning his question back on him, and that the issue in question later became the foundation of all his theorizing. The peasant didn't respond with a theory of his own so much as to describe how things seemed to him, what seemed to be important, and then sending the question back at Harris. There was no debate, no agonistic academic ritual, but simply two people listening to each other and trying to understand what the other meant, and how the other understood the matters in question. The theoretical positions that eventually arose from that encounter were not those of the peasant for he had no need of theory; rather they were Harris's theoretical demolition of western linguistic theory. Twenty-five years after the peasant spoke, we find his own words put forth as the "best evidence" in support of the critical perspectives for which Harris was arguing.

When reading this passage in Harris (1990), what most struck me was the contrast between Harris's attitude towards the theories he knew—what he had been taught in school—and the world of orientalism against which Edward Said turned all his attention and intelligence. I don't know what Said ever said or wrote or thought about Harris—if anything—but surely had he read this passage with a knowledge of how much western theory

Harris rejected in accepting the peasant's reply, he would have gushed with appreciation and admiration. Certainly I do. The passage is clear evidence that theory was abandoned precisely because Harris regarded the peasant's understanding of his own situation *as the only one that made any sense.* And this regard for the peasant later became one of the pillars of Harris's perspective on language: the primacy of the lay perspective. What I wish to stress is that Integrational theory did not lead Harris to engage the peasant with respect, attention, and an openness to learn and to be changed by the encounter. Instead, it was the reverse: it was Harris's attitude toward the peasant that enabled him to learn from the peasant and pursue his extraordinary theoretical explorations. Positive social change and social justice come from respectful, loving attention to the Other, not from social theory.

It is perhaps also worth noting that this passage may be the only passage in the entire corpus of Harris's writings in which he acknowledges that someone else was right and he was wrong. Harris, like many intellectuals, was rarely willing to acknowledge the value of another's opinions even when they thought they were agreeing with him. And it does seem to be the case that the normal attitude of intellectuals is "I talk, you listen" which is somehow presented as dialogue or the quest for truth and justice, if not boldly declared to be "speaking truth to power." Taking differences seriously requires listening to and understanding dissenting voices from all sides, making room for all our differences with the hope of *our* being changed during the process into something better; it does *not* mean just listening to one side condemn the others.

The passage from Harris means far more to me than it may mean for many others because of the differences between my experience and Harris's. Harris, the professor doing research among peasants and trying to understand that world, and David Bade, the child of pentecostal Bible Belt American farmers who wanted their son to study at a school in which the Bible was the only textbook but who was somehow accidentally admitted into an atheist public university. (A neighbor woman who worked in the university's admissions office was probably responsible for this little 'accident' but I will never know. My mother believes it must have been God's will, while my father thinks the Devil did it.) My path was more or less the reverse of Harris's: a deeply religious teenager trying to overcome religious prejudices in order to understand modern science and linguistic theory. That young boy also had an intense longing to learn about and eventually live in an Asia known only from a childhood filled with missionary tales of pre-Christian Africa and Asia, the television series Kung Fu, biographies of Albert Schweizer, Tarzan books and an old atlas in which Africa consisted of a few very large areas 'belonging' to some European nations, and a few countries with actual names.

Ich bin kein Berliner: Embracing the Other without Debasing Oneself

Religious conversion frequently involves embracing some exotic Other—for Mongolians this is often some form of Christianity, while for Americans this is often some form of oriental religion—while turning away in contempt from the world within which we have been born and formed as children. This is as common in the world of intellectuals as in the world of religion, and we should probably best understand these religious and intellectual conversions as instances of the same development: beliefs about the world, whether described as religious, philosophical, ideological or theoretical, are abandoned in favor of other beliefs. When Chomsky's as yet unpublished Pisa lectures began to circulate as photocopies, all the generative semanticists in the department abandoned Lakoff and McCawley overnight and scrambled to put themselves in the vanguard of the Pisa program. This is the usual course of events when science has become one's only religion, for there is no other perspective available from which to challenge it. Harris and the peasant followed a different trajectory: learning to appreciate the other perspective while also coming to understand their own worlds from outside as well as from within. Harris did not become a peasant, nor did the peasant become a professor; I imagine that neither would have been happy in the other's shoes but they were able to have an extremely productive conversation.

How does a white, Christian boy from a farming/working class family in central Illinois learn to embrace the Other without debasing the world which made him what he is? Is it true—as some believe—that our origins preclude us from ever doing anything other than upholding and reproducing our class, our gender, and our national and racial origins? Must our perceptions be determined by our nationality and race as Said claimed? I do not think so and here is why: I adored my professor of Chinese linguistics C.C. Cheng and my Palestinian Arabic instructor Nicola Talhami (as well as his sister Aida). I thought Cornelius Muthuri, the Meru farm boy who was the language source in my field methods class, stood shoulder to shoulder with the finest human beings known to me. In graduate school it was fellow student Daniel Bitrus and roommate Mobil Kolbon, and still later my ESL student Nam-ju Lee. Then in the library a Thai co-worker whose name I have forgotten but whose gift I still wear 40 years later and Mamadou Niang for whom I cataloged 11,000 volumes of Northwestern University Library's collection of books in African languages in order that he would know what they had. Later on in middle age Khotgoid ovogt Makhburiadyn Purevbadam taught me the songs of her grandmother from Khuvsgul AND how delicious were the wild cherries in my parents' front yard, cherries that I had never even known were edible. Through these encounters I learned of the real Africa and Asia, while at the same time understanding that Tarzan, Kung Fu and missionary tales were just what they were, and not the real story, much less the whole story. I am still grateful for Edgar Rice Burroughs, ABC Television and all those missionaries who gave me a child's pleasures and started me dreaming about the Orient, but I cannot imagine how anyone could or would prefer those images of Asia and Africa over C.C. Cheng, Aida Talhami and Cornelius Muthuri. When you delight in a friendship, cherish a relationship or love someone, all prejudices, images from popular culture, theories and even religions can be modified, set aside or tossed in the trash for being of less importance than the person who is here.

The other side of those encounters is how I renegotiated my relationship to my own past, my own family, the world I knew and loved prior to those encounters with other worlds. One significant moment for me involved a conversation with a professor who held most of us in awe at his academic reputation and verbal wizardry. In speaking to him once, I mentioned that his remarks on religion had made a profound impact on me and he responded by saying "Had I known that, I would have made much more concerted efforts to destroy your faith." His response was entirely unexpected and I immediately lost all respect for him. Why? Because I had understood that science and scholarship were solely interested in understanding the world, in discovering the truth (i.e., I had believed the usual self-serving propaganda disseminated by universities and scientists). In order to feel that one has a right, even a duty to destroy someone's faith, one must believe that one's own beliefs are unquestionably true while the other's beliefs are unquestionably wrong. Yet all that professor knew of my beliefs—something we had never discussed—apparently came from something he had heard from a third party. That professor learned nothing from me because he assumed there was nothing to be learned; and in the end I learned from him only that closed mindedness, hubris, prejudice and the desire to dominate and control the next generation's mind and soul were as much a part of the academic world as of the religious and political worlds. Trying to destroy someone's inherited culture, beliefs and orientation in the world seemed to me then, as it does now, to be beneath contempt. I was trying to understand that world into which I had been born, and still am; turning my back on it all in contempt would have made understanding myself forever impossible. If you compare that professor's response to me with Harris's response to the peasant, you will understand why reading about the latter sent me into ecstasy.

I did not become a missionary linguist as planned. Instead, I fell in love with a woman who was of the wrong religion. A follower of the Anti-Christ my parents would have said had they ever known of her. After having abandoned my religion in favor of her (*nota bene*: not her religion), she informed me that she was not interested in me. Such is life: we have only the love in our hearts. "My weight is my love, by it I am borne whithersoever I am borne" wrote Augustine, the African Christian. And so it is with theory: it is oriented by our loves. Unfortunately theory is not only oriented by our loves, but often also by our hatreds. Therein lie the crucial questions to be directed at all theories and religions and those who profess them: Who do you love? And who do you refuse to love? (For some, of course, the questions would have to be 'Whom do you love?' etc. but among those influenced by Roy Harris you can get away with either way of expressing yourself. The important issue is the bit about love.)

Amo, Amas, Amat, ...

> *On comprend que les intellectuels soient en première ligne, et à l'origine de tous les délires totalitaires.*
> —*Bernard Charbonneau*

In an earlier discussion of Said (Bade, 2013) I suggested that the main complaint and accusation in his *Orientalism* is that we intellectuals have read too much and loved too little. Theories about peoples and cultures founded upon what we have only read and elaborations of such second-hand learning, when unchecked by our direct experience, usually blind us to the social realities of our world. More reading and more theory can never deliver us from our imagined unrealities; only a different kind of relationship to our Others can accomplish that. A relationship in which we reveal ourselves to each other, learn from each other and are changed by each other is the necessary condition for producing a world in which north/south, male/female, black/white are experienced as romances or marriages rather than as wars or as separate worlds in mutual excommunication. Carvalho's photographer, not Carvalho's diplomat, should be our guide.

Southern Theory is in origin and in intent an attempt to help realize social justice by theoretically disestablishing the justifications for perceived injustices, specifically those injustices which correlate with the divide between a northern hemisphere that embraces science and capitalism, and a southern hemisphere that is dominated and exploited by the northern. Yet justice is understood quite differently in the north and in the south. Any theory that is oriented by one perspective and is not engaged with others as necessary partners in learning is doomed to create a theoretical world of injustice in half the world, if not in most of it. A just theory must come from an encounter in which all are continually shaped by attending to the voices of all around us. All of those voices, even those we have been taught —at home, through religious instruction, at school—to despise and condemn.

"Love your neighbor as yourself" is a Jewish exhortation in origin, affirmed by Jesus though oft ignored by his Christian followers (for a marvelous discussion, see Mendes-Flohr, 2007). A few thousand years ago somewhere in the region of Iraq-Palestine-Sinai-Egypt an old man urged upon his people this orientation as a path towards social justice. That man, portrayed as an old man with white hair and a beard, became both the iconic image of God and the demonized father of patriarchy. Yet as a guide to social justice, his was a very, very good idea. I know of none better. The Christianization of Europe was the Oriental refashioning of a new world from the ashes of empire by means of that vision. It is that Oriental heritage from the distant past that formed my childhood, and by returning to reaffirm this element of my own past, the world of my parents, my place and my time, I also embrace the world of Asia 3000 years ago. How could I, why would I, turn against "Love your neighbor as yourself"? I embrace this ancient commandment not as a religious believer or member of any class, group or organization, much less as one colonized, dominated or oppressed by a foreign religion, but as one who acknowledges and appreciates that inheritance. In loving the world as I encounter it I find the only orientation that does justice to it. I find this to be an orientation that allows and even encourages me to embrace and learn from those worlds that were not given to me at birth, nor at home, nor at school. I have been Oriented.

In the end (or at least at the present moment), after my encounters with professors who would dominate me (if they but could), preachers who would cast me into an eternal lake of fire (if they but could), neighbors who would assault me (and did) and friends from around the world who have loved me in spite of my gender, my race, my class origins, my nationality, my ignorance, my beliefs and my unbeliefs, I am neither young nor beautiful, neither Republican nor Democrat, neither Jewish nor Christian, neither Buddhist nor Muslim, nor even—to my great chagrin—a Chinese sage (I am still enthralled by this image from my childhood). My encounters with the real worlds of men, women, black, white, sexual assault, racial violence, inner city, desert solitude, homelessness, day labor, white- and blue collar employment, farming, graduate school, tenure, science, scholarship, Mexico, Africa, Asia, Communism, anti-Communism, Judaism, Islam, Buddhism, marriage, separation, fatherhood, justice, injustice, dancing with joy, weeping alone, and mourning the deaths of some of those whom I have loved have led me to radically rethink my own heritage and to understand it anew and differently. How could I not?

Changing and deepening our understanding of the worlds into which we are born in light of our encounters with the worlds of the Others need not lead to rejecting and reviling the worlds of our mothers and fathers in contempt (turning them into the justifiably despised Others so common in social theory), but can and should lead each of us, as in my case, to a deeper appreciation of our own heritages, a recognition of the multiple relations between cultures that have formed *all* the worlds we inhabit, more tolerance towards and appreciation of other ways of living, and a good deal of humility in the face of a world that is surely a far more fluid and creative polylogue of futures in the making than any empirical science could ever imagine, much less mathematically model or delimit in theory. A theory that is based upon and oriented by only one experience, one perspective or one 'revelation'—whether that is the world in which we were born or the world of our professors, heroes and gurus—banishes all else to a world apart, ignored or condemned or persecuted. Let us have instead theoretical discussions that will be oriented by that Jewish exhortation to love one another and the Buddhist doctrine of the Bodhisattva: no one achieves enlightenment unless and until we all do. That will not make any of us Jewish or Buddhist, much less social scientists, but it will probably enhance the social value of our theories immensely.

I leave you with a passage from one of North America's greatest Southern writers, Carson McCullers in her 1942 short story "A tree. A rock. A cloud":

I see a street full of people and a beautiful light comes in me. I watch a bird in the sky. Or I meet a traveler on the road. Everything, Son. And anybody. All stranger and all loved. Do you realize what a science like mine can mean?

Now *that* is my kind of Southern Theory.

References

Augustine. *Confessions*, 13.9.10. Translation from: Hannah Arendt (1978). *The Life of the Mind. Volume Two: Willing*, One volume edition, First Harvest Edition. New York etc.: Harcourt Brace & Company, p. 95.

Bacon, Francis (1964). "Temporis partus masculus" In: Benjamin Farrington, *The Philosophy of Francis Bacon*, p.60-72. Liverpool: Liverpool University Press.

Bade, David (2013). "Imaginary travels in post-socialist Mongolia" *Inner Asia* v. 15 nr.1, p.135-164.

Carvalho, Bernardo (2003). *Mongólia*. São Paulo, Brazil: Companhia das Letras.

Charbonneau, Bernard (2019). *Quatre témoins de la liberté: Rousseau, Montaigne, Berdiaev, Dostoïevski*. Paris: R&N Éditions. (Ars longa, vita brevis)

Galileo Galilei (1960). *On Motion and On Mechanics*. Comprising *De Motu* (ca. 1590) translated with introduction and notes by I.E. Drabkin and *Le meccaniche* (ca. 1600) translated with introduc-tion and notes by Stillman Drake. Madison: The University of Wisconsin Press. (The University of Wisconsin Publications in Medieval Science)

Harris, Roy (1990). 'The dialect myth' In: *Development and Diversity: Language Variation Across Time and Space: a Festschrift for Charles-James N. Bailey* / edited by Jerold A. Edmondson, Crawford Feagin and Peter Mühlhäusler. (Dallas : Summer Institute of Linguistics ; Arlington : Univ. of Texas. Summer Institute of Linguistics publications in linguistics, 93). p.3-19.

Hawking, Stephen (1988). *A Brief History of Time*. New York: Bantam.

Hobbes, Thomas (1839). *The English Works of Thomas Hobbes, of Malmesbury*. Now first collected and edited by Sir William Molesworth, Bart. London: John Bohn.

McCullers, Carson (1988). "A tree, a rock, a cloud" in her *Collected Stories*. Boston: Houghton Mifflin Company. First published: *Harper's Bazaar*, 76 (November 1942), 50, 96-99.

Mendes-Flohr, Paul (2007). *Love, Accusative and Dative: Reflections on Leviticus 19:18*. Syracuse: Syracuse University Press.

Said, Edward (2003). *Orientalism*. London: Penguin.

X

To Those Who Do Not Smile

This letter was written to the University of Chicago's student newspaper The Chicago Maroon *in response to the letter by Nora Niedzielski-Eichner "Don't ask me to smile" published in that paper May 18 2001. The reader may wish to read Niedzielski-Eichner's letter first:*
https://www.chicagomaroon.com/article/2001/5/18/letters-to-the-editor-68/

Dear Ms. Niedzielski-Eichner:
You may be unaware that your life is in the constant care of millions of human beings who work together to make sure your life of solitary misanthropy is both possible and comfortable. We make your shoes with which you walk down the street for no one's pleasure but your own, we make the sidewalks on which you walk, the clothes you wear to protect your holy body from the rude glances of children and old ladies, we plow the fields and plant the vegetables you eat, tend our fruit trees to provide you with delicious fruits and juices, make buses for you to ride when your way takes you too far to walk, make stop signs to protect you when you are in a vehicle. We police the

streets and wait in ambulances in case of any accident or crime that may happen to you. We clean the streets and sidewalks to make sure your walks are pleasant and we keep your accounts at the bank and at the bursar's office. We teach you in class, write books and make music for you, build houses and apartments for you, and we remove your garbage, dispose of your excreta, repair your plumbing, fix your roof and millions more activities every moment of every day. We are not, however, your whores and slaves who may speak only when spoken to. We expect to be treated like human beings; instead we are regarded as rapists. If we have to beg for people to acknowledge our existence, to treat us like human beings, to smile at us in public as a simple acknowledgement that we are here on this earth together, then something is terribly wrong with our world.

Culturally trained to accept misandry, rendered inarticulate by your anger that a black man should expect to be treated like a human being and even ask for such treatment, you blame the victim of your hostility by accusing him and condemning him as a (potential) rapist. Such sexist treatment of the man on the street is exactly the same as a man treating all women as sexual prey: All men are rapists, all women are whores. Two peas in a pod, you and the rapist create a world of fear, anger, and injustice with your refusal to acknowledge another's humanity, your sexist prejudices and hatreds. Instead of being treated like human beings with our common forms of civility—polite greetings, smiles—you regard us as rapists, our smiles and our expectation to be smiled at as sexual assaults. If you regard that man on the street (and all other men on the street) with such hostility and contempt, what kind of an attitude toward you (and women) will that create in response?

That black man on the street is your brother; instead of treating him in a human manner, you justify your refusal to acknowledge his existence, your hostility and your sexism with the sloppy logic of a juvenile philosopher. Like a child who has overheard everything and understood nothing, you babble on in justification of your inhumanity and your prejudices. You have read too much and loved too little. It is time you stop treating people like slaves and whores, to be ignored or paid and discarded, and start looking people in the face, caring for this world and all of us in it. A smile is a good place to start.

P.S. I assume we are discussing the same man, for he also asked the blank-faced unfriendly author of these lines "How 'bout a smile at least?" Unlike you, I felt ashamed and angry at myself for walking through the world as though nothing matters but me. You and I have the problem, not the fellow who always greets everyone with a smile.

David Bade
Another man on the street

www.ingramcontent.com/pod-product-compliance
Lightning Source LLC
Chambersburg PA
CBHW071952070526
44583CB00015B/1167